A Hardy Breed

A Hardy Breed

Sheep Farming in Wales

BRUCE CARDWELL

SEREN

Seren is the book imprint of
Poetry Wales Press Ltd.
Suite 6, 4 Derwen Road, Bridgend,
Wales, CF31 1LH

www.serenbooks.com
facebook.com/SerenBooks
Twitter: @SerenBooks

ISBN 978-1-78172-721-8

A CIP record for this title is available from the British Library

The publisher works with the financial assistance of the Books Council of Wales

Printed by Bell & Bain Ltd, Glasgow.

Contents

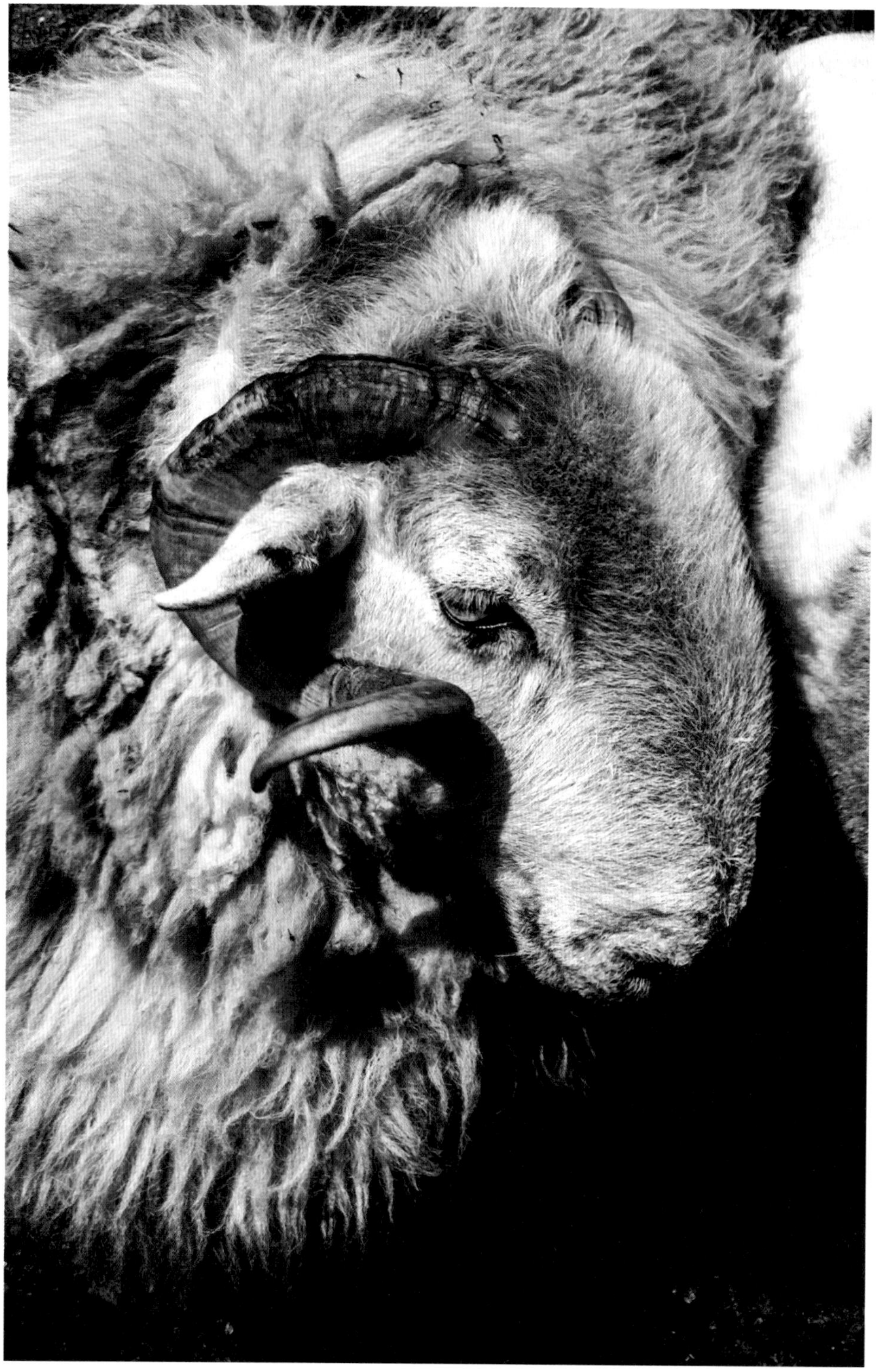

Forewords

A Hardy Breed: Sheep Farming in Wales is unique. Although sheep farming was a regular subject for that great of Welsh photography Geoff Charles, his flat capped hill farmers were photographed more than fifty years ago. By necessity his work for the newspapers of the day distilled sheep farming into a series of photo opportunities – new-born lambs, gathering sheep on a sunlit summer hillside and shearing were regular features. His male dominated studies, though important and sometimes detailed, are fragments of the whole. Quad bikes and mobile phones unheard of fifty years ago now make a difference to the work but can only complement the tried and tested shepherd's crook, sturdy boots and faithful sheepdog.

In *A Hardy Breed* Bruce has covered the entire contemporary sheep farming 'ecosystem' – the finely balanced interwoven dependencies which create and underpin the shepherd's way of life. There is no better illustration of this than in the communal sheep shearing – a time of hard work, camaraderie and hearty meals, also a time for skill, lore and knowledge to be passed on. Like a tightly knit jumper, the landscape, farmer, sheep and sheepdog are intertwined in the photographs. Each photo reveals an interconnection, like the threads Gill is weaving on her peg loom in the Welsh Woolshed.

Included here are highs and the lows – Arwyn helping a ewe down from Cwm Llan in the cold penetrating drizzle possesses an almost biblical quality. A relaxed Teleri and her wary sheepdogs, one cautiously circumventing a farm cat, the other keeping an eye on the photographer, is a reminder that shepherding is no longer the male preserve of fifty years ago.

Do I have a favourite? – perhaps the two young Ceredigion lads grooming a ram brings out their youthful enthusiasm and delight in aiming for perfection. Their exhibit is immaculately groomed, pampered (for a day or two at least) to almost Hollywood perfection in the quest for that first prize rosette at the Royal Welsh Show. Or maybe Cameron dipping in the remote shed at Neuadd Fawr, his day's task there for all to see. Then again maybe it's….

– *Will Troughton, Curator of Photography, National Library of Wales*

It's hard to imagine Wales without sheep – and you can't have sheep without shepherds. These are the men, and increasingly women too, for whom caring for sheep is not a job. It's a way of life.

We all know that agriculture is constantly undergoing change. In my own lifetime we have 'discovered' how saturating our precious soil with chemicals can produce yields our forefathers could only have dreamed of. We have also learned that there is a very high price to pay for those yields.

What this book so beautifully demonstrates is how caring for sheep brings its own rewards, not just for those who have been doing it for countless generations, but for all of us who believe that our countryside is about so much more than simply farming for profit.

Good luck with the book!

– *John Humphrys, Broadcaster*

Introduction

A hardy breed, they have adapted specifically over many centuries to their particular and demanding environment, and are able to subsist happily there when many others might perish.

We could be talking about Welsh Mountain Sheep, or indeed about the people and communities who share a lifestyle with them – the shepherds of Wales. In both cases there is an ongoing reciprocal process of influence at work; the shepherds and sheep are being moulded by the nature of their surroundings, while the appearance and development of the landscape they inhabit is continually being modified by shepherding usages and activities.

This process of mutual interaction has created families and communities with a deep and passionate regard for their place in a time honoured system. To be a shepherd in Wales is not merely to gain a living from grazing and looking after sheep, it is also to feel an intrinsic part of a historic Welsh pastoral tradition, and to be content to be largely defined by it.

The worldwide stereotype of Wales leans heavily on images of sheep and rugby, and as in most cases of stereotyping, there is plausibility and an element of truth in this one. Wales is a country which in the 1990s had a sheep population of 12 million, and even by 2016 sheep still outnumbered the human population by a ratio of three to one. In 2022 at the Royal Welsh Show it was announced over the tannoy that on that particular day there were more than 2,200 sheep present, making it … "the biggest sheep show in the world."

The practice of transhumance, that is of moving stock from low level pastures up onto the higher ground during the better summer weather, takes place in many rural communities worldwide. It is deeply ingrained in the historic fabric of Wales, and there are many references to it in place names. The Welsh word "hafod" is an amalgam of "haf" meaning "summer", and "bod" which is the verb "to be". So a hafod is where you would be when shepherding your flocks in the hills during the summer season, and originally it was most likely a simple stone and earth-sod bothy. "Hendre" is the other side of the transhumance equation; from "hen" meaning "old" and "tref" meaning "home". This would be where you spent the winter, lower down in a milder location. The widespread and frequent occurrence of place names including "Hafod" or "Hendre" in Wales is testament to how general this practice has been over a very long period of time.

Low level subsistence pastoralism had been carried on in Wales from time immemorial before the twelfth century, when the Cistercian Order were granted huge tracts of land in Wales by both the Anglo-Norman settlers and Lord Rhys ap Gruffydd of Deheubarth. It was the Cistercians who organised and expanded sheep husbandry in Wales into the hugely lucrative wool trade which became the mainstay of the nation's economy. The massive profits which flowed into the coffers of the monasteries would not have escaped the attention of the Royal Exchequer, and the resultant envy must surely have been a factor in the eventual Dissolution of the Monasteries by Henry VIII.

The Medieval period in Britain was characterised by an enormous generation of wealth created by the wool trade, and the economic importance of sheep subsequently lasted for centuries. The ascendancy of wool in the textile industry persisted until cheap cotton was produced using slave labour, or grievously underpaid sharecropping farmers. The development and mass production of synthetic materials in the twentieth century was the final blow to wool's dominance in the international market place.

This could well have spelled the end of an epoch as regards the value of grazing sheep, and the need for a shepherd to manage them. If "free market forces" had prevailed at that time, this could have been what transpired. The considerable political clout of farmers and landowners, however, allied to the strategic necessity of maintaining a secure national supply of food, resulted in a different outcome. Although no other industry had ever been supported in such a way, a system of grant aid was instigated whereby an annual sum was paid by the government for every ewe that was kept. This created an unintentional incentive for numerically over intensive stocking rates, which were soon vilified for the effects of overgrazing. The uplands of Wales, which are species poor acid grassland lacking in diversity in any case, were soon characterised as "Green Deserts." The sheep farmers, who had regarded themselves as guardians of the countryside, then faced criticism from the conservation lobby, and resentment from the unemployed miners and steel workers, who had not themselves been thrown a financial lifeline by the government. Media commentators, and others who some derided as "laptop conservationists" or " eco-warriors", then lined up to propose alternative claims and priorities for land usages. Some of these suggestions were reasonable, some well-meaning but ill-informed, and others more fanciful than realistic.

The departure of the UK from the European Union in 2020 then presented a further crucial challenge to an ancient way of life in Wales. The system of grant aid to farmers in the EU had been controversial for many years, but had been adamantly defended by France, where most families had relatives somewhere in the country benefiting from the subsidies. This prevented any radical reform. After Brexit agricultural grant funding here, and the conditions of how it was awarded, became the prerogative of UK governments.

There has since been intensive lobbying by environmental bodies and others to use this financial leverage to achieve greater species diversity, create more abundant wildlife habitat, and reduce carbon emissions.

This wide range of interests and demands does not always combine together comfortably however. Governmental policies require nuanced application to avoid doing more harm than good, as any over concentration on a single-issue interest often leads to inadvertent collateral damage elsewhere. Blanket prescriptions such as those aimed at moderating climate change by indiscriminate or overwhelming tree planting might have some beneficial effect in that particular regard, but could be positively detrimental to many other important considerations. Not the least of these considerations is the human, and social, dimension...people.

An important lesson, only recently absorbed by conservationists around the world, is that failure to get a resident population "onside" inevitably results in a project which fails to deliver the desired outcomes. Planning for changes of land use in Wales should take into account the full spectrum of possible effects which might ensue, and "Think Welsh" as well as "Think World". Many of the upland shepherding communities are primarily Cymraeg speaking as their first language, and although much is made of the increasing numbers of Welsh speakers in Wales many of those are basically learners, and primarily English speaking. It is the number of first language speakers of any language that is the key indicator of its relative strength and resilience. Ireland has, sometimes controversially, financially supported the Irish speaking communities of the Gaeltacht areas, and seen a cultural return on their investment with an upswing in the growth of the native Gaelic tongue.

With Welsh national consciousness already scarred by the drowning of Tryweryn to slake the thirst of Liverpool, and the eviction of farming families from Mynydd Epynt to create a military training area, the prospect of multi-national companies buying agricultural land in Wales on which to plant trees in order to offset their carbon emitting activities elsewhere is a grim and unwelcome outlook – socially, economically, and culturally.

Reflecting on this portmanteau of ideas set me thinking that a photographic record of the current shepherding situation might be a constructive project, hopefully as a celebration and not as a eulogy. Whatever the future may bring, posterity will be curious as to how this long-established world looked in the early years of our third millennium. I was unsure how, or where, to start with such a complex challenge until I thought of an old friend called Erwyd Howells, who was himself a shepherd. It was to prove a lucky starting point, and to be the basis of my initiation into the world which I planned to record photographically ... shepherding in Wales.

Erwyd howells

Erwyd Howells originates, very appropriately, from Ponterwyd in Ceredigion, where his family have been shepherds and smallholders in that area for three hundred years. It is impossible to separate his sense of self from his occupation as a shepherd, for his language, anecdotes, hobbies, friends and social life – in fact every component of his personal identity – have been derived from that connection. It is he who explained to me the reason why there is that characteristic little upturn on the hook of the shepherd's crook, it was where a lantern would have been hung in the past when lambing at night out on the hill.

He is the author of a book called *Good Men and True*, which chronicles the lives and histories of the shepherds of Mid Wales, and demonstrates his encyclopaedic knowledge of the subject. By describing their way of life, and the hardships they had to contend with, he evokes a vanishing reality which is becoming increasingly dissociated from the technologies of the digital age. He recalls that all of his early shepherding work before his marriage was on a "live-in" basis, sharing the triumphs and tragedies of the farming family for whom he was working, and that the consequent bond of shared experience forged lifelong friendships which have continued through four generations. The social cohesion still apparent in Welsh shepherding families and communities today is of an order no longer common in urban situations. The shared lifestyle and common values are, Erwyd says, " the ties that bind and bond like-minded people."

Erwyd likes to contextualise his anecdotes and general lore with a quote from Newell Dwight Hills, "These recollections are embalmed and transmitted as social capital, legacies unspeakably precious." Neither is he short of the odd pithy comment of his own.

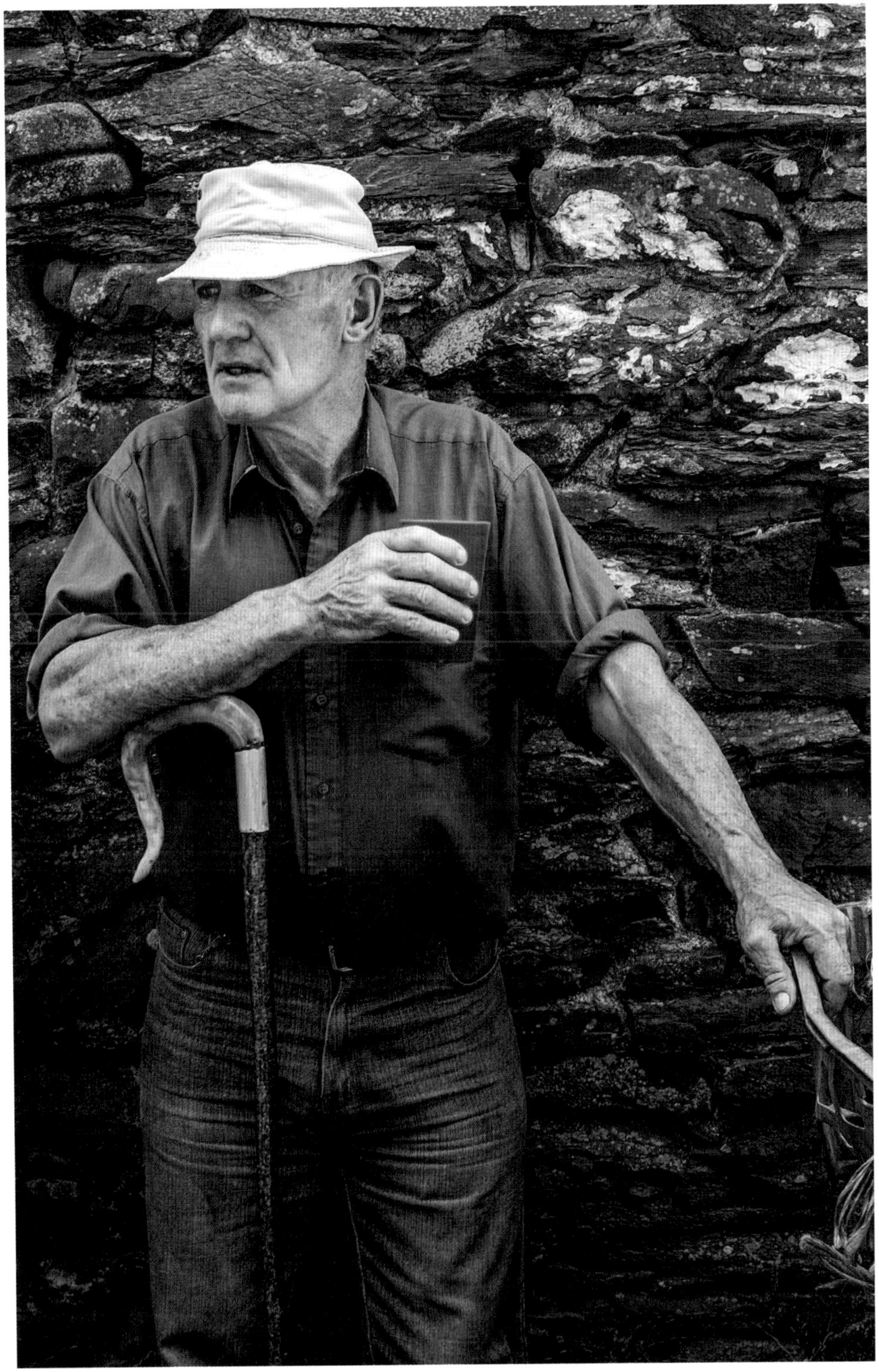

A cup of tea which he might be offered without an accompanying bite to eat is "an urban cup of tea". As a graduate of the school of learning on the job it is his opinion that… "education is not a substitute for intelligence". He cherishes the memory of his own tutelage under the redoubtable, though often irascible, Alfred Edwards of Cwm Ystwyth, who instilled in him the habits of observation and thoughtful analysis.

He has a collection of old shepherding hand tools, and of those specially designed books which recorded the hundreds of individual unique ear-markings which once differentiated the various flocks grazing together on the open hills, together with many other interesting and intriguing related objects. These are, however, increasingly taking on the status of curios, or museum pieces. Plastic ear tags and other more "convenient" practices may have superseded many of the traditional ways and techniques, but as he remarked, "A plastic ear tag can be removed, or changed, in a way that was impossible with the old ear clipping system."

A shepherd's most essential resource is a working sheepdog, and Erwyd trained his own first dog at seventeen years of age. His preference has always been for the native Welsh type, and his pedigrees for those he has owned go back eleven generations. "Dogs are of supreme importance for me, and for shepherding," he says. "Border Collies are good on the outrun, but the Welsh dogs are pushier with big flocks of sheep, so they complement each other very well". He has an impressive array of trophies won at sheepdog trialling events, but maintains, "Dogs are really important for working, and the trialling is just a sociable bonus." When Erwyd works his two dogs together he has one who is trained to work to Welsh commands, and the other one to English commands. This ensures that there is no confusion about which dog he is directing with each command.

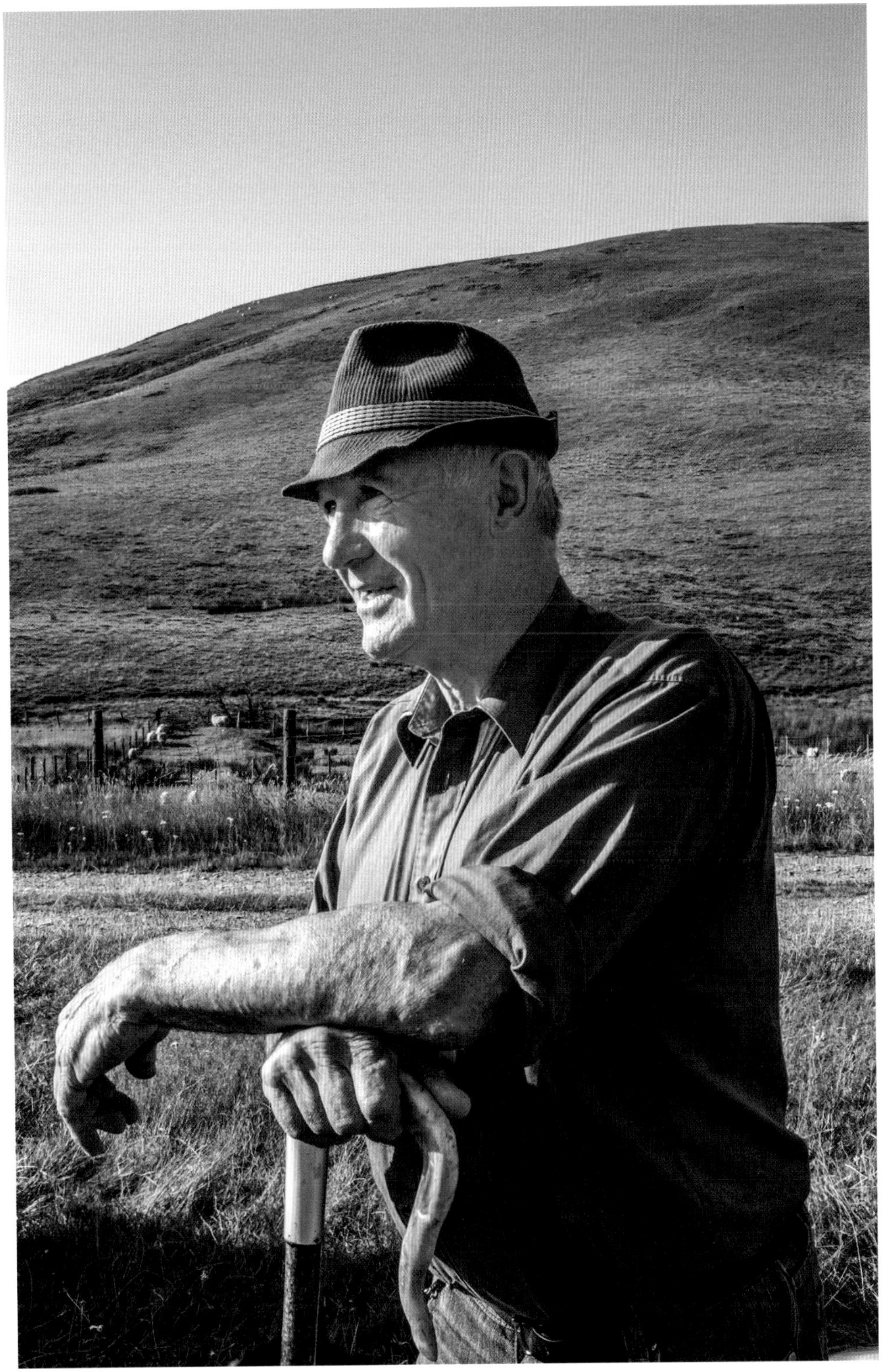

The regard in which the working sheepdog is still held can be illustrated by the fact that 157 dogs were sold online from Dolgellau on the 16th of November 2022. The top price paid for one fully trained dog was £10,400, although obviously partly trained animals and pups would go for a lot less. Another professional trainer sold five dogs for a total of £30,000. The rugged landscapes in which much of a shepherd's work is carried out in Wales means that no algorithm or ingenious mechanism has yet been invented that can compete with the intelligence and abilities of a well trained dog in dealing with sheep.

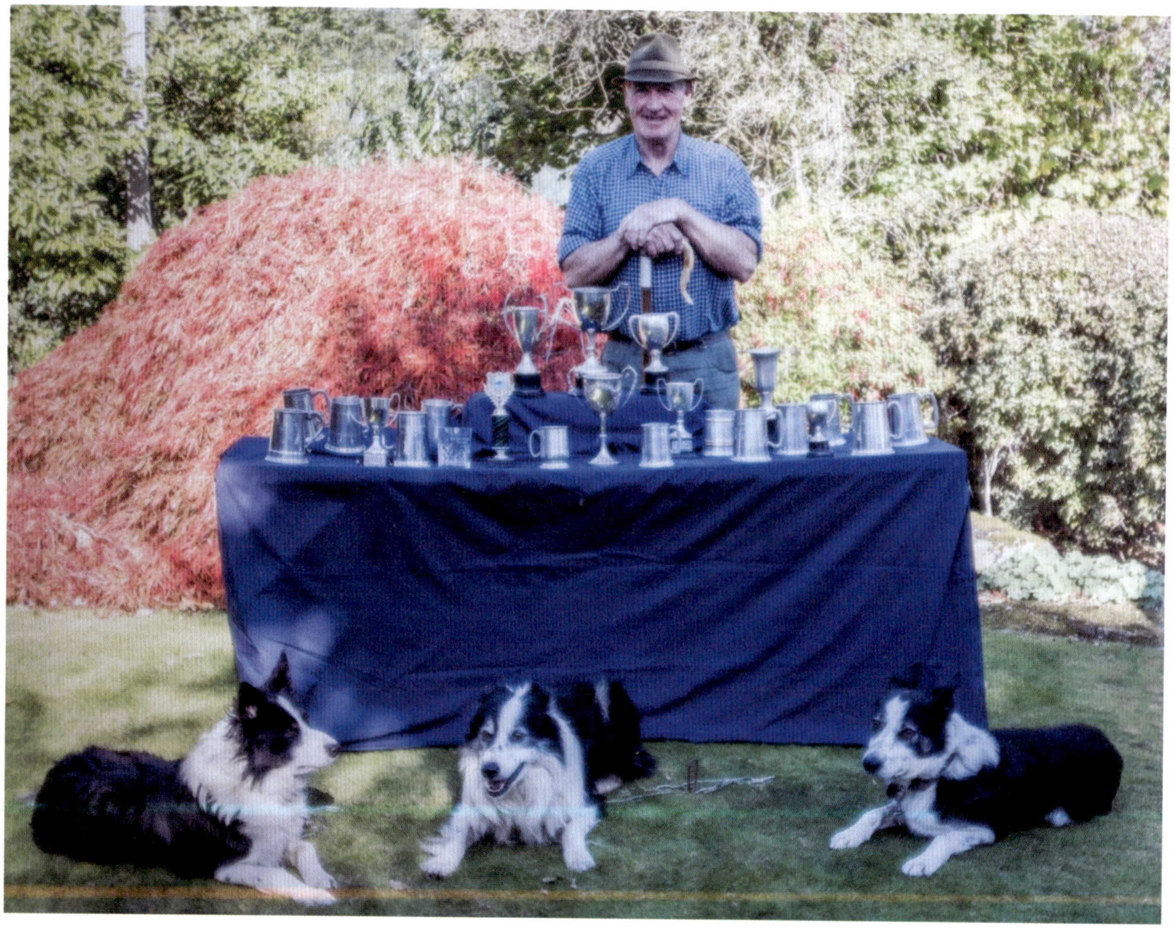

Gathering

Keri Davies

Keri Davies was born at Wernheulog, home to his father and grandfather before him. He runs sheep on 280 acres of land which he owns, 260 acres which he rents, and parts of 3,500 acres of assorted common lands which he shares with other local graziers.

Gathering sheep in these deeply gullied uplands is an epic challenge. It requires numbers of horses, dogs, and skilled shepherds in order to effectively sweep the difficult terrain and bring the whole flock safely down from high ground to the farm itself. "The shepherds here today helping with the gather came from Ystradgynlais, Brecon, the Cambrian Mountains, Merthyr, and other upland areas," Keri explains, "so they have the necessary skills and experience. In fact Simon Mogford, Gwyn Protheroe, John Griffiths and Ross Games are a bit of a 'dream team' for this kind of work, they are about as good as you can get. It is an important social network for us, so the loss of a hill flock anywhere in Wales has detrimental effects that ripple through all those remaining. As a stand alone business shepherding profitability is dependent on the Single Farm Payment scheme, so over the last fifteen to twenty years there has been a decline in the number of traditional hill flocks, those which keep the sheep out on the hill for nine or ten months of the year. It is these hardy hill stock that are the bedrock of all the different sheep cross-breeding projects, they are critically important for the genetic health of the entirety of the the national flock."

Considering the web of interconnectivity that informs the grazing of the uplands in so many subtle ways, any proposed change in financial support would need to carefully assess the potential for unintended negative consequences.

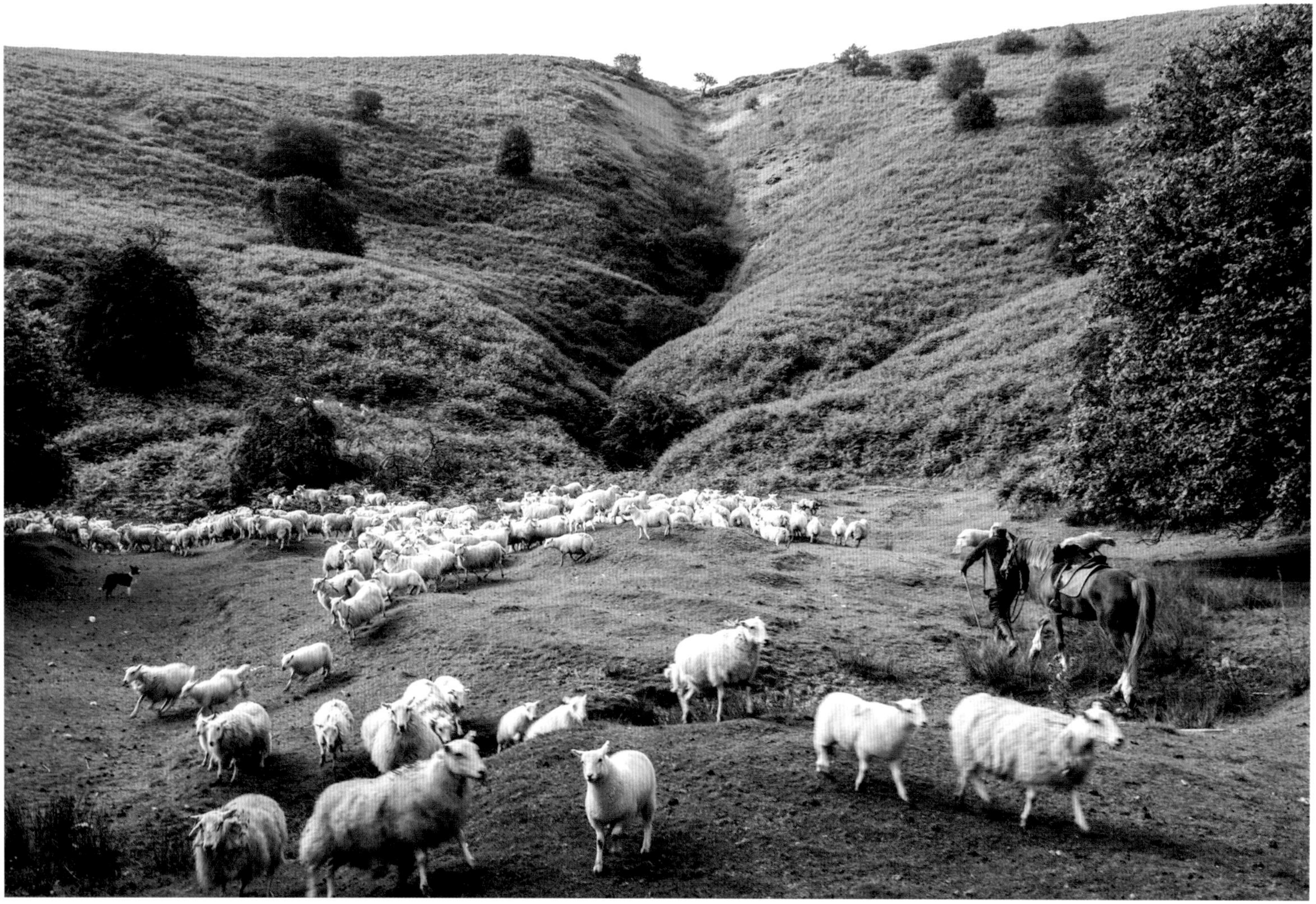

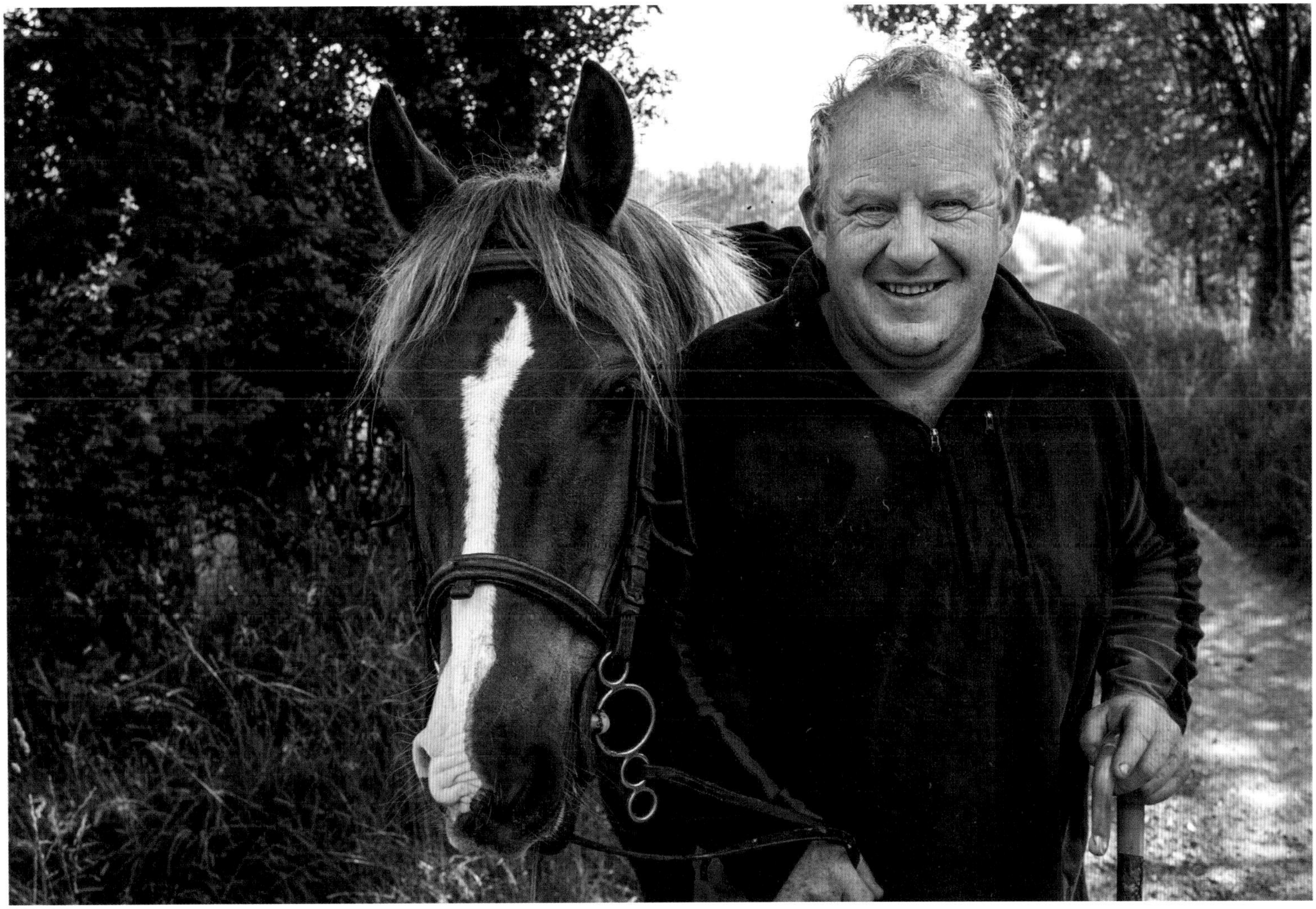

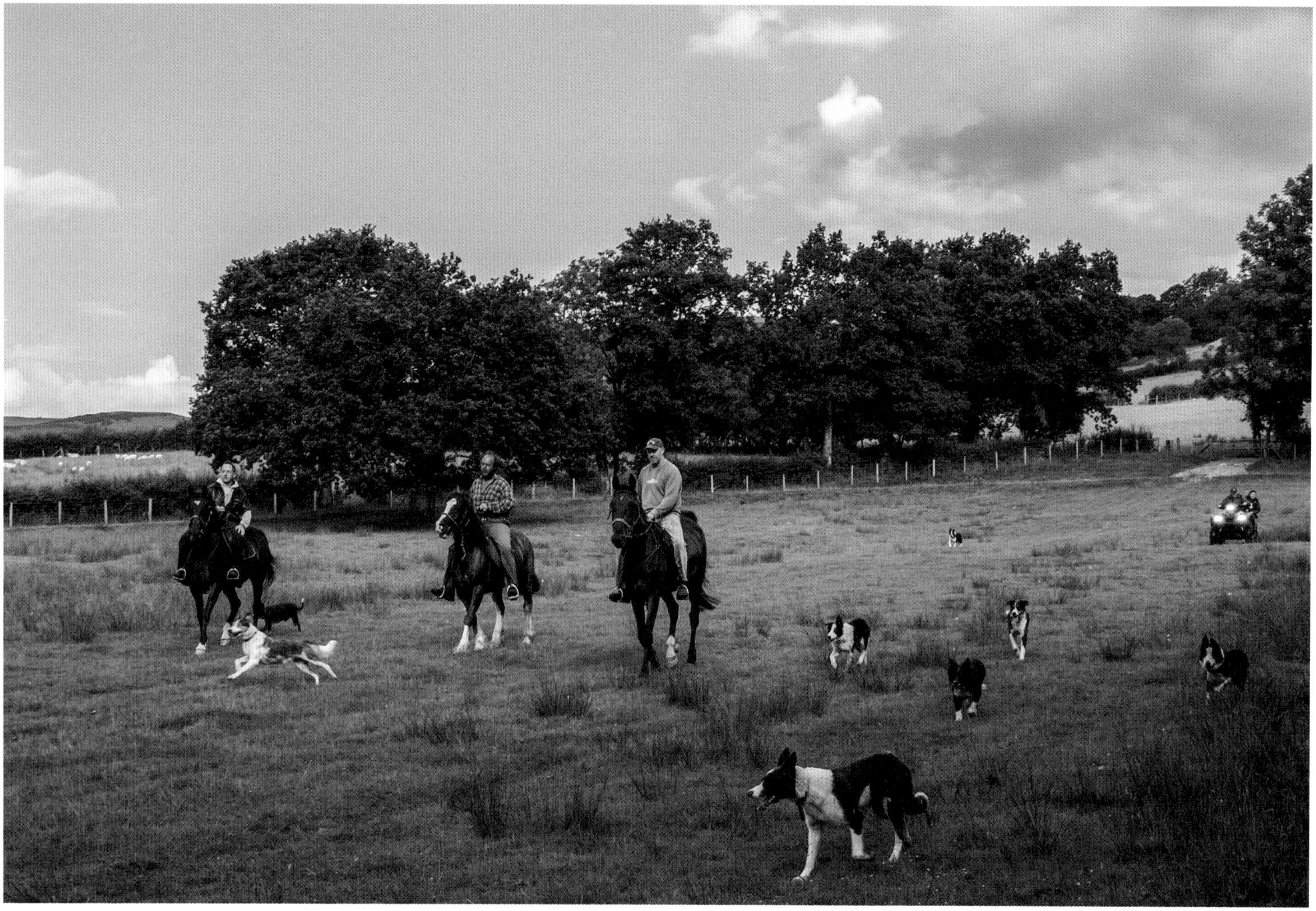

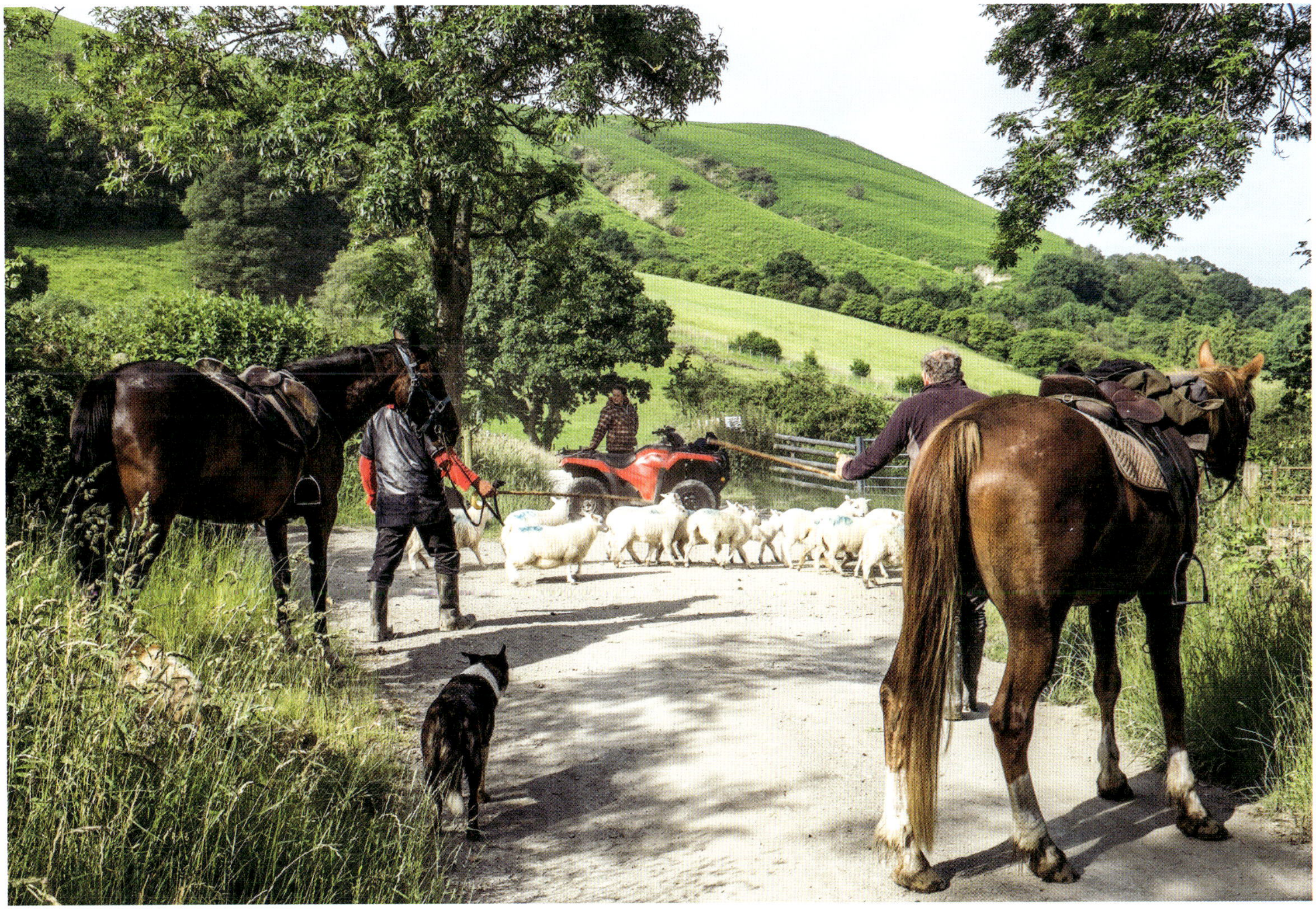

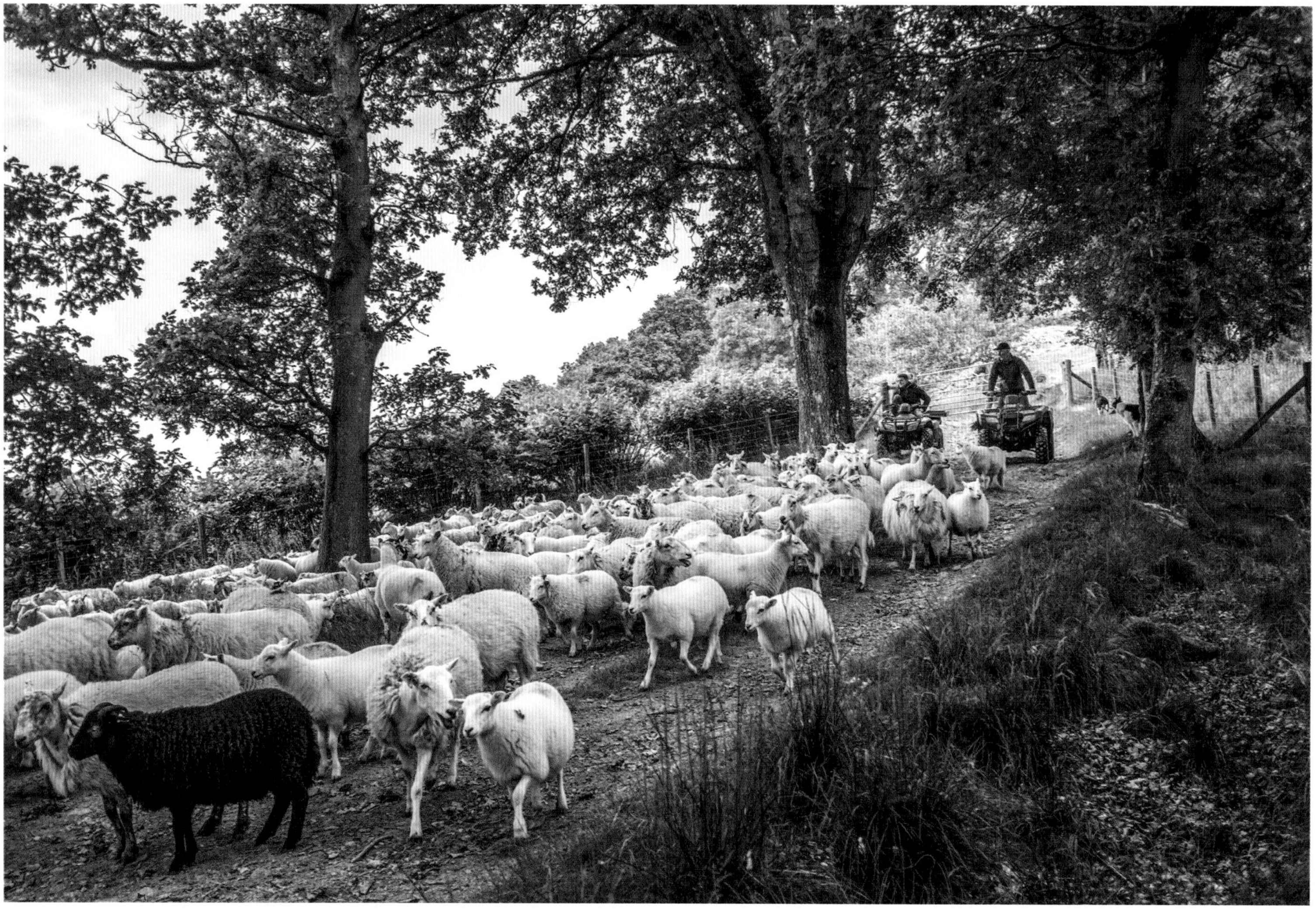

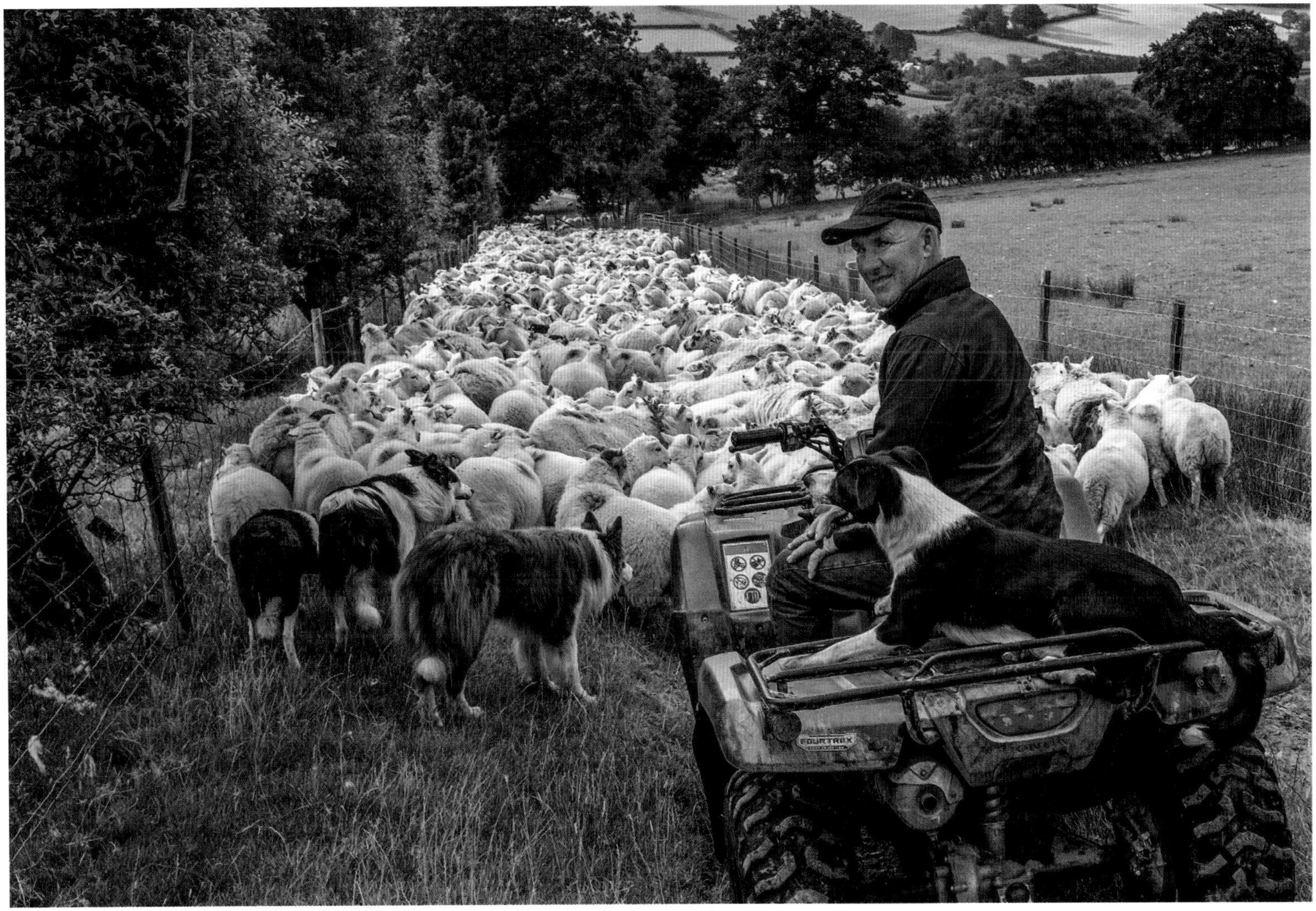

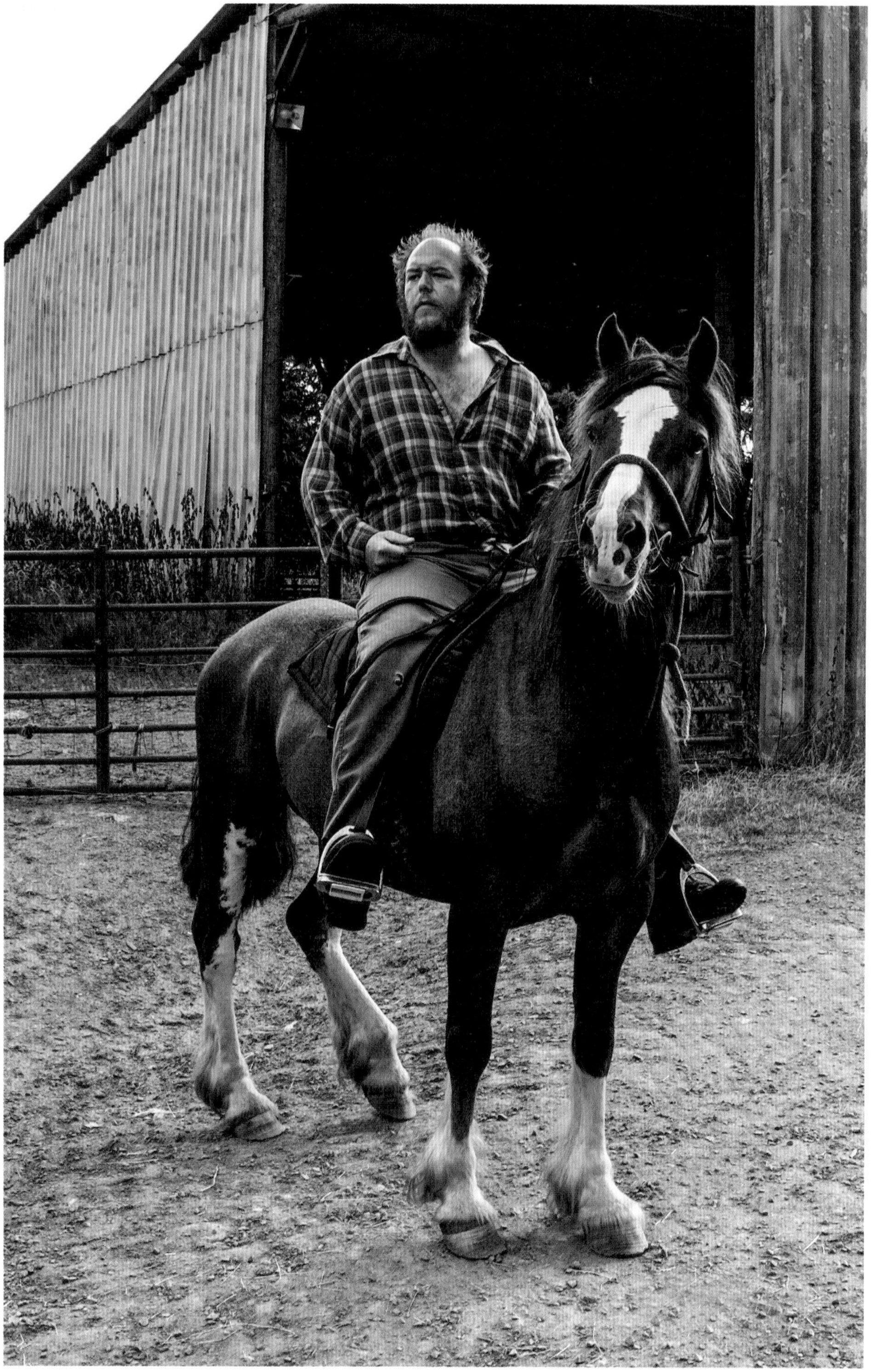

Robert and Janet Hughes

In 1892 Birmingham City Council acquired 180 sq. kilometres of the Elan and Claerwen valleys, damming and flooding the area to create a water supply for the city. They dispossessed one hundred people of their homes, demolishing three manor houses, eighteen farms, a school and a church to accommodate the reservoirs. The land is now in the keeping of the Elan Valley Trust, who manage seven farms in hand with just two shepherds. In 1957 the additional drowning of the Tryweryn Valley provoked the iconic painted graffiti "Cofiwch Dryweryn" by Meic Stephens, which became a rallying cry for both Welsh nationalists and environmentalists.

Aber Glan Hirin farm is 1,800 acres of upland grazing in the Elan Valley, and Robert Hughes was born there in 1950, the third generation of his family to tenant the holding. Robert himself is widely respected in shepherding circles as a "good yard man", someone who can quickly and accurately sort out sheep from a flock according to their ear-markings. The farm carries 1,300 sheep today, significantly down from the 2,000 of twenty years ago. "The grant schemes have focused on reducing sheep numbers," Robert explains, "but the reduced grazing pressure has resulted in the expansion of Molinia, or Purple Moor Grass, which becomes too coarse and rank for the sheep to eat. So it is not a good outcome either for shepherds or environmentalists. We could try to manage that problem by using Welsh Black Cattle to keep it grazed down, but then we would have to feed them over the winter. We can't get a hay crop of our own up here, and buying it in would be ruinously expensive. Theoretical advice is well and good, but you have to live on the land to know how it works."

Robert's wife Janet shares his love of the shepherding life, "While the socialising side is not all that much, there is always something to be doing on the farm, it is the best life ever." On the morning of the gather she is hard at work in the kitchen, saying, "A good cooked breakfast will keep them working for the day."

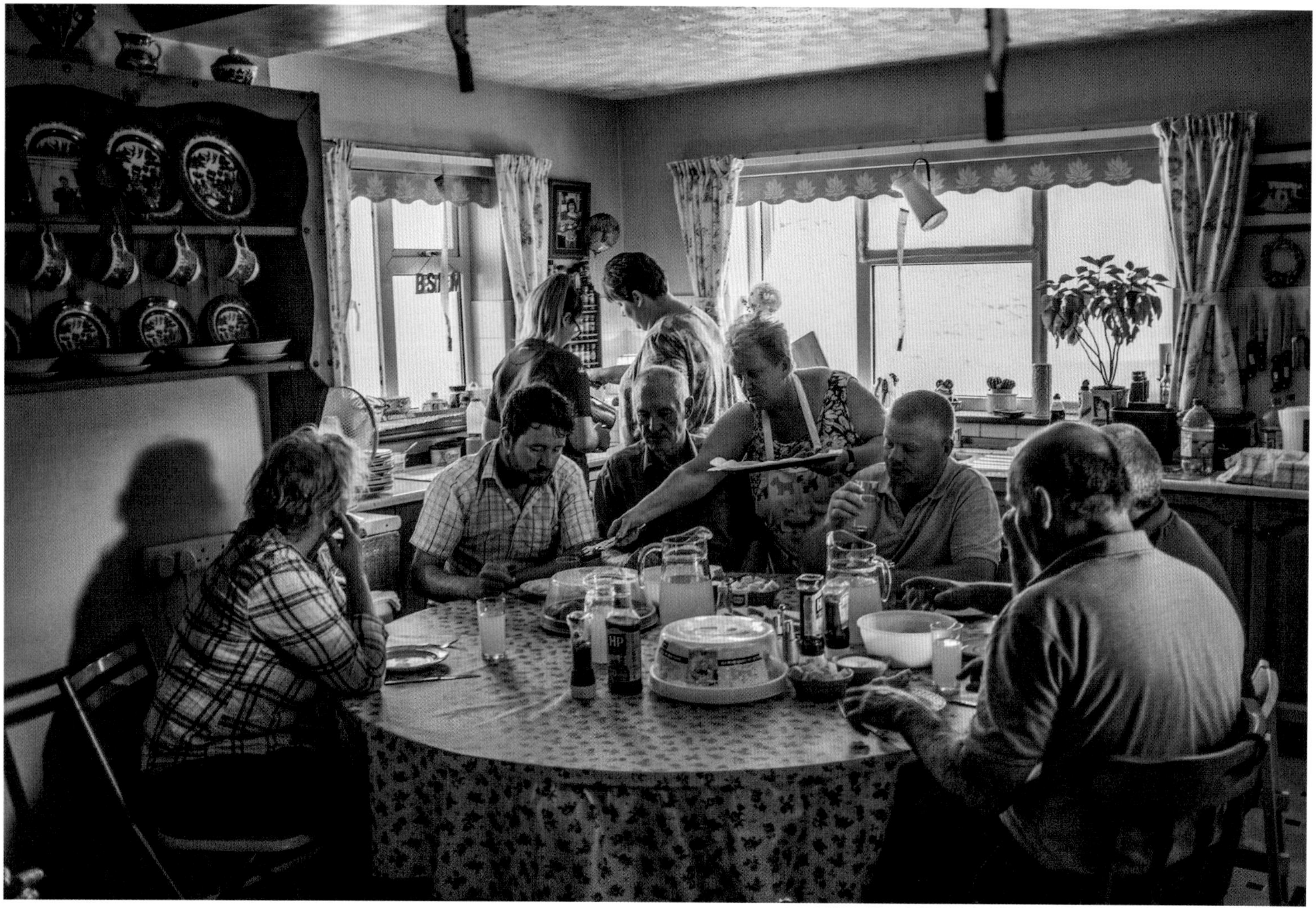

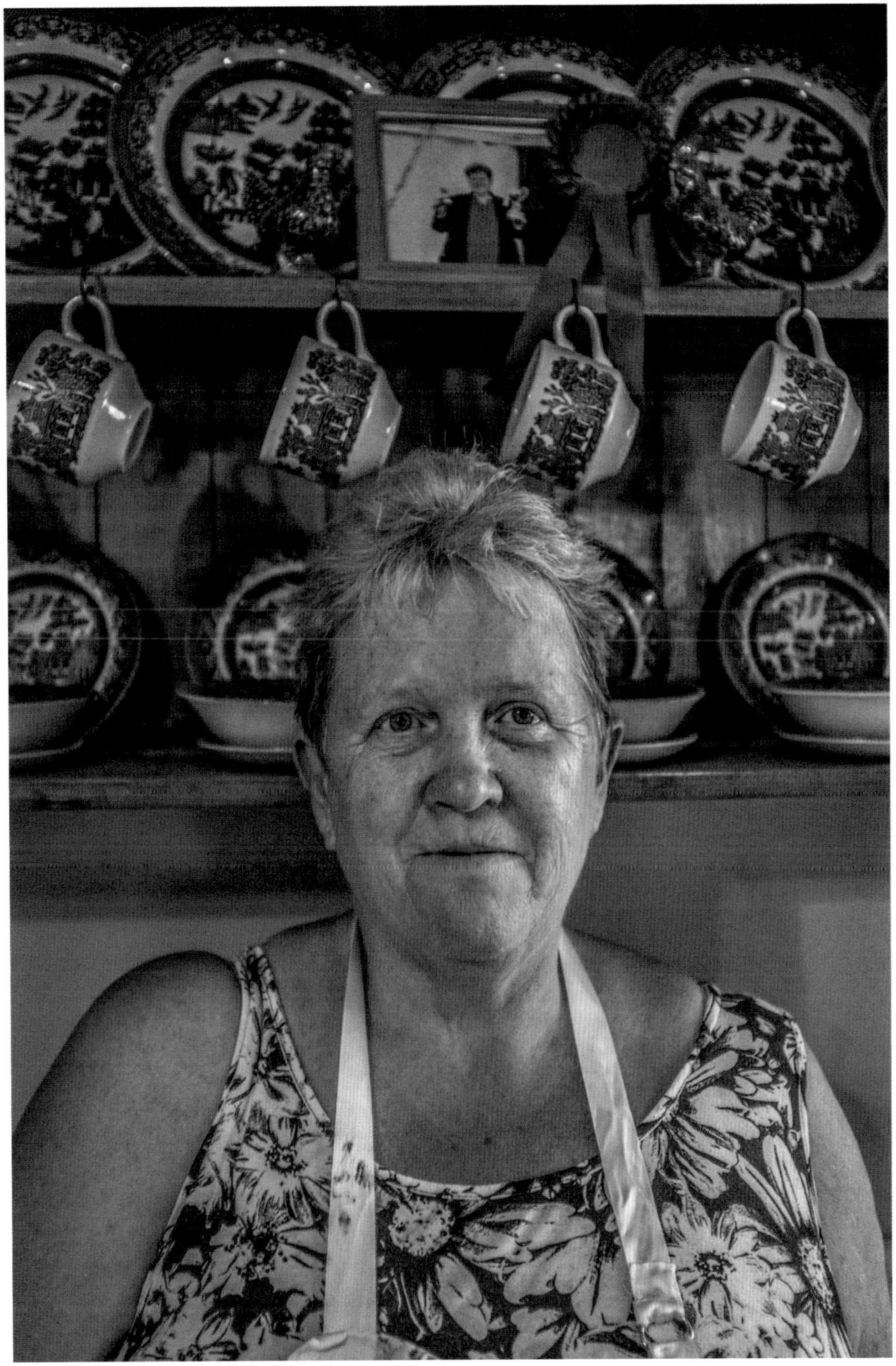

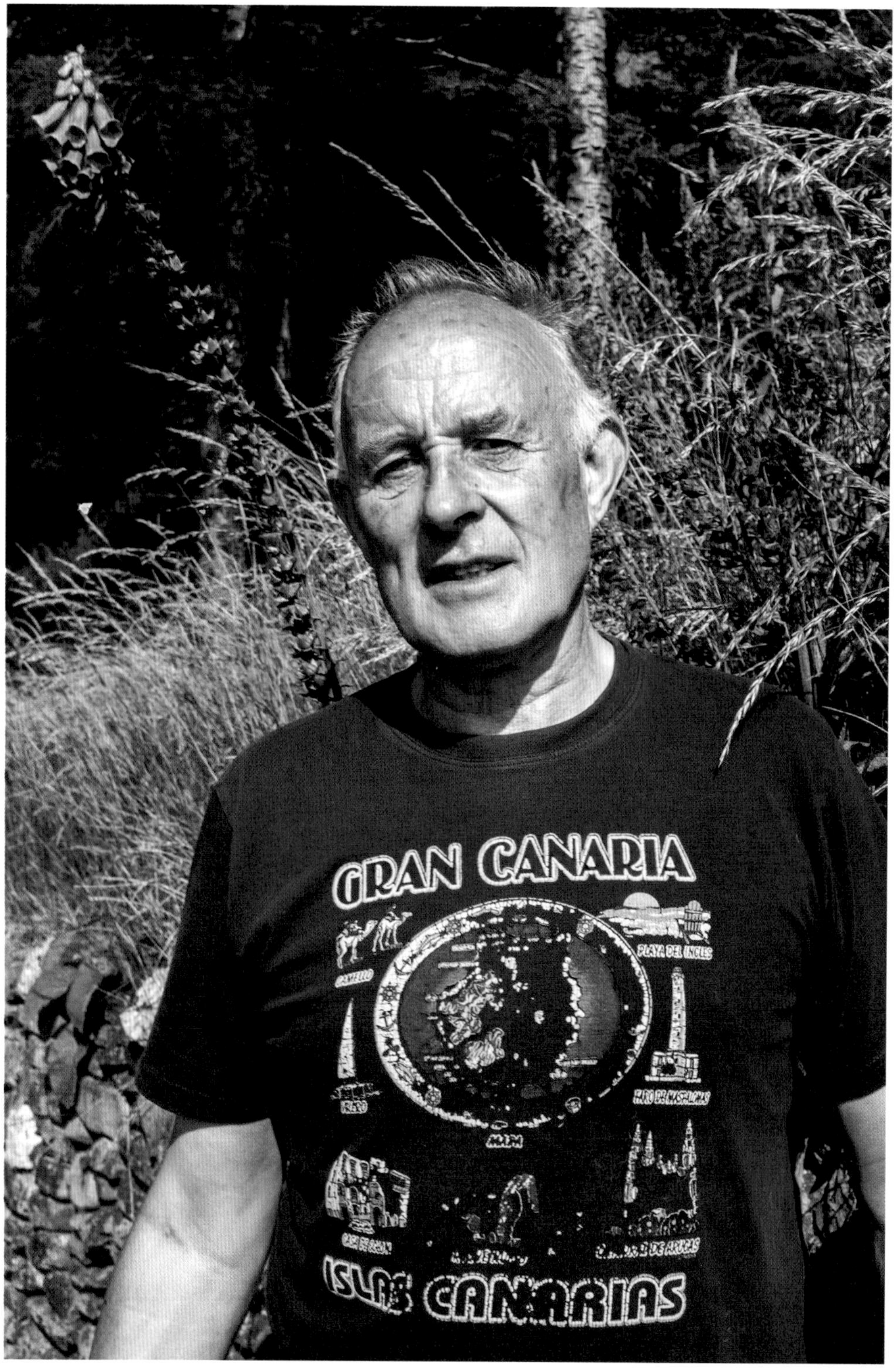
GRAN CANARIA
ISLAS CANARIAS

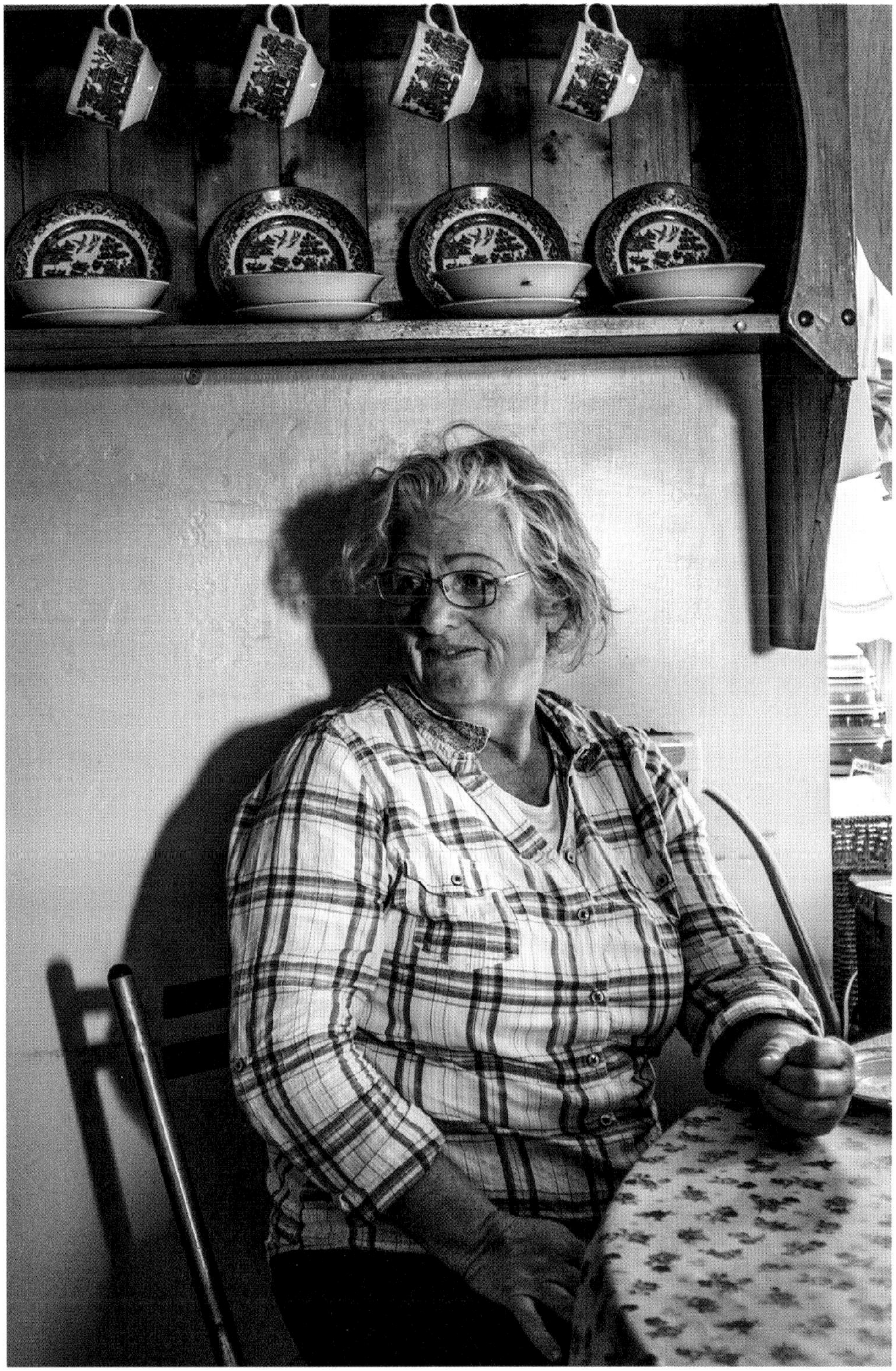

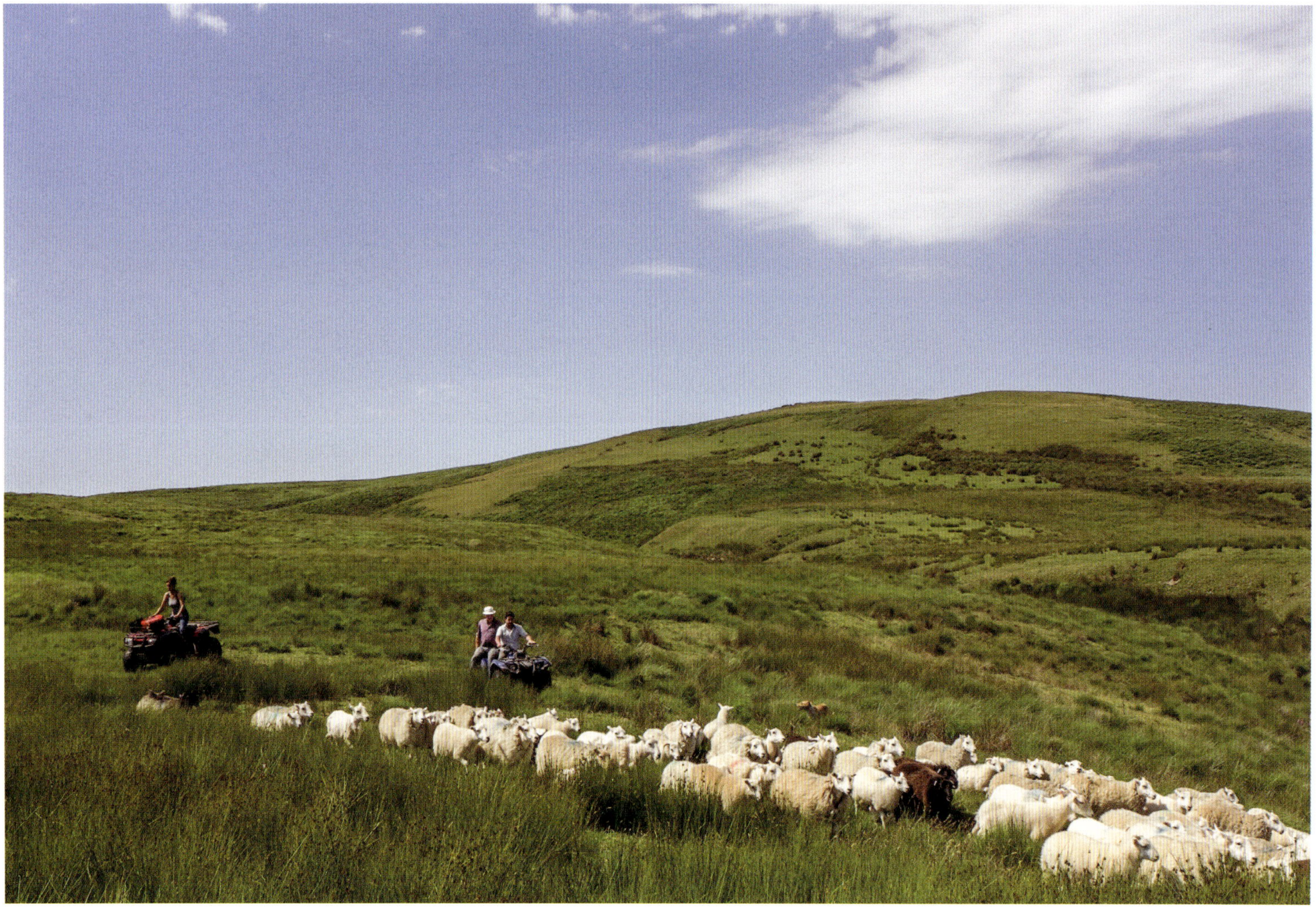

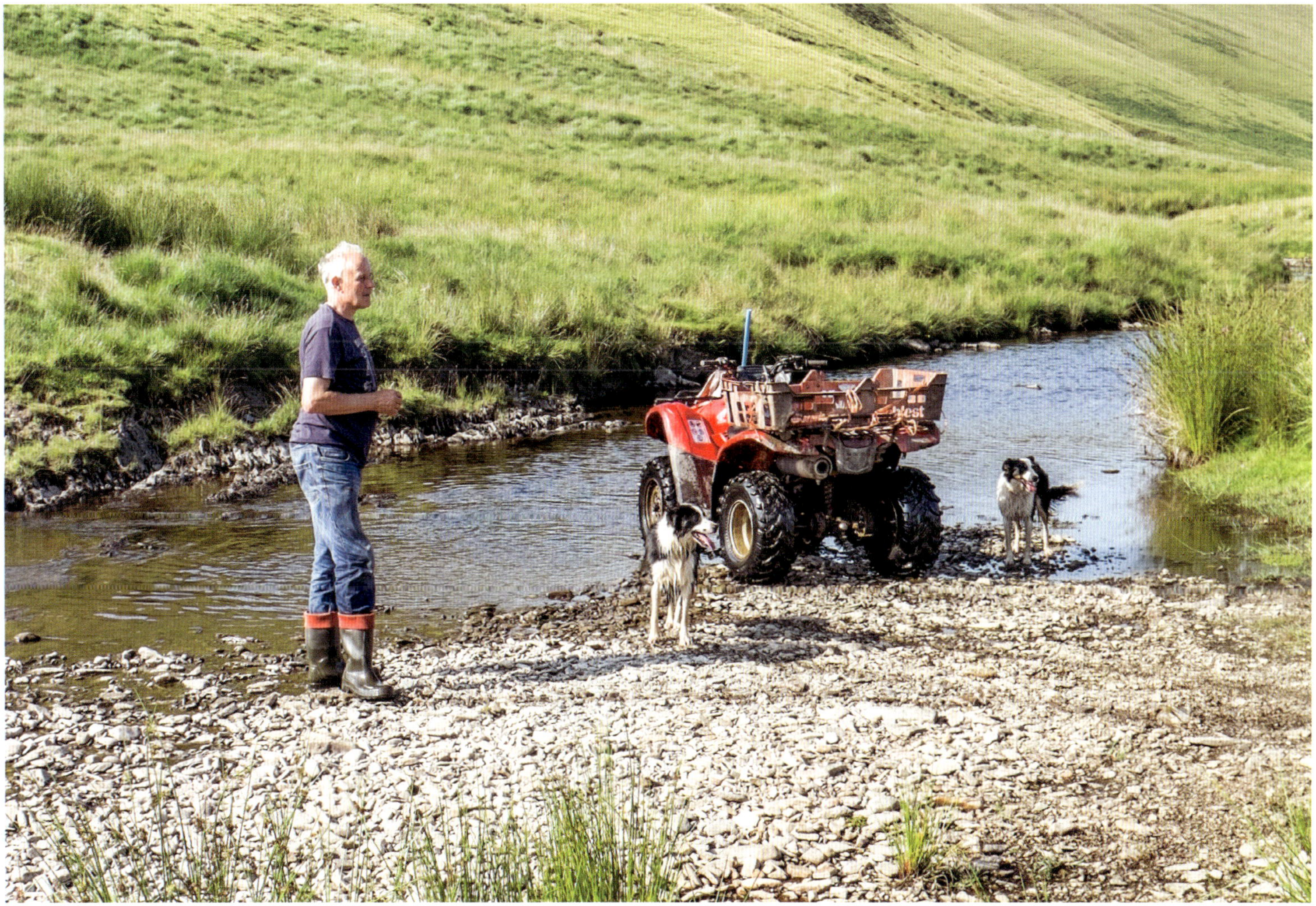

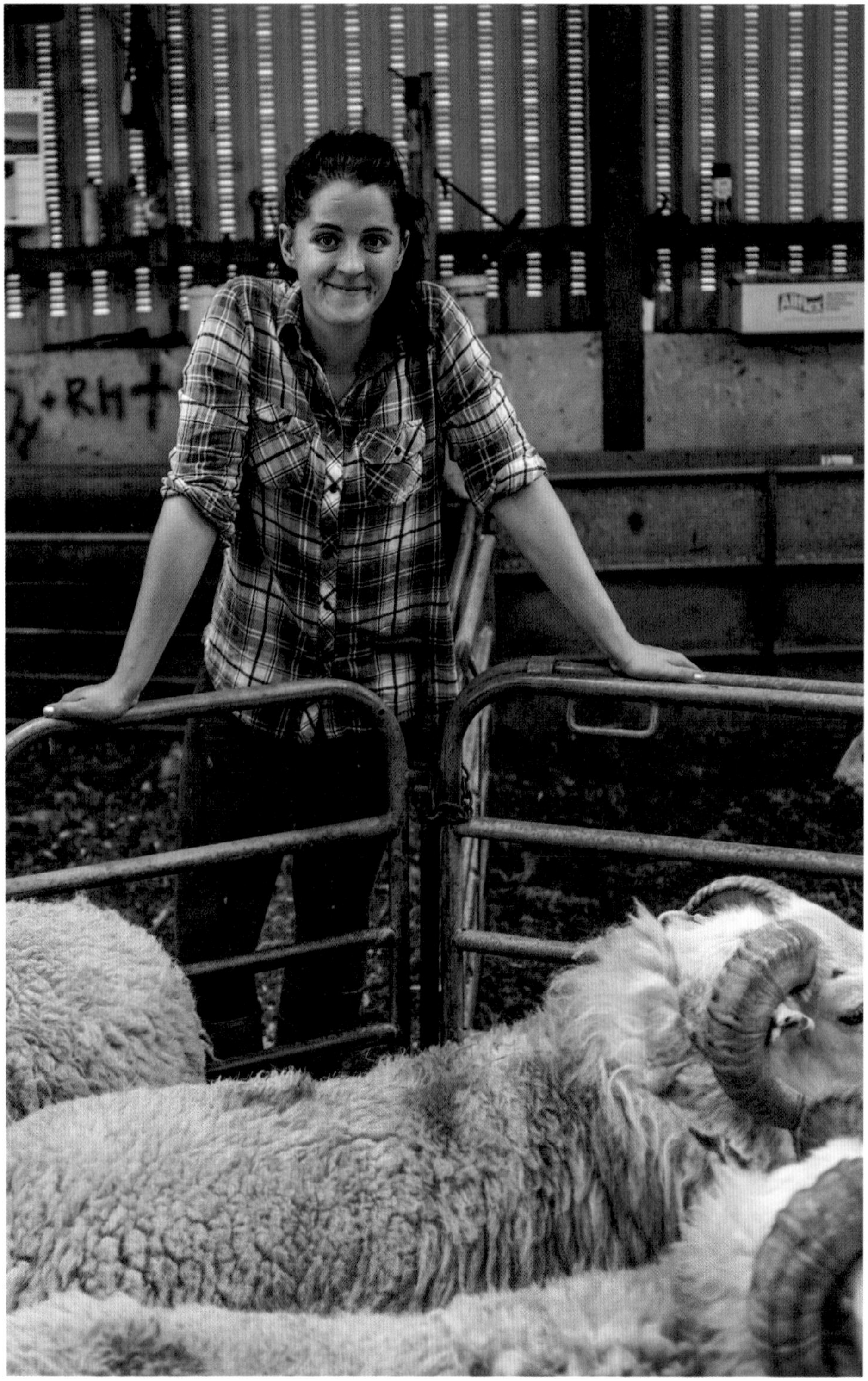

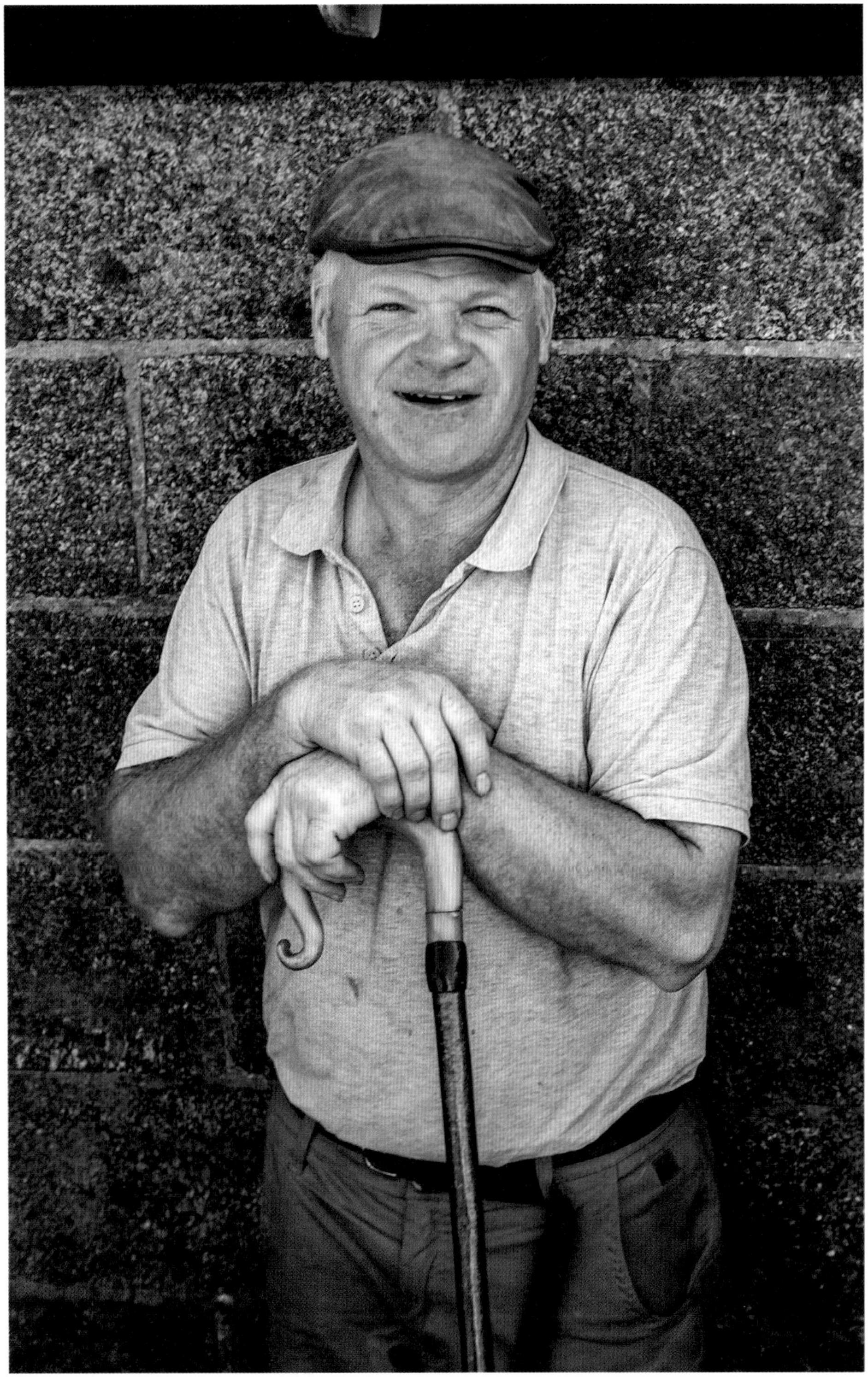

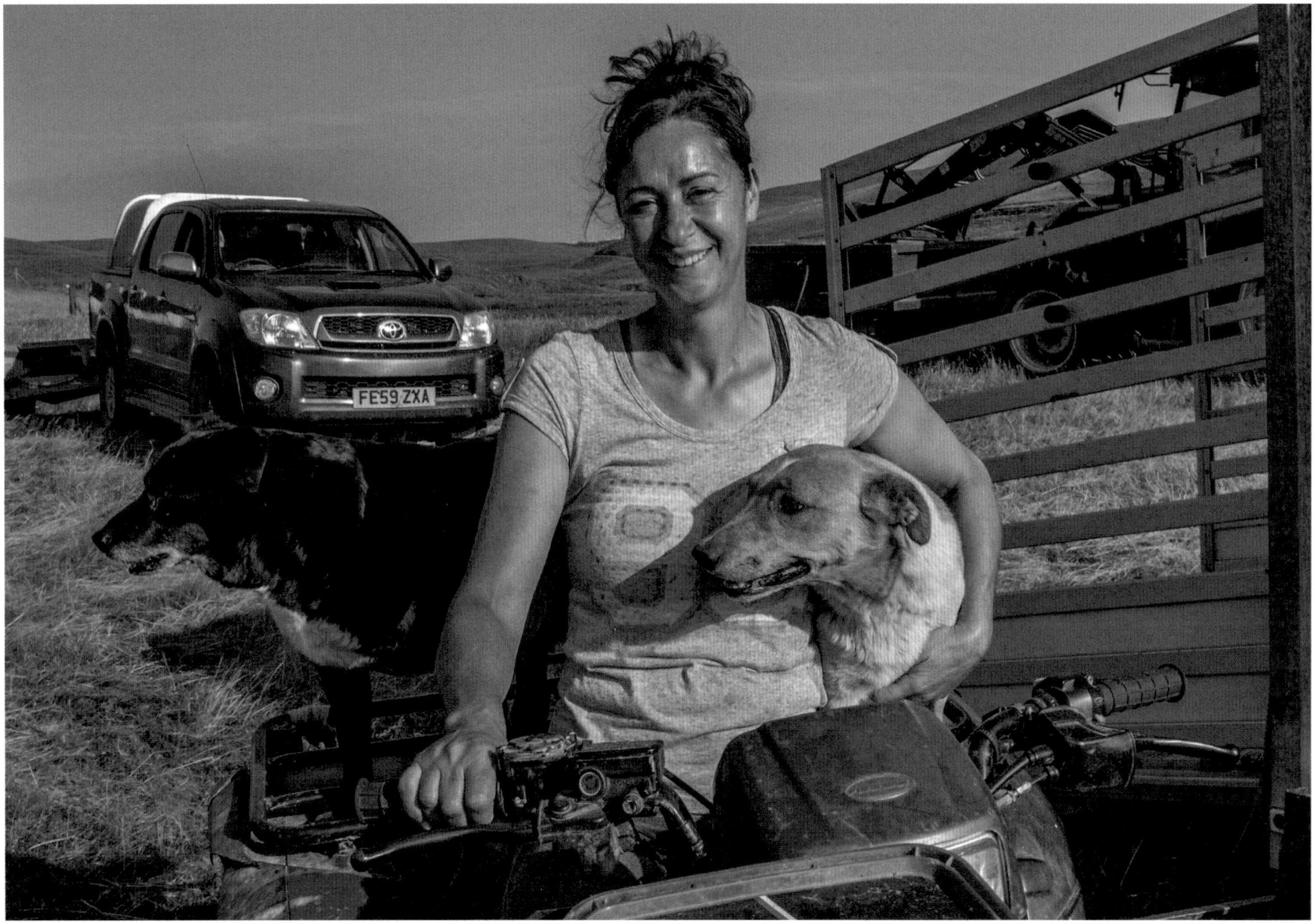
FE59 ZXA

Lambing

Heledd and Prys Davies

Prys can trace his shepherding forebears back to 1775 in Penrhyncoch, and is sure that they were thereabouts long before that. His grandfather and father before him farmed in the Bontgoch area, and his grandmother raised six children on her own after the grandfather died very young, probably from an infection caused by a blackthorn puncture wound. She raised turkeys to help with the family's finances through those very hard times. One of her children, who would later be Prys' aunt, was actually baptised over her father's coffin while it was still in the house, before he was buried.

Prys himself was born in the family farm of Tyncwm in Capel Dewi, starting work with the stock at the age of seven or eight, and never really considering doing anything else. Heledd's parents, on the other hand, were teachers. She is quick to point out that … "I help out, but I wasn't born into it. I do want to learn more though, and I can be a real help with the onerous digital admin work that goes along with farming today." Her pleasure and recreation is playing the harp, a very traditional and appropriate pastime in the context of the Welsh countryside.

Including the land at Coedllys and the original holding back in Capel Dewi, they run between 1,400 to 1,500 sheep altogether. At lambing time they expect to birth about 2,000 lambs, which is accomplished just with the help of Prys' brother Aled, and one helper hired for a fortnight. That is an intense work commitment, and if the weather is not helpful it becomes even harder. Ironically, though, the ewes drop the lambs more easily in moderately wet weather rather than in the heat. Cold, wet weather is the worst combination.

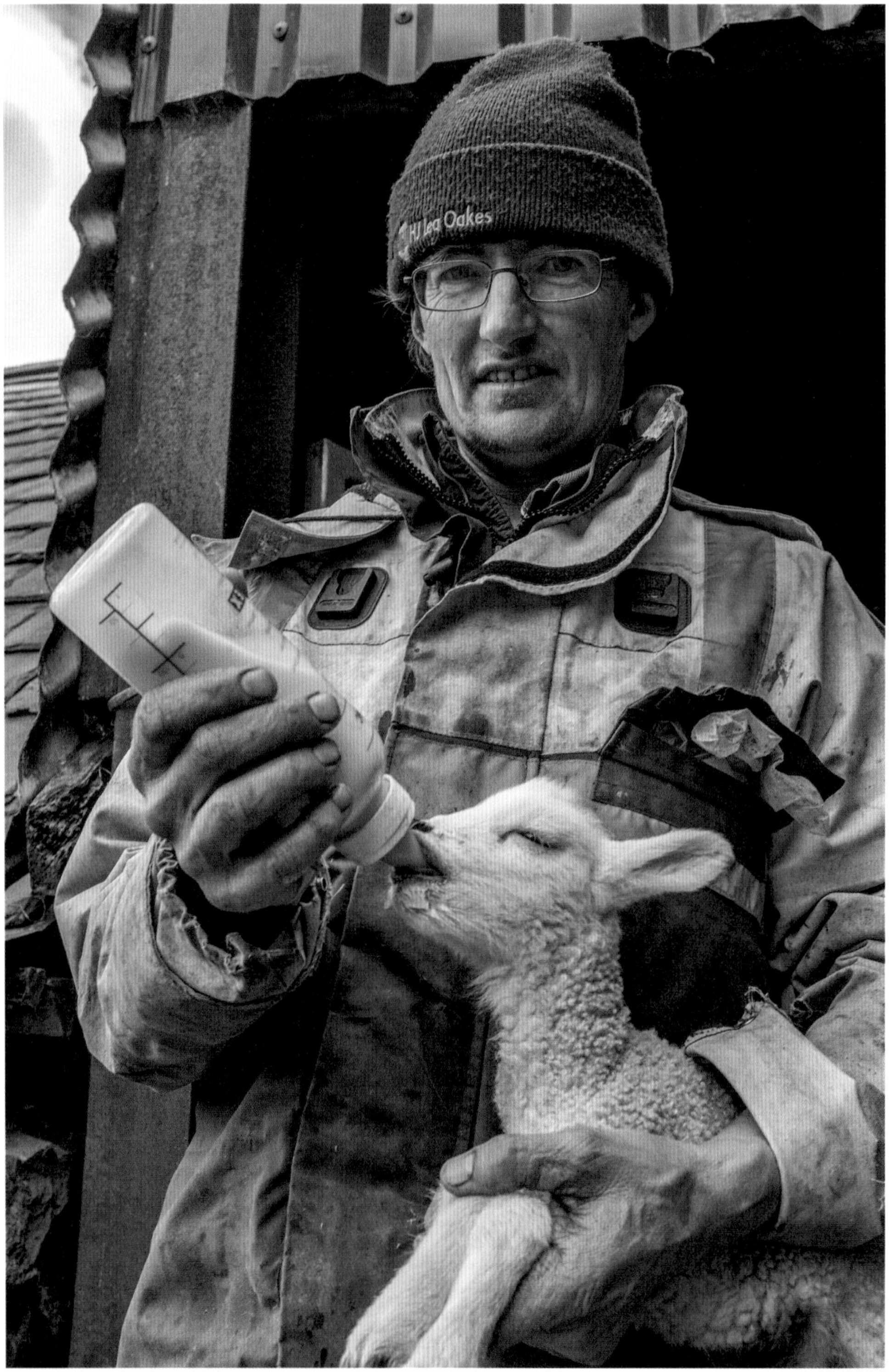
HJ Lea Oakes

Prys enjoys the shepherding life, saying, "Every day is different, and it is never monotonous or boring." Their boys take an active interest, and have helped deliver lambs from a young age. He is adamant though, … "it's up to them what they want to do. I would never pressure them into it."

A concern for Prys at the moment is the recent Free Trade Agreement struck by the UK with New Zealand and Australia. "There are farms in Australia the size of Wales, so we can never compete with them. The land here in Ceredigion is shallow soil on either clay or shale, and it cannot be as productive as those places with deep fertile soil. They can quickly ramp up production there at any time if they manage to avoid drought."

Each year Prys plants up sections of hedgerow, double fenced to prevent rabbits eating the tender young growth. This increases biodiversity and wildlife habitat, while creating useful shade or shelter for stock. "If you want to do that as part of a government scheme, though," he says, "they insist on the hedges being three metres wide, which is unnecessary and wasteful of productive grazing. The people who make those rules are not in the same world as us."

He maintains an optimistic outlook, however, and intends to remain shepherding for the long haul.

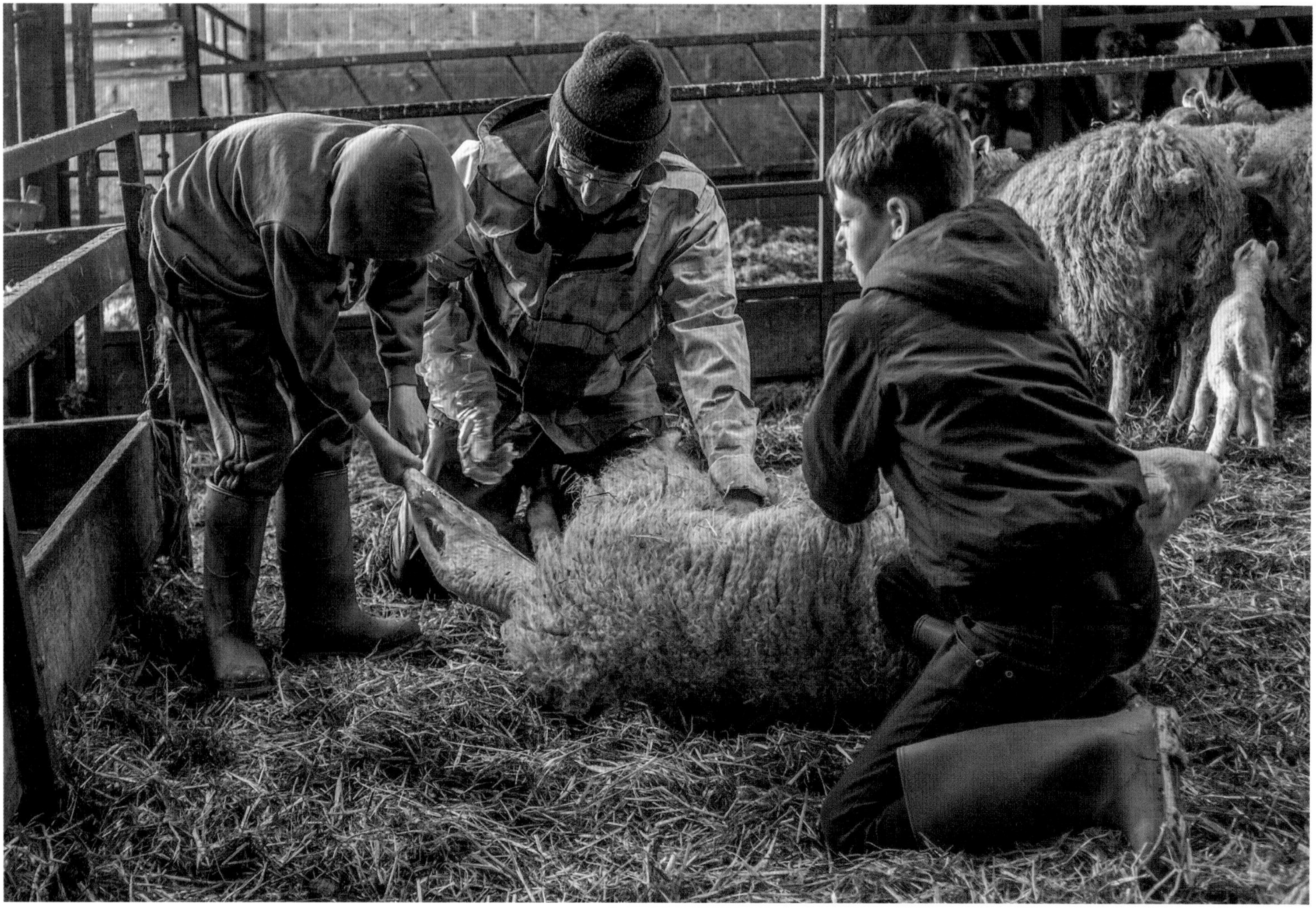

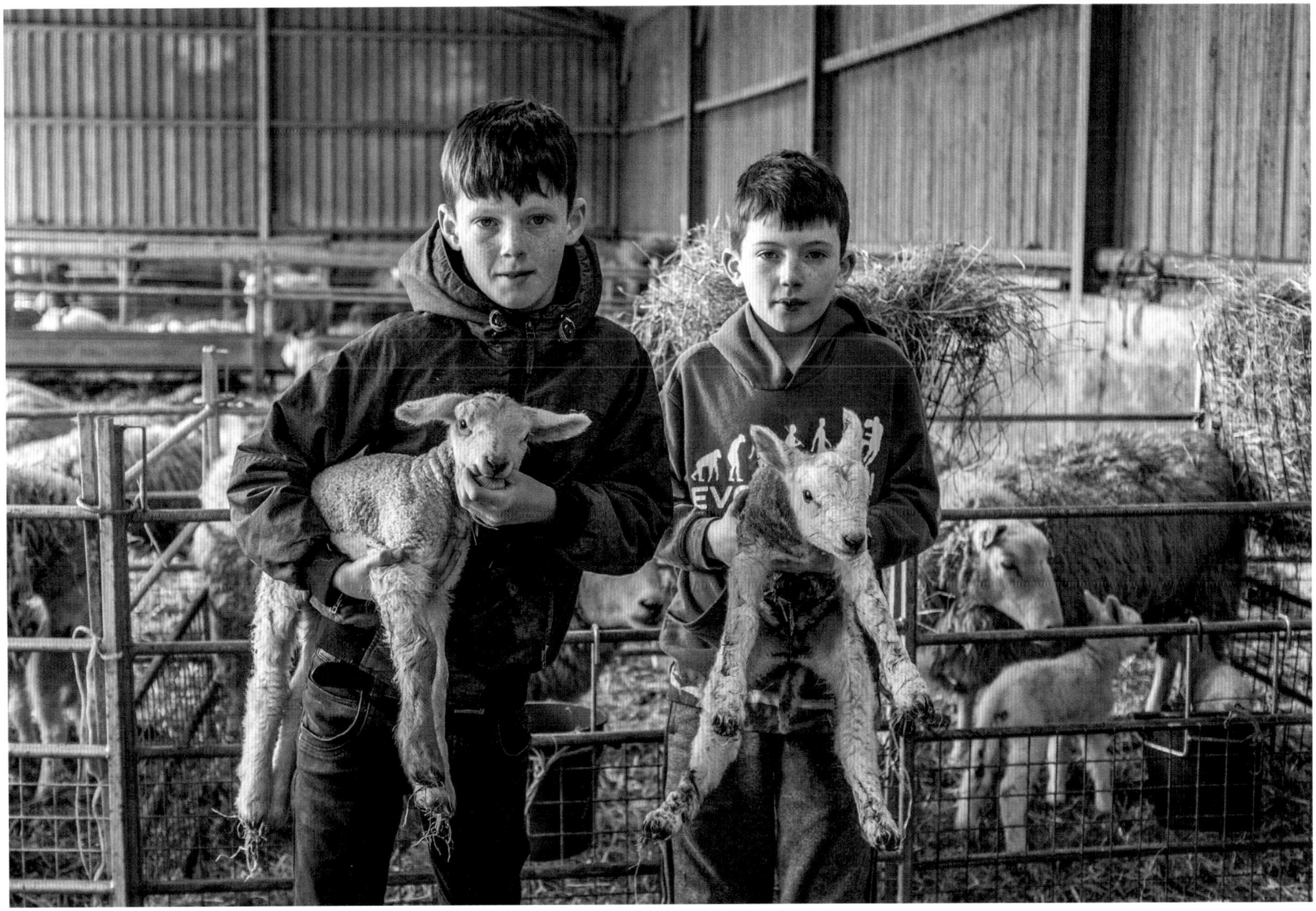

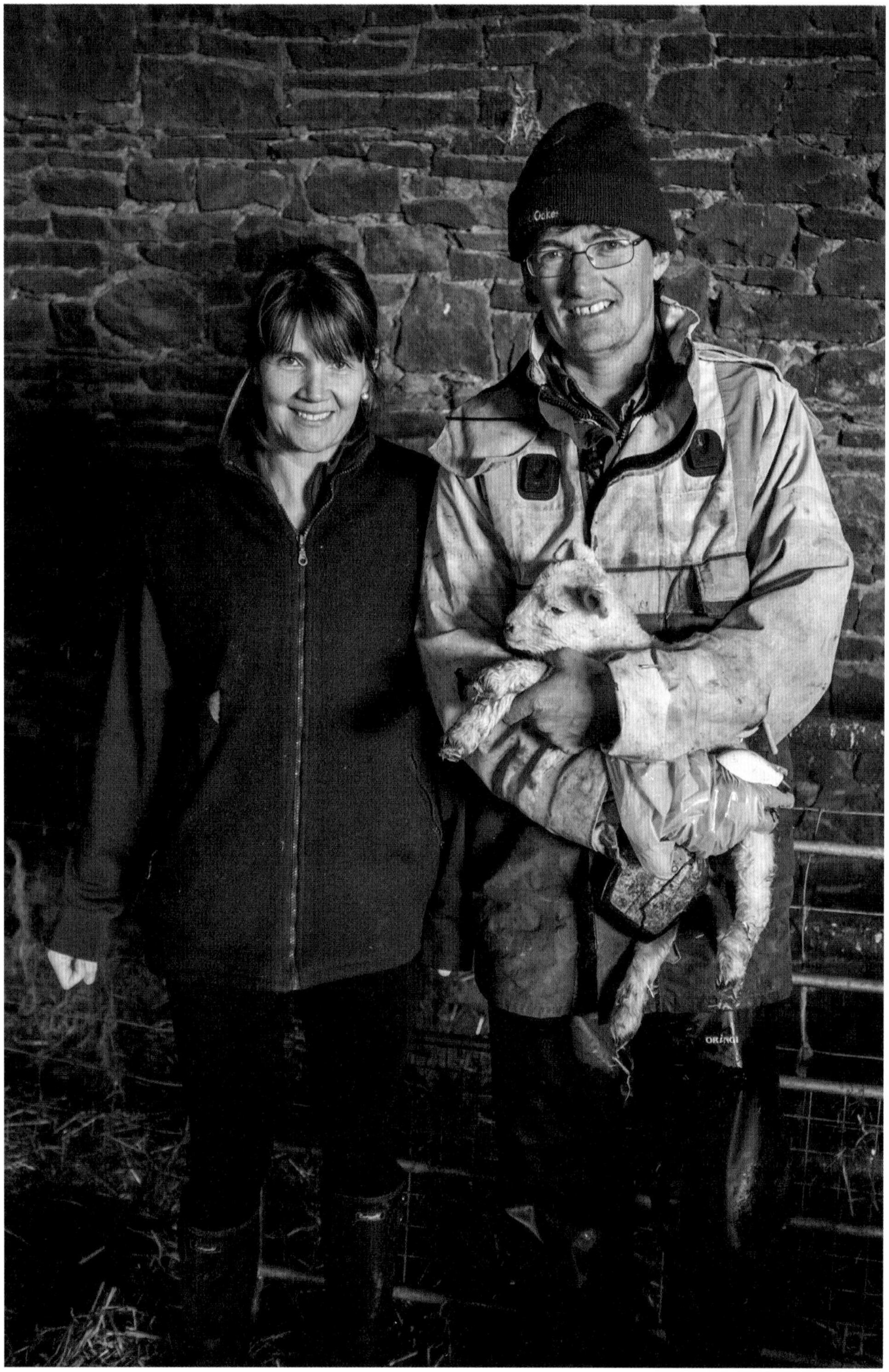

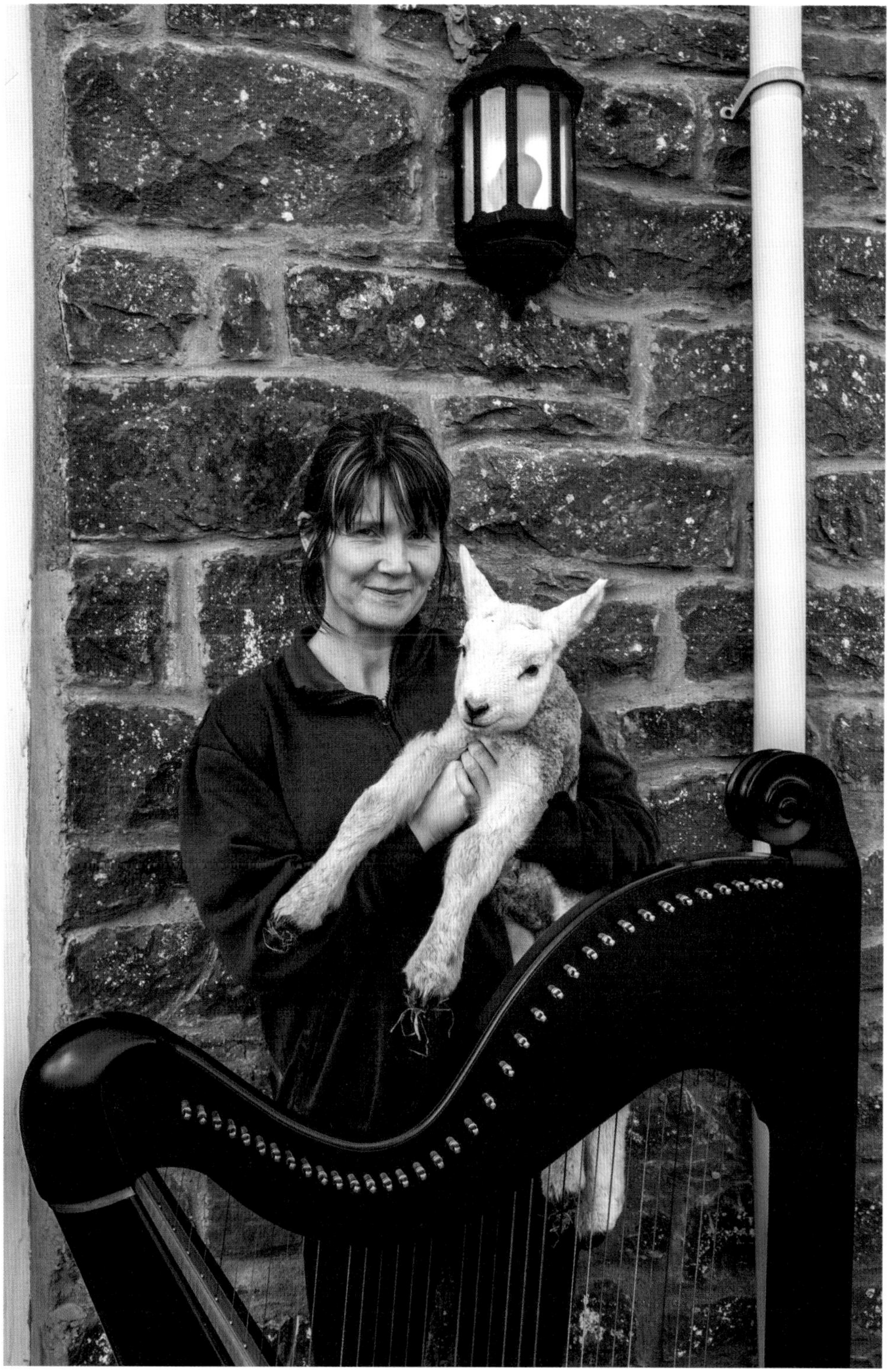

Shearing

Dai 'Coed' Evans

David Evans was born at Coed Gruffydd Farm in Ceredigion, in an area where there were perhaps half a dozen other David Evans who were also involved in the sheep farming business. To avoid predictable confusion the community reverted to a time honoured custom, and included his home farm as part of his name. He became Dai Coed, and that is how he is known to this day. His father and grandfather before him had shepherded in the Bontgoch area, so that name identifies not only him, but generations of his forebears, to those who can understand the code. On his 60th birthday his family bought him a personalised licence plate for his pick-up truck, DA I 60ED. "I love it," he says, "but now when I'm driving around so many people are waving to me, and their vehicles are not so easy for me to recognise for waving back!"

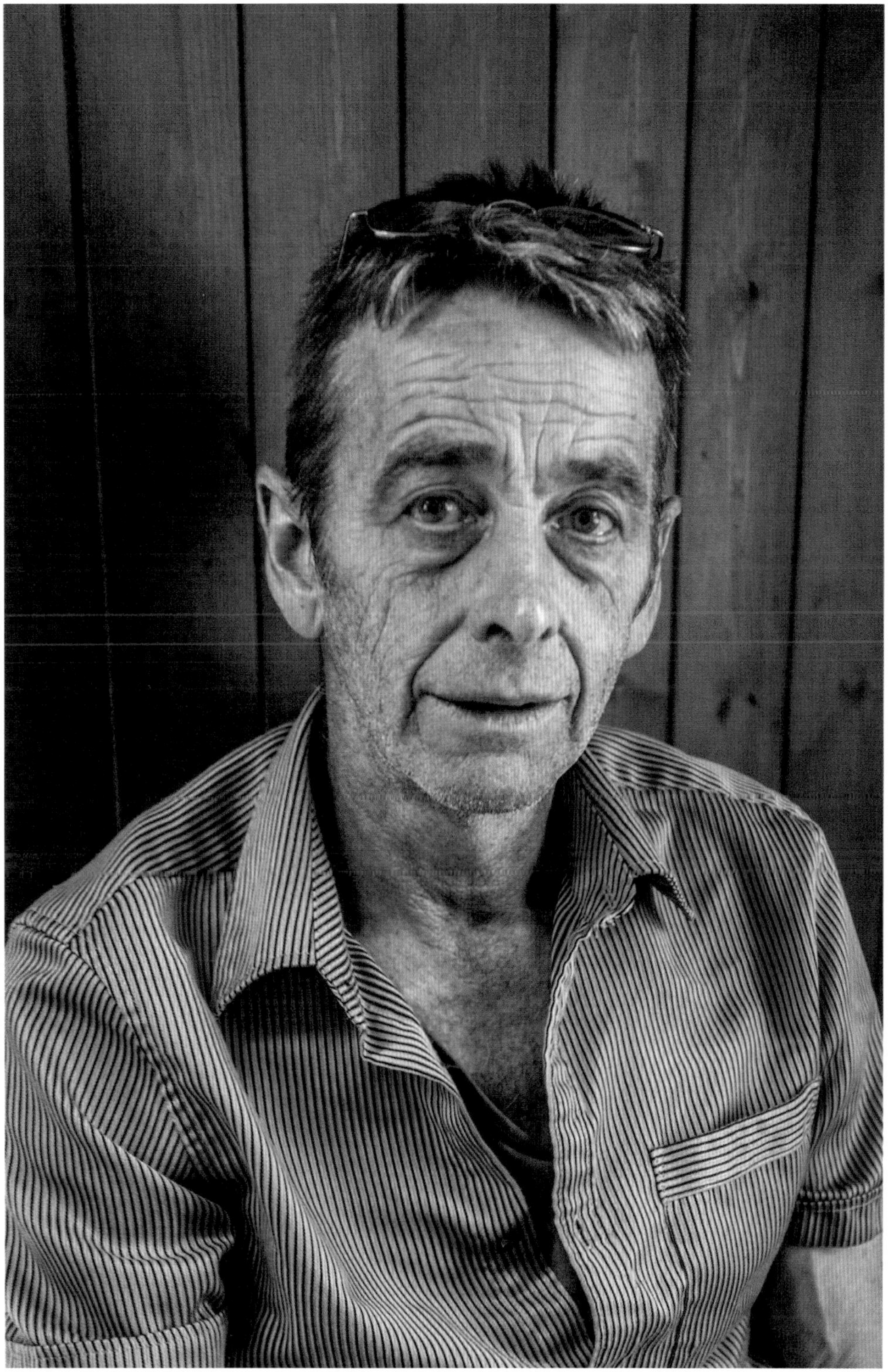

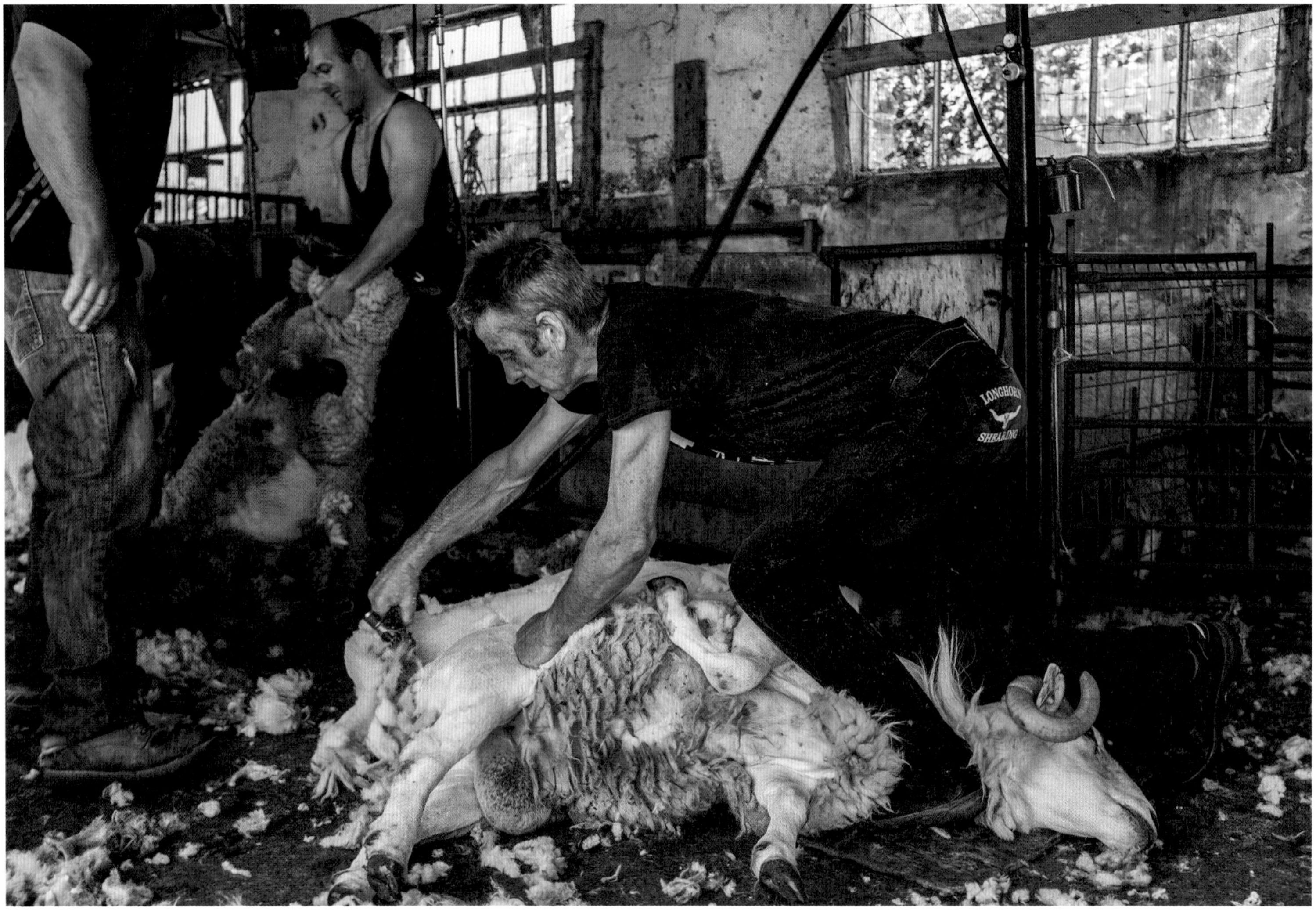
LONGHORN
SHEARING

Dai has put in an amazing shift at shearing sheep; he has not missed a single season in the forty year span leading up to his retirement. This is seriously physically challenging work; watching the gangs the sweat is not running down them, it is flying off them from the speed of their movement. "I thoroughly enjoyed it, and thankfully my health kept going," he says, "because it can be very hard on the back and the hips. It is in my blood, and it gives me great pleasure that my son Rhys is taking it on after me, he will be the fourth generation in our family of gangers in charge of the shearing gangs." There are two distinctly different styles of shearing. In the traditional method favoured by Dai the back is kept straight, while in the new style developed in New Zealand more recently, which Rhys favours, the back is bent and the shearer uses soft shoes for "footwork" in managing the sheep. Dai acknowledges that the new style is quicker... but then his "old school" approach has served him well for forty years.

Contract shearers are paid £1per sheep, and they aim to get through 100 a day, but it is not easy money. Dai himself runs about 800 ewes on three farms, two of which belong to the family and another which they look after for an expatriate Welshman living in England. Together with his son Rhys, Dai also takes on contract fencing. His wife Wendy has contributed to the family finances by working for thirty-eight years in the Aberystwyth jewellery shop owned by the popular Mr T.J. Davies. "The government is too hard on the backbone workers, while those on benefits seem to get a much easier time," Dai complains, "we have had fifteen years of less and less money, along with ever increasing paperwork. Detailed reporting requirements for fallen stock is an awful time-wasting process, when ninety-nine point nine per cent of all shepherds take such good care of their sheep. After all, their quality is what pays you in the end."

“Sheep farming has gone more lonely than it was twenty years ago,” Dai reflects, “as farmers have mechanised and become more independent of each other. Forty years ago you would get fed on every farm where you went to shear as a contractor, and because we were being paid by the farmer at a price per sheep regardless of time we took, the lunch break was a leisurely sociable time. That custom is disappearing, especially in the last fifteen years, with all the pressures now to earn money. People used to have more time to enjoy life.”

“I have a grand daughter now, though, and perhaps she will be the fifth generation at the work....”

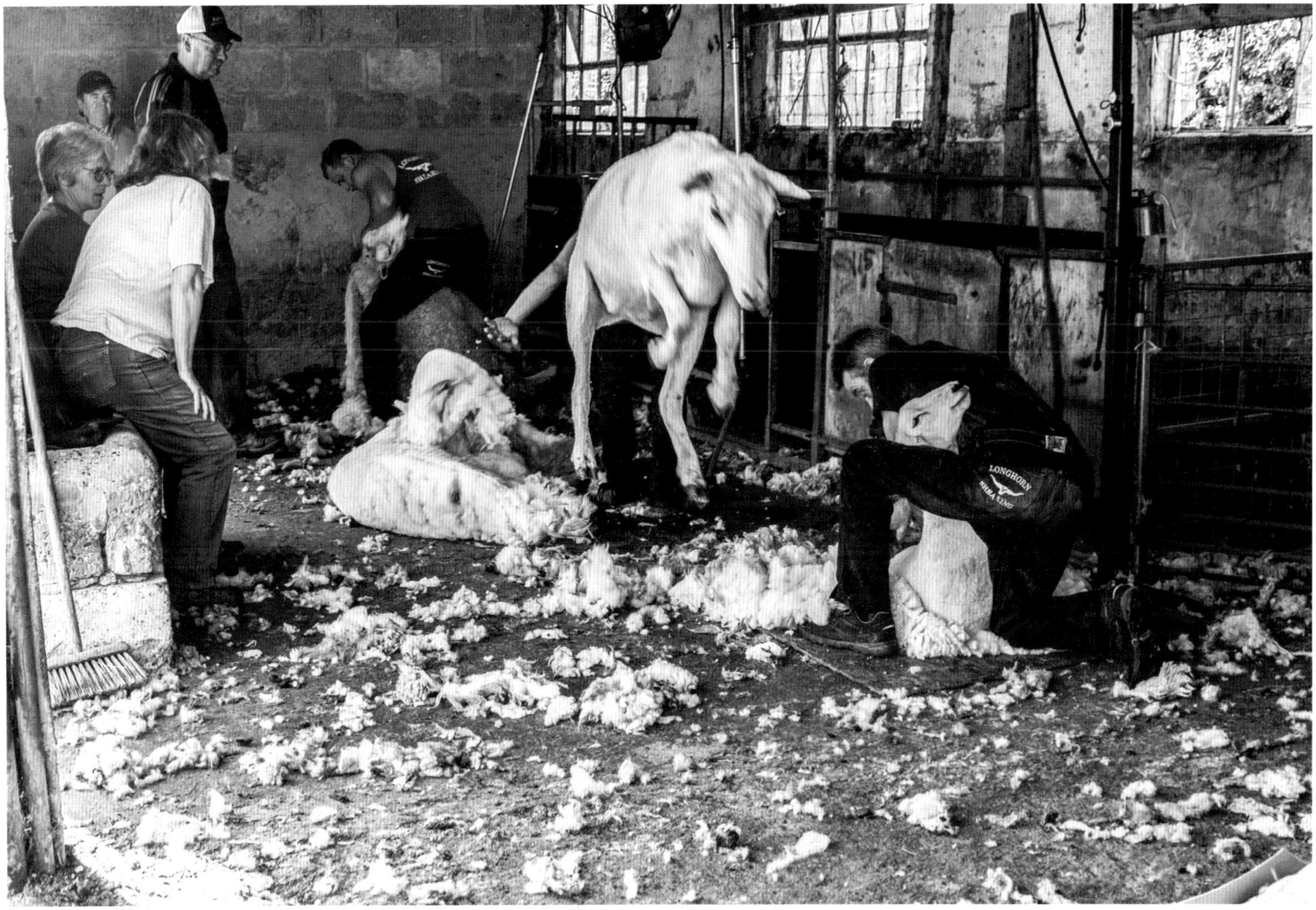

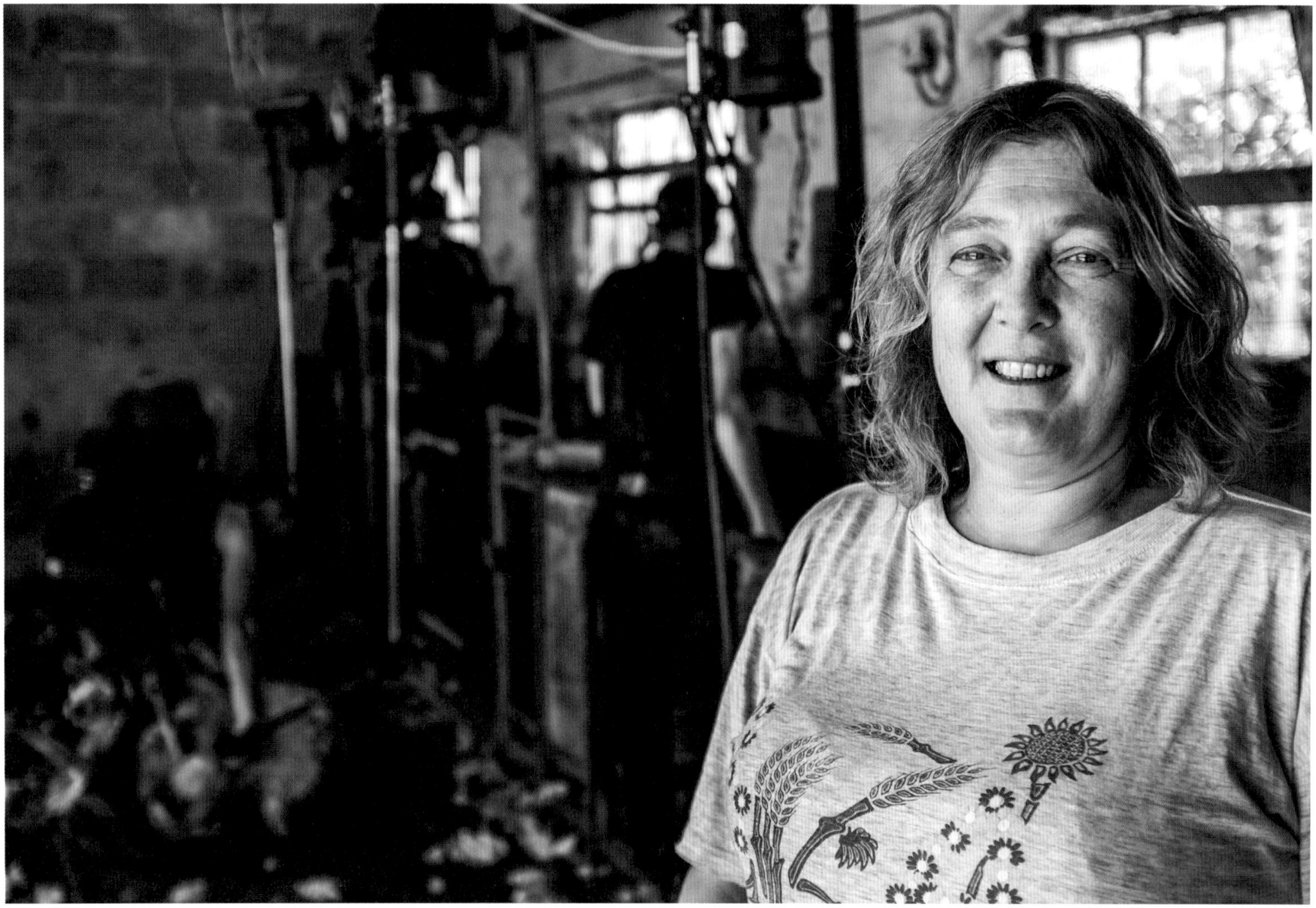

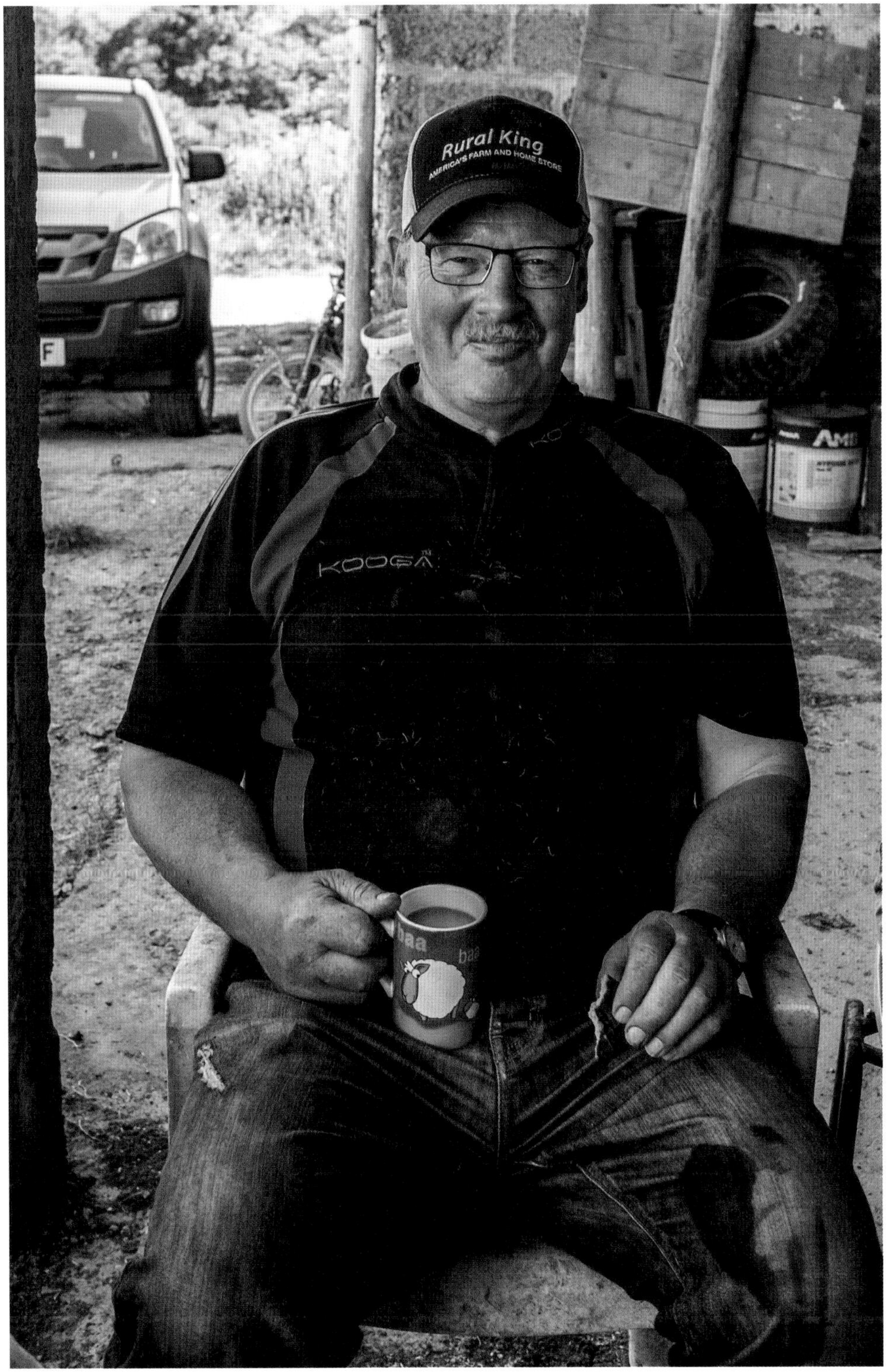
Rural King
AMERICA'S FARM AND HOME STORE
KOOGA
baa
baa

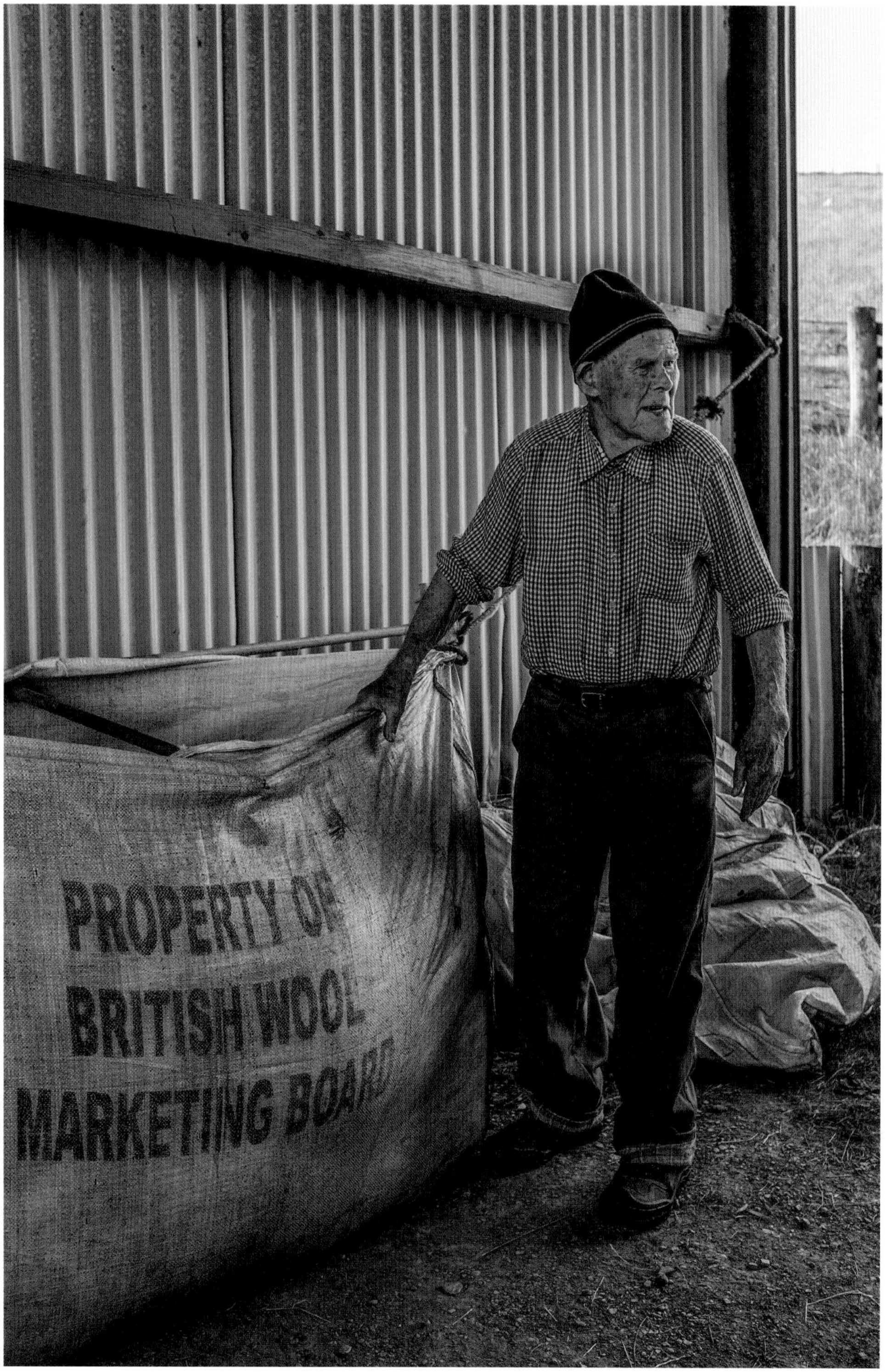
PROPERTY OF
BRITISH WOOL
MARKETING BOARD

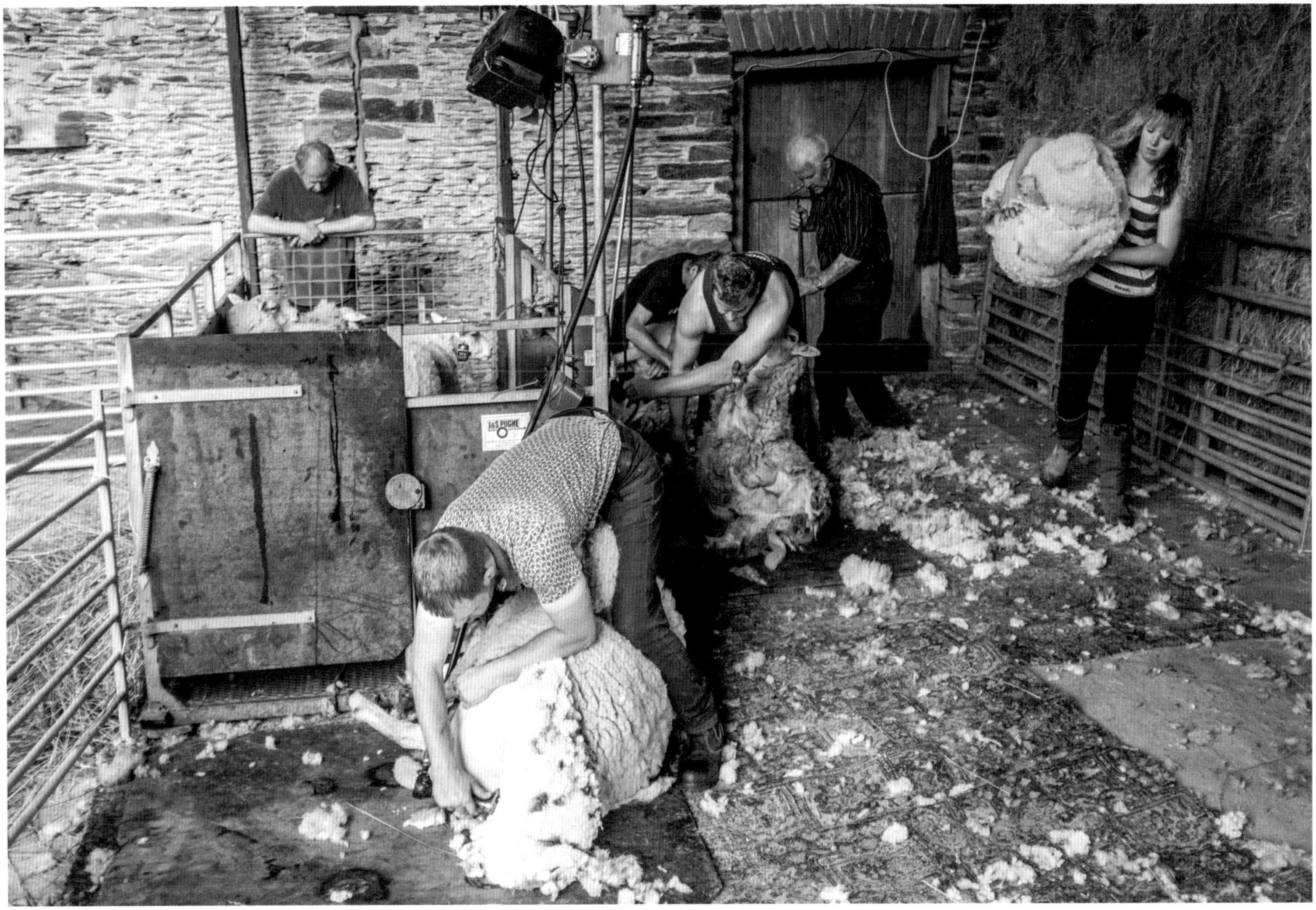

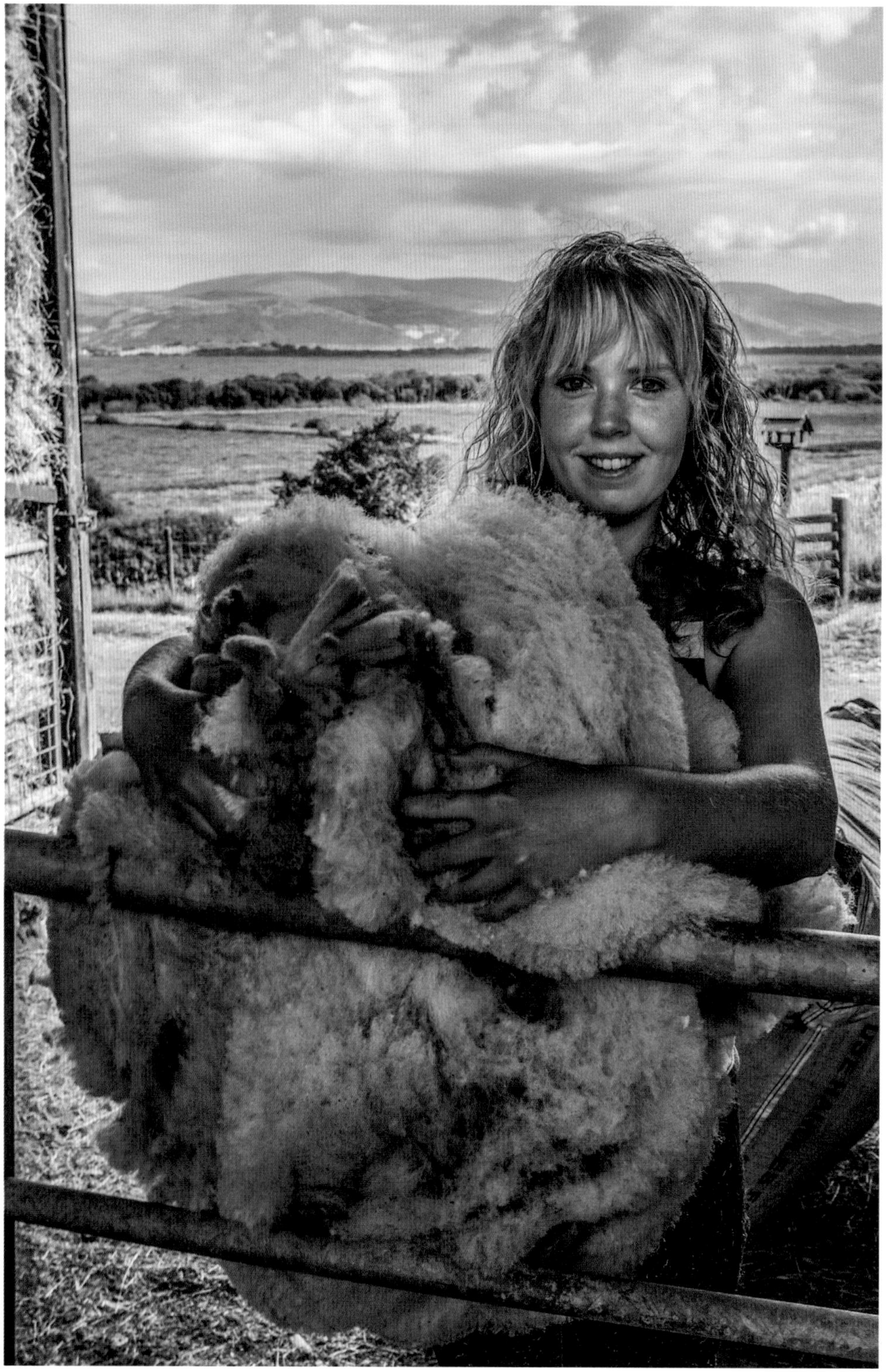

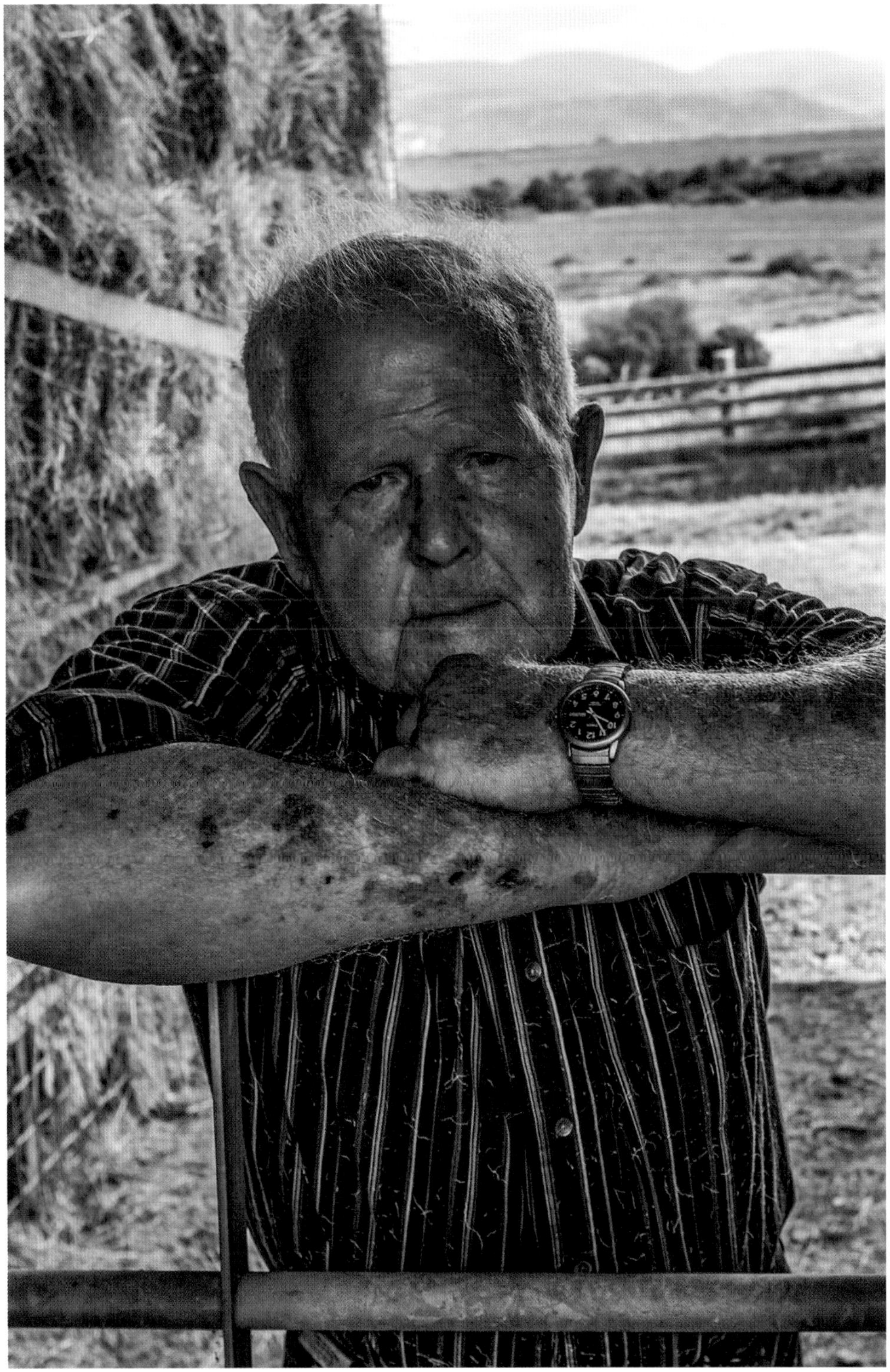

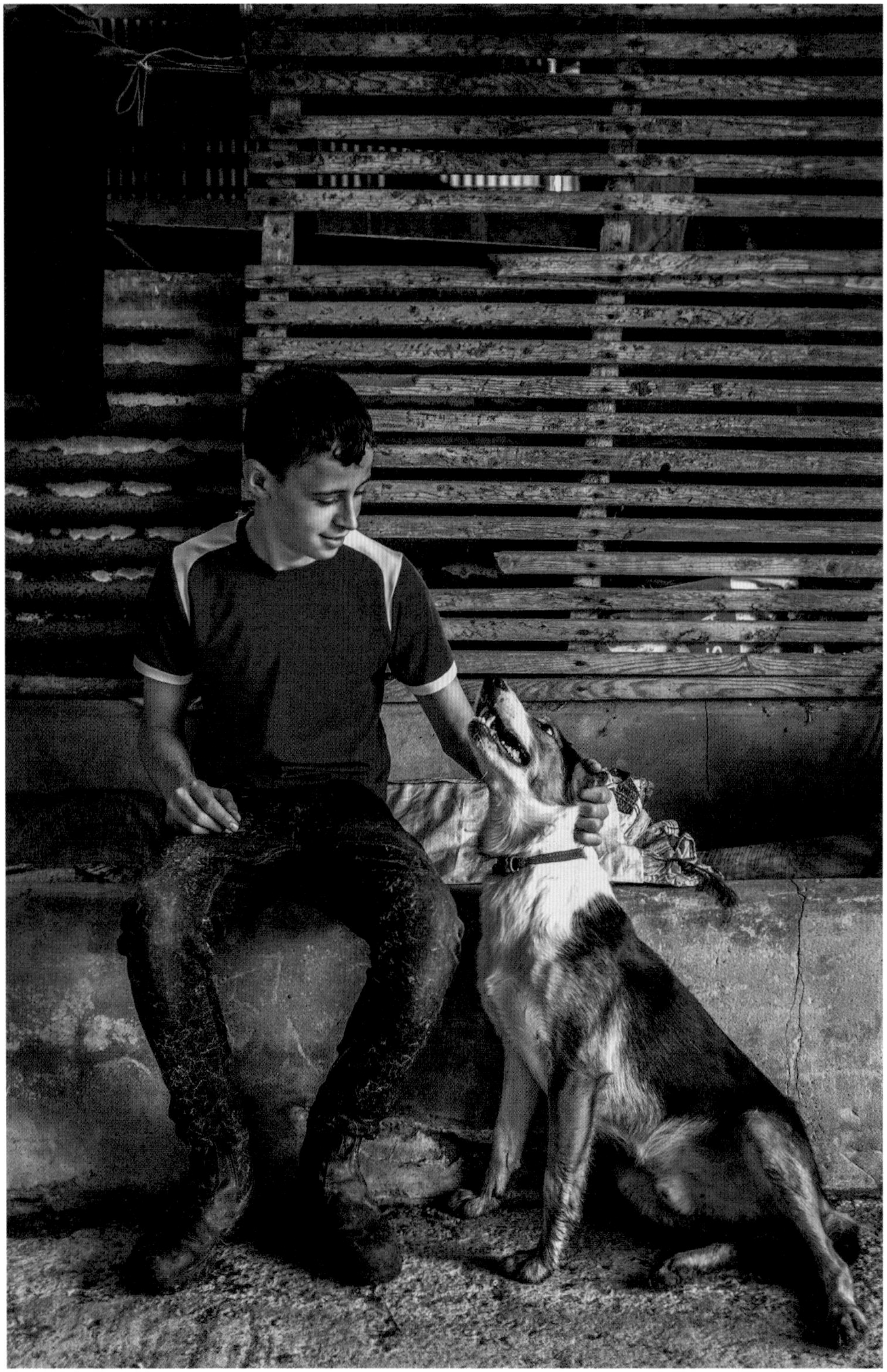

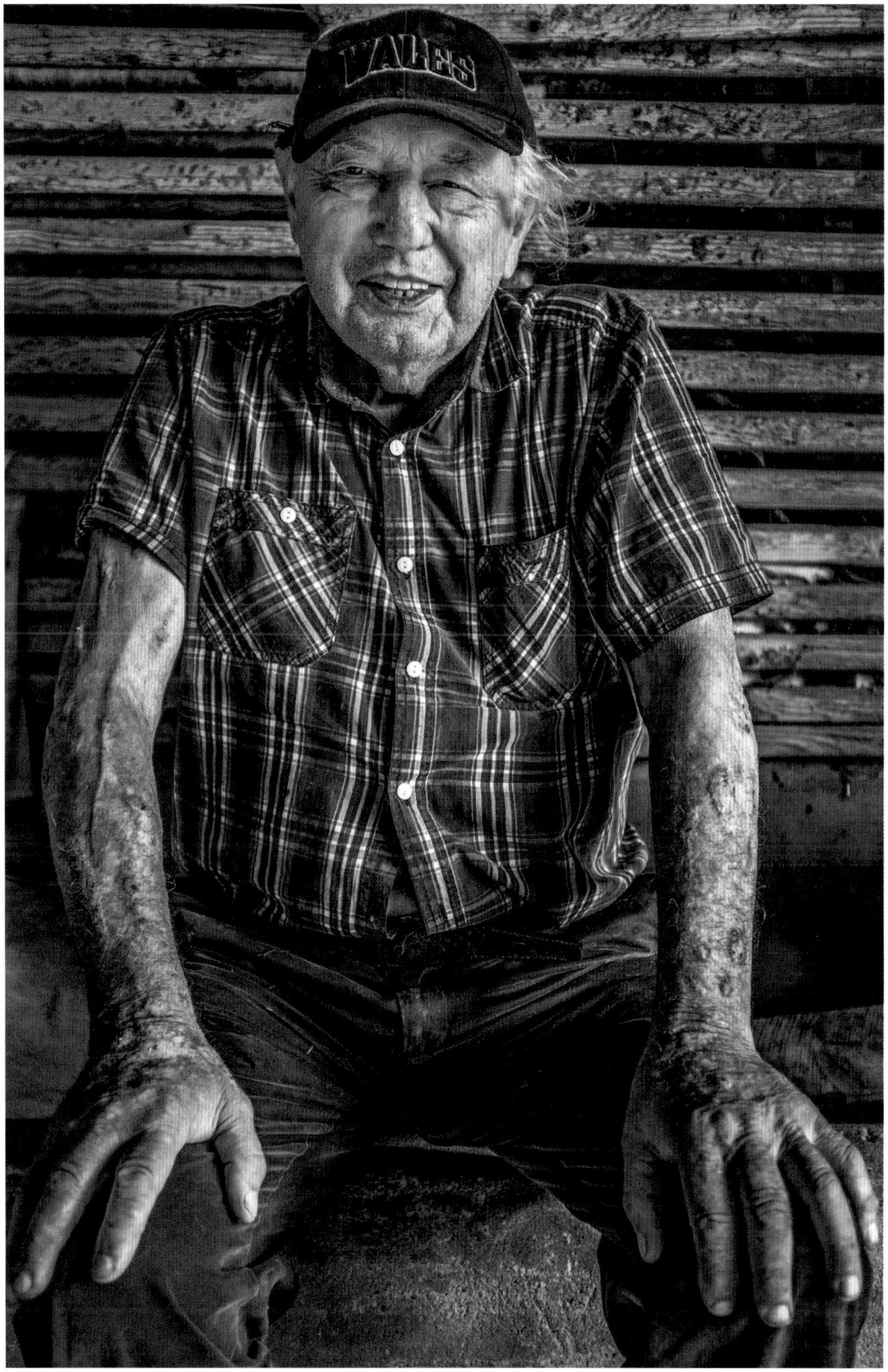
WALES

Dipping

Hefin, Siôn and Cameron, Neuadd Fawr

Dipping is an essential procedure in the humane and practicable management of sheep. If it were not carried out in a timely and effective manner the health of the animals would deteriorate in a quite distressing way, as they become prone to a variety of nasty conditions caused by mites, blowflies, ticks, and lice. Immersing the sheep in a bath containing a mixture of insecticides and fungicides treats the animals against these.

Historically in Wales farms had a dipping bath dug into the ground through which sheep were funneled to be treated, but due to genuine environmental concerns about the toxic waste liquid finding a way into water courses when it was disposed of, an alternative arrangement such as the method pictured here is now usual.

Cameron works for a contracting company, towing a mobile dipping unit around the local farms, and the dipping mix which fills the bath is stored in large plastic vats with metal frames for use on the next occassion. This does away with the need to dispose of the dipping wash after each usage.

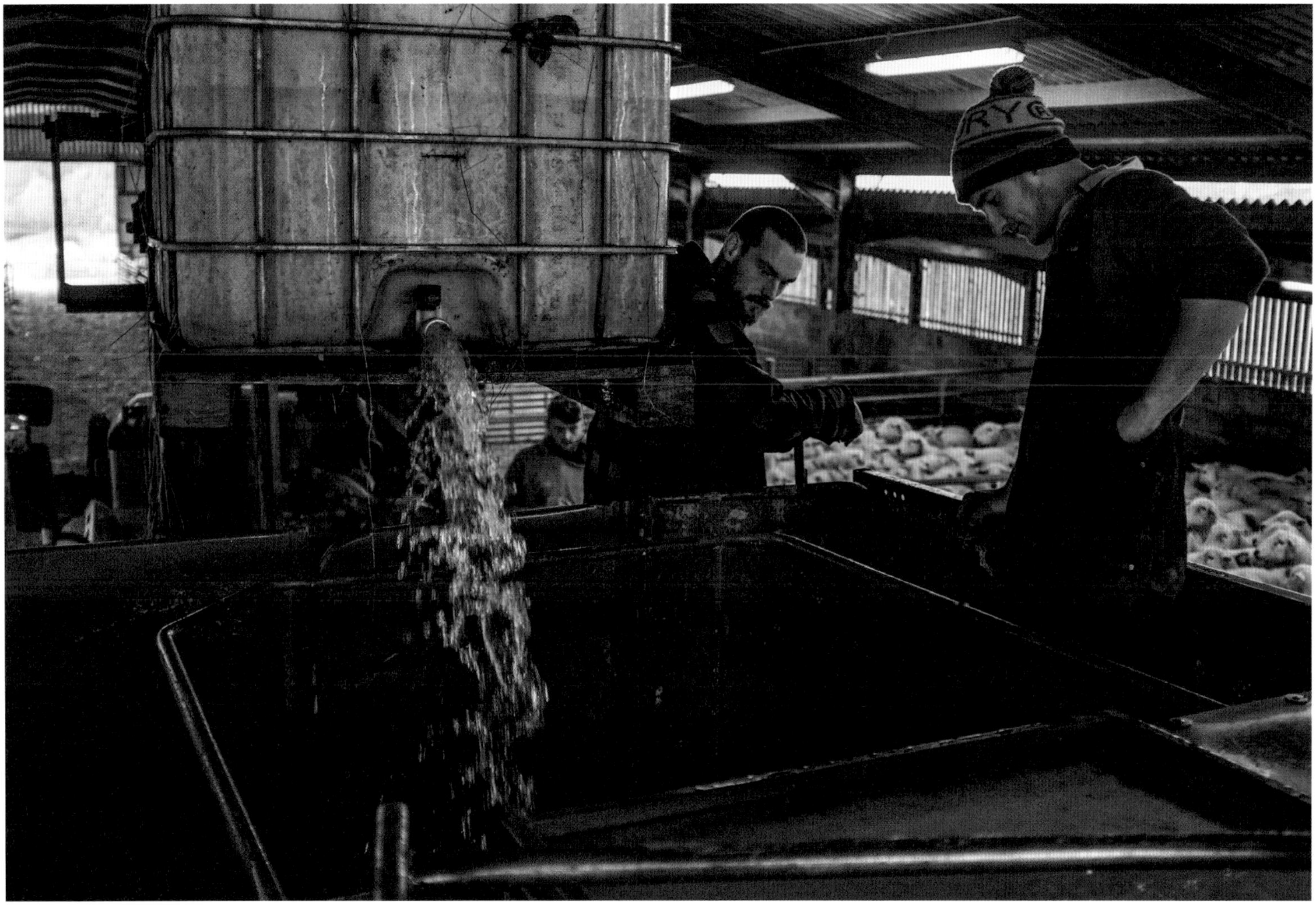

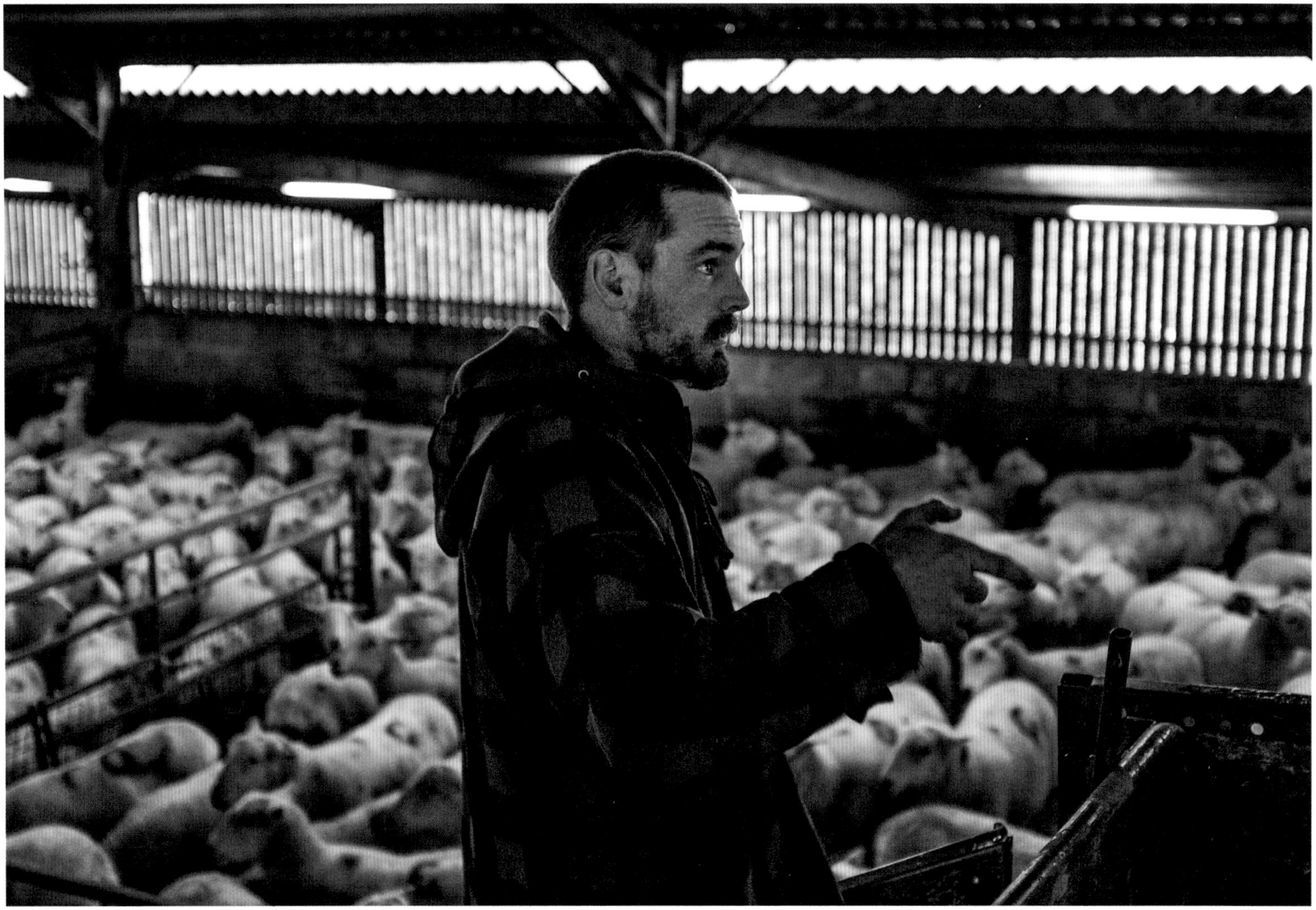

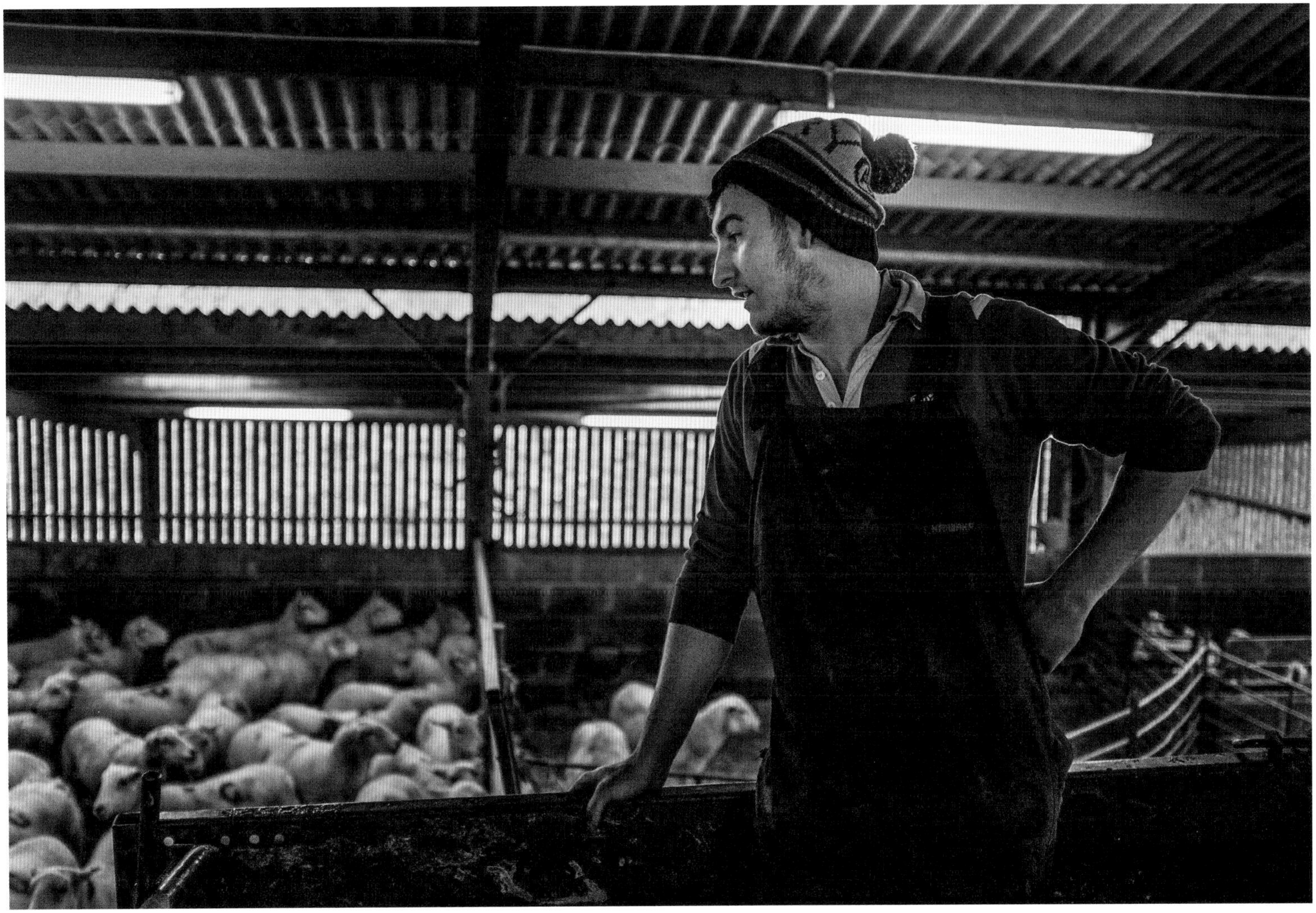

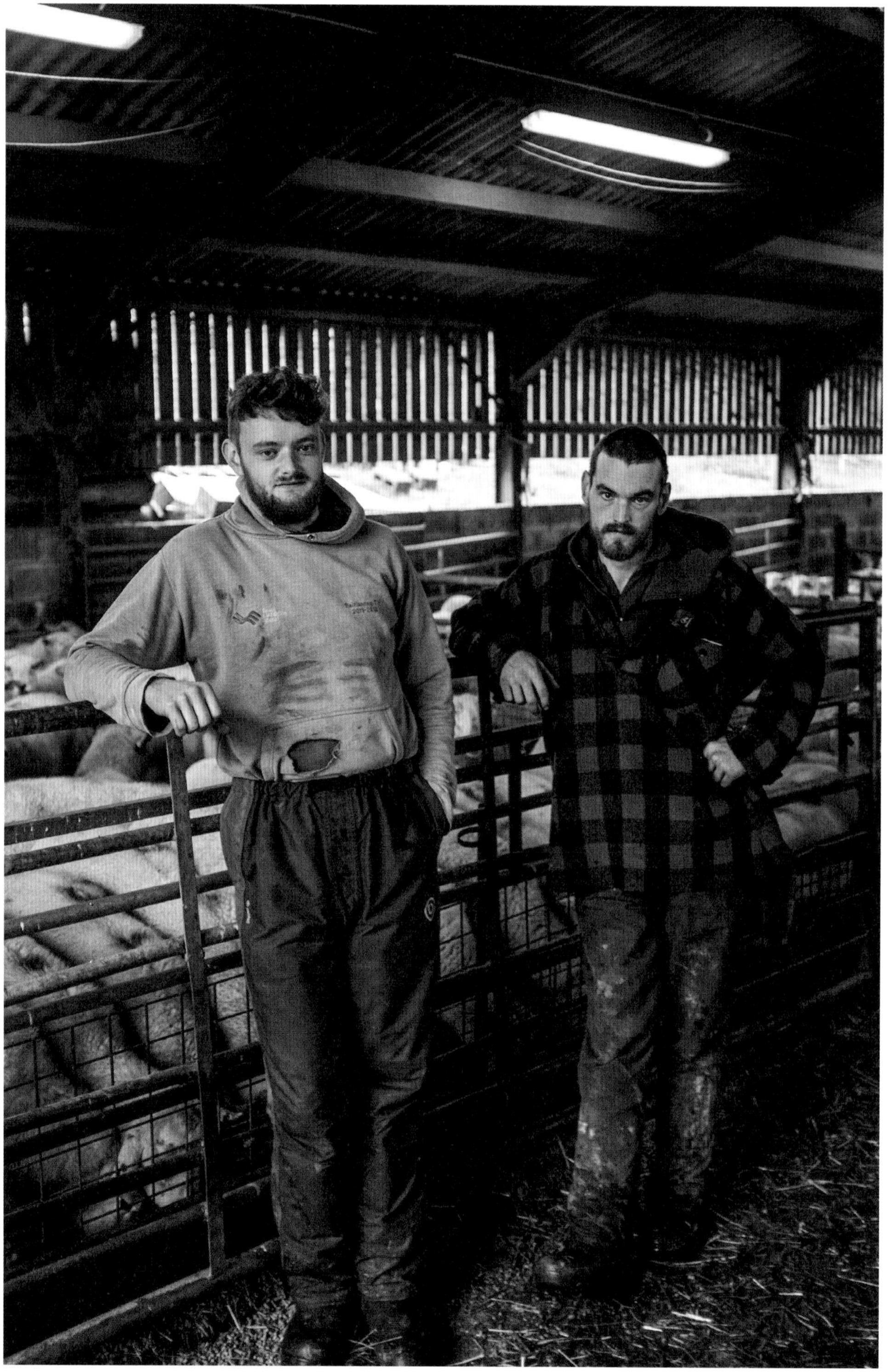

Trialling

I was introduced to Elin Hope by Dai Nutting of the Welsh Mountain Sheep Society, and was subsequently invited to an informal training day for young trials dogs which her family organised at their Gilfach Y Fran farm. Although young in years, Elin has a well respected ability in the training of sheepdogs, both for trials and general work. Interestingly she feels that her training style is not so compatible with the harder and pushier Huntaway style of dog, but better suited to the Border Collie type.

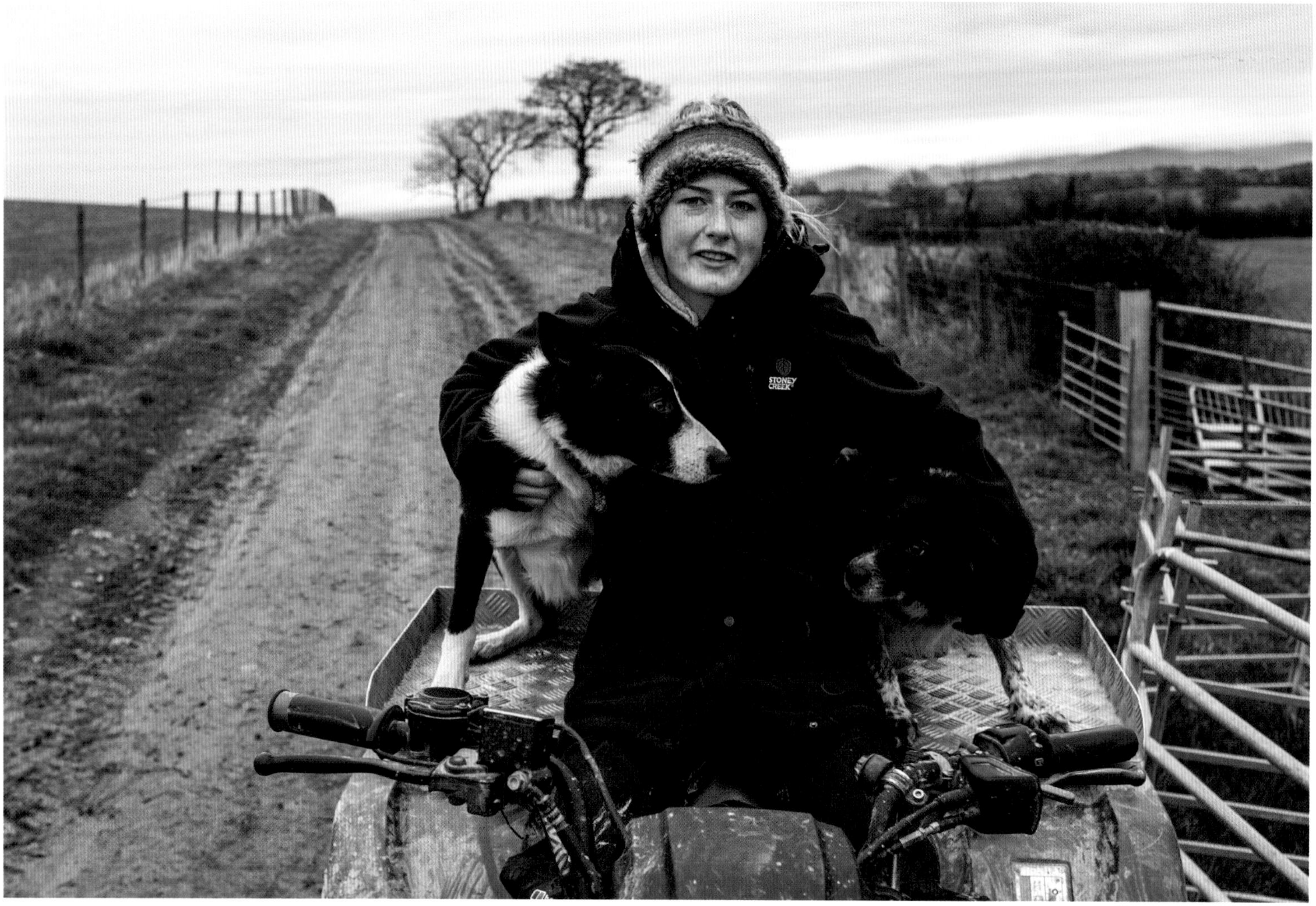

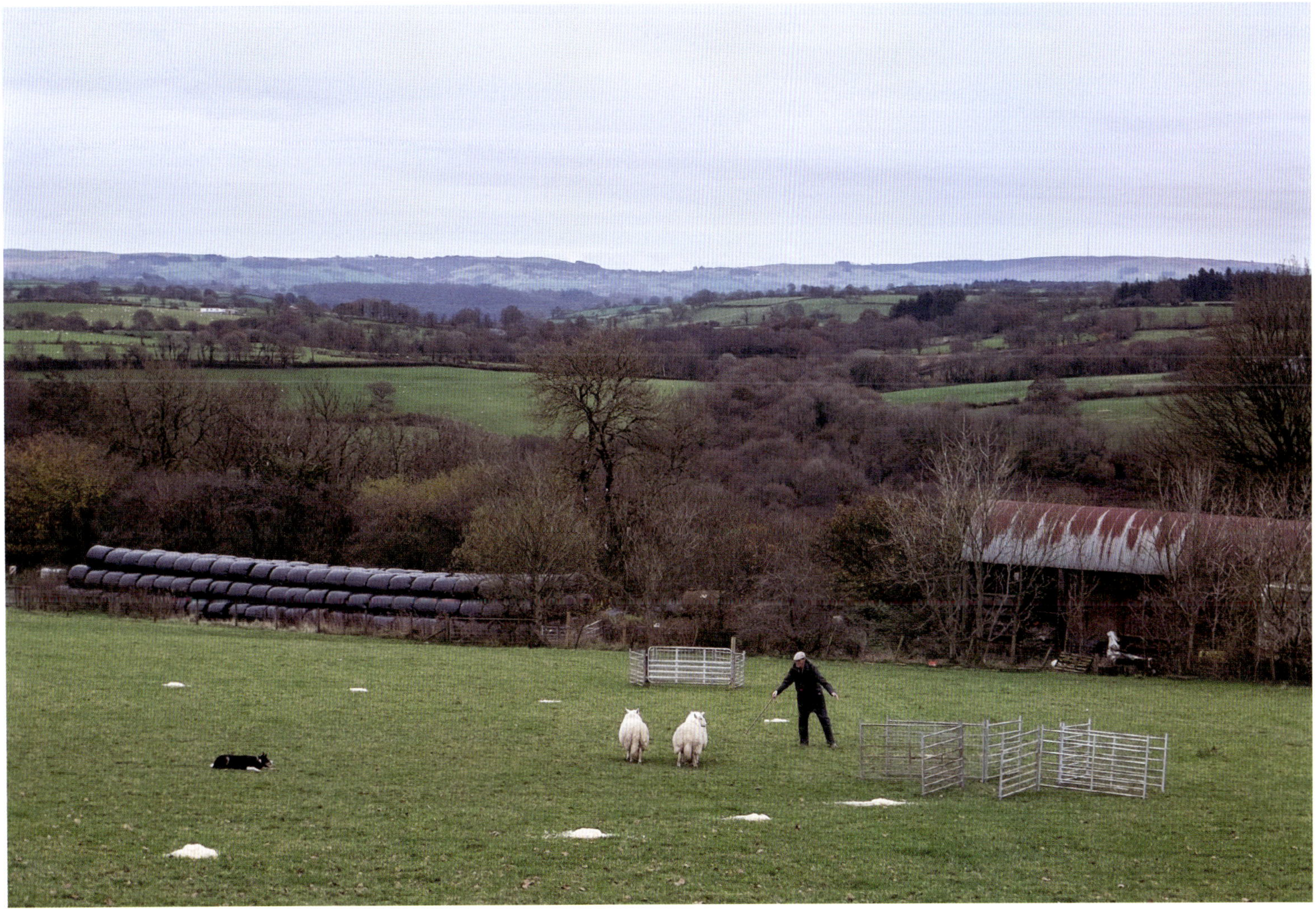

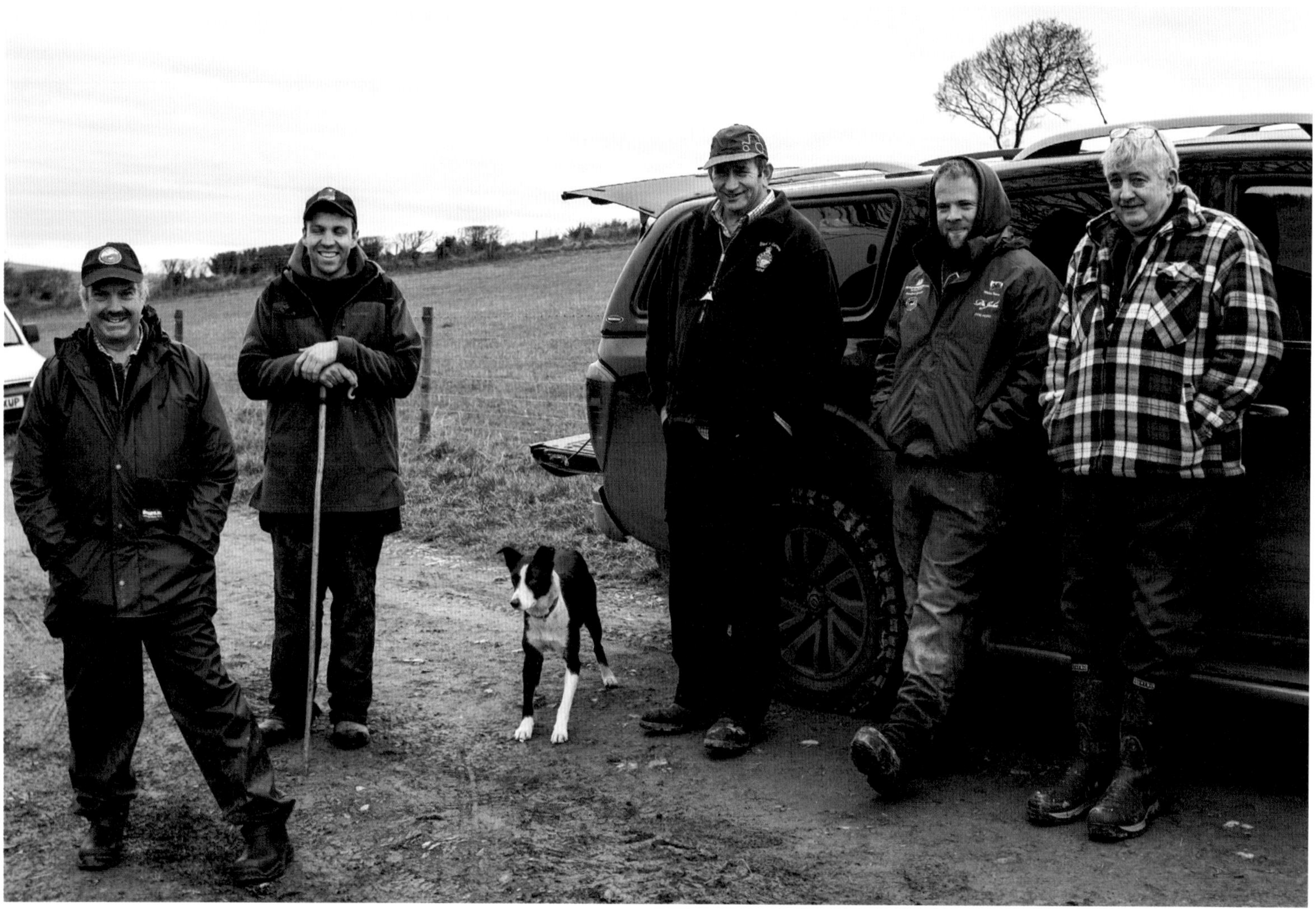

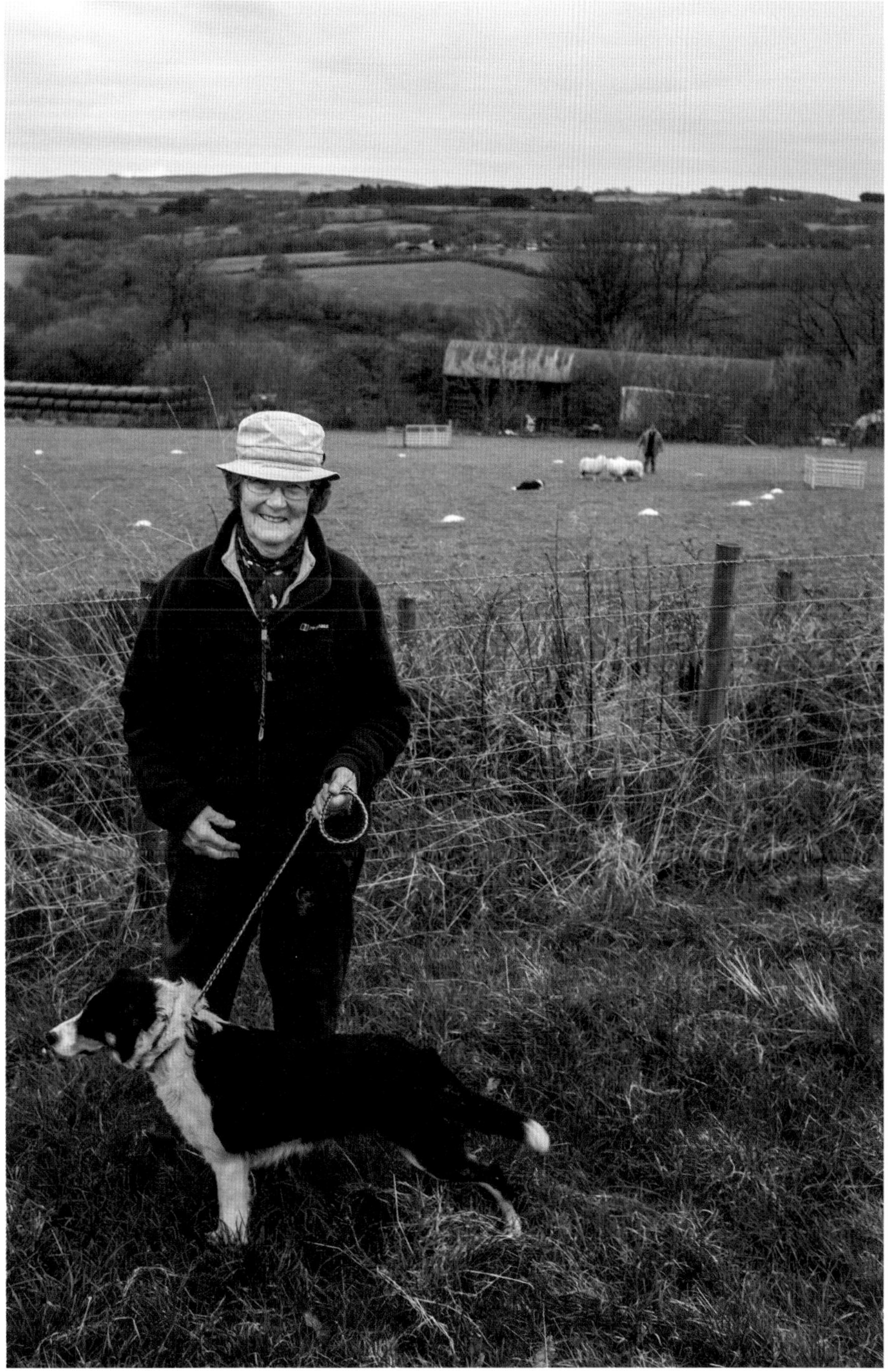

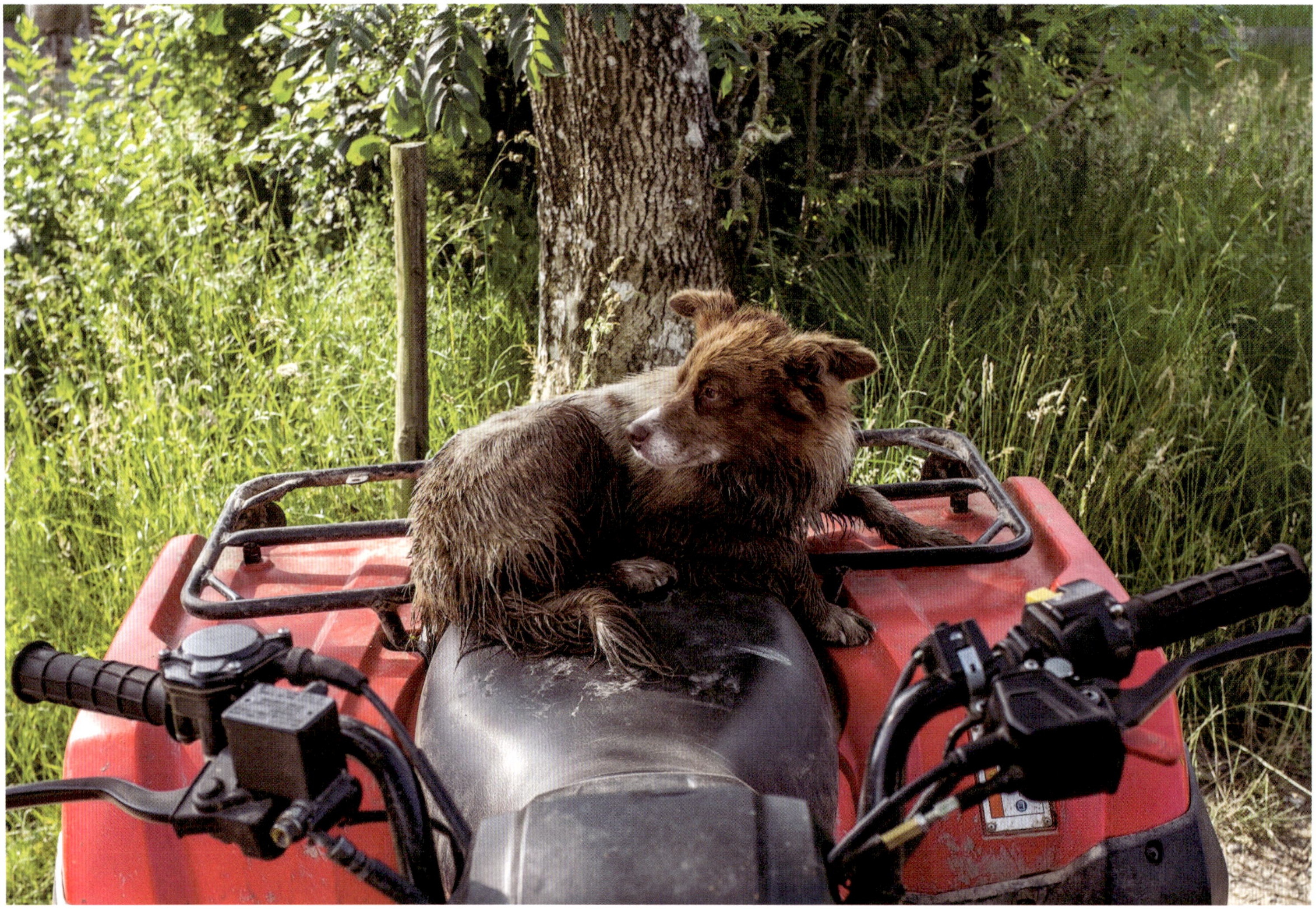

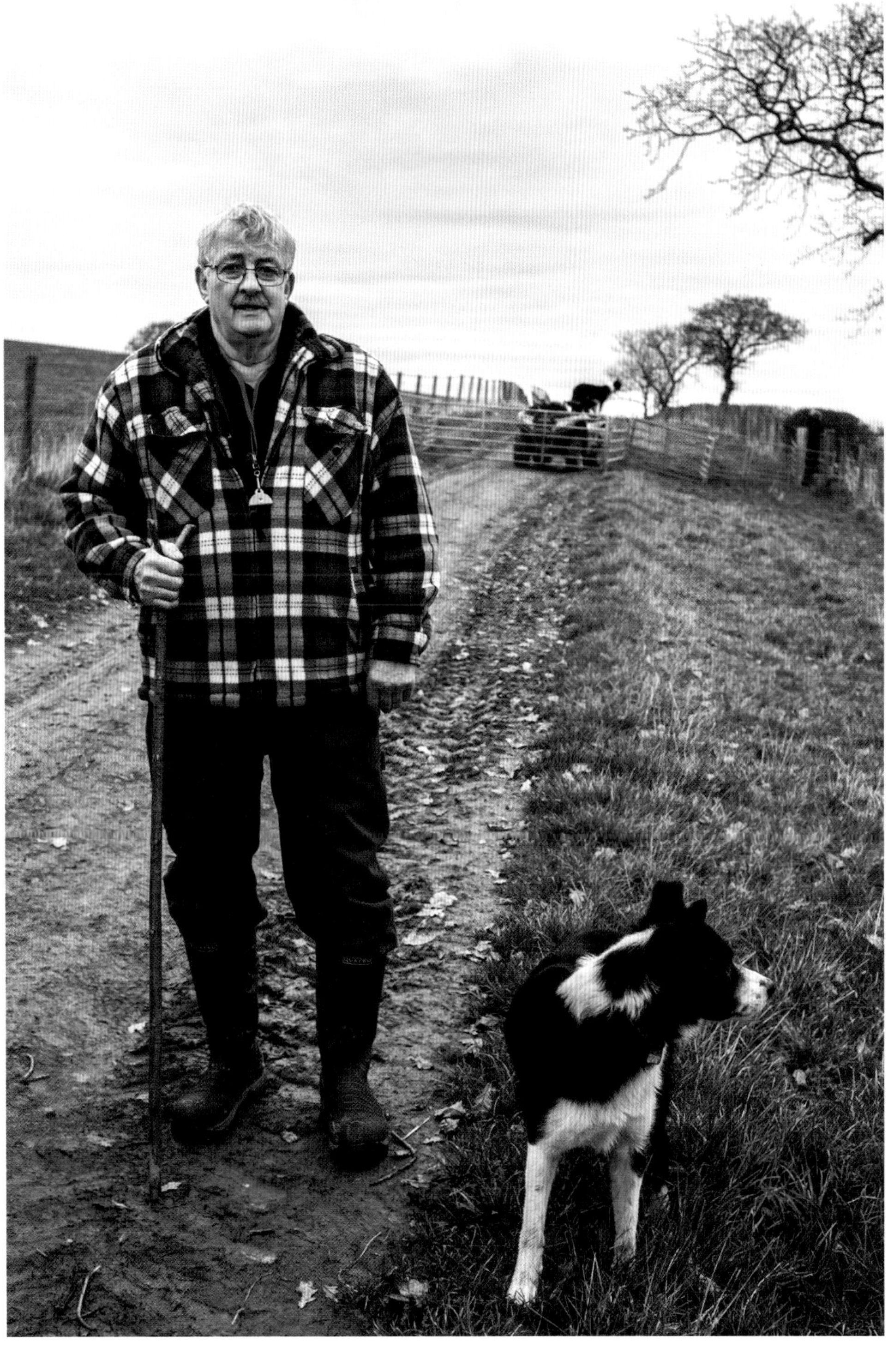

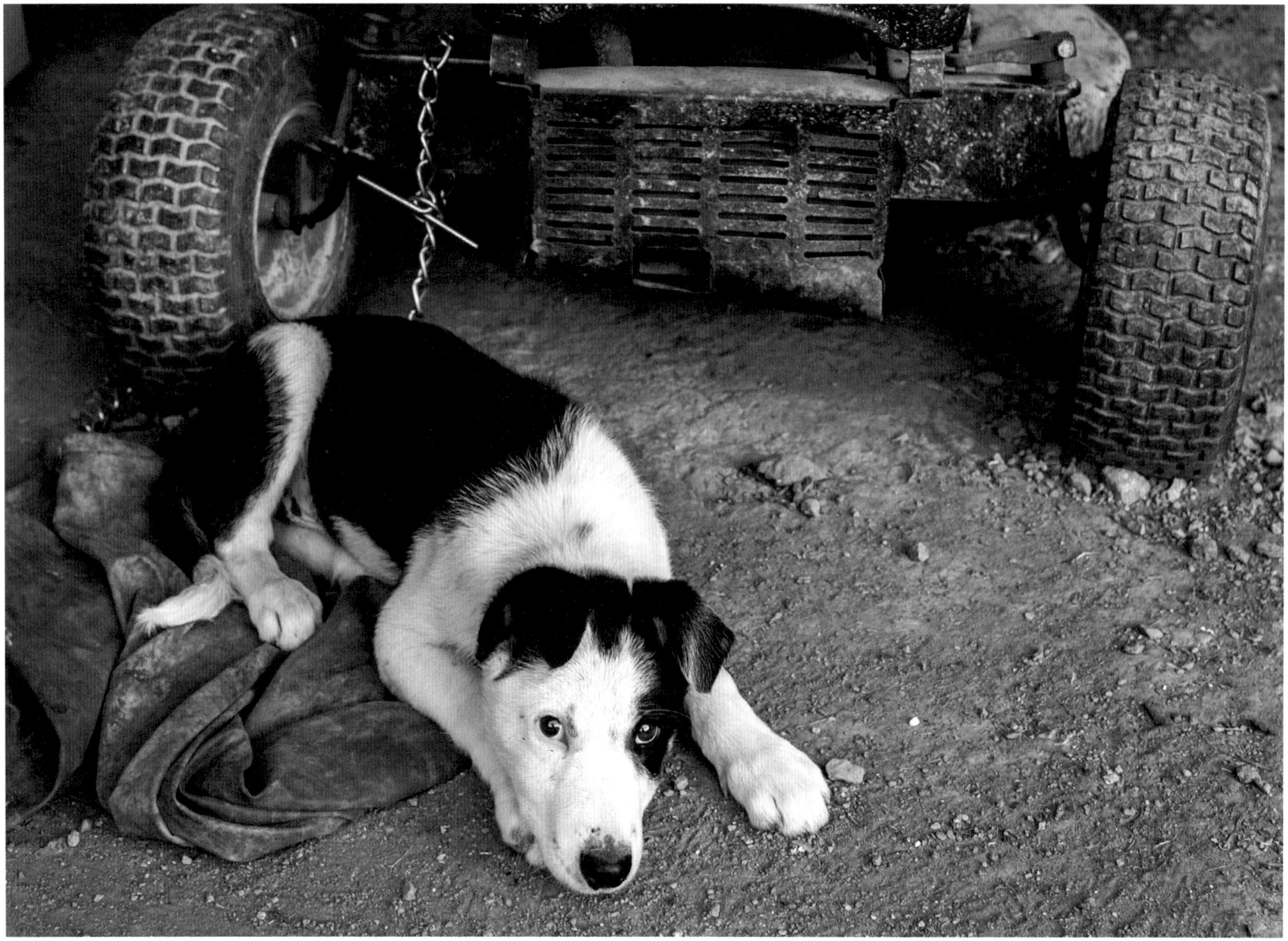

Showing

Sheep farming can mean working in an isolated rural location, either alone or with a small family group. However picturesque your surroundings, and however convivial that group, there still exists the need for occasional outside socialisation. Showing provides the livestock breeding community with an opportunity to travel elsewhere, and to meet other like-minded people. It also provides an important chance to compare notes with other well-informed practitioners regarding bloodlines, market prices, and the general state of the industry.

Across the country there is a network of small local shows, many of which retain an "Olde Worlde" charm reminiscent of the James Herriot television shows. As well as the many classes of livestock judging there are homely competitions for flower arranging, jam making, vegetable growing, stick making and many other rural domestic skills.

The showing highlight of the year in Wales is undoubtedly the Royal Welsh Show, held every July at Llanelwedd near Builth Wells, and for many shepherding families the Royal Welsh week is their annual holiday. The huge permanent showground hosts a wide variety of commercial stands, retail stalls, refreshment kiosks, and spectacular shows in the main rings, with too much going on to really take in over the space of one day.

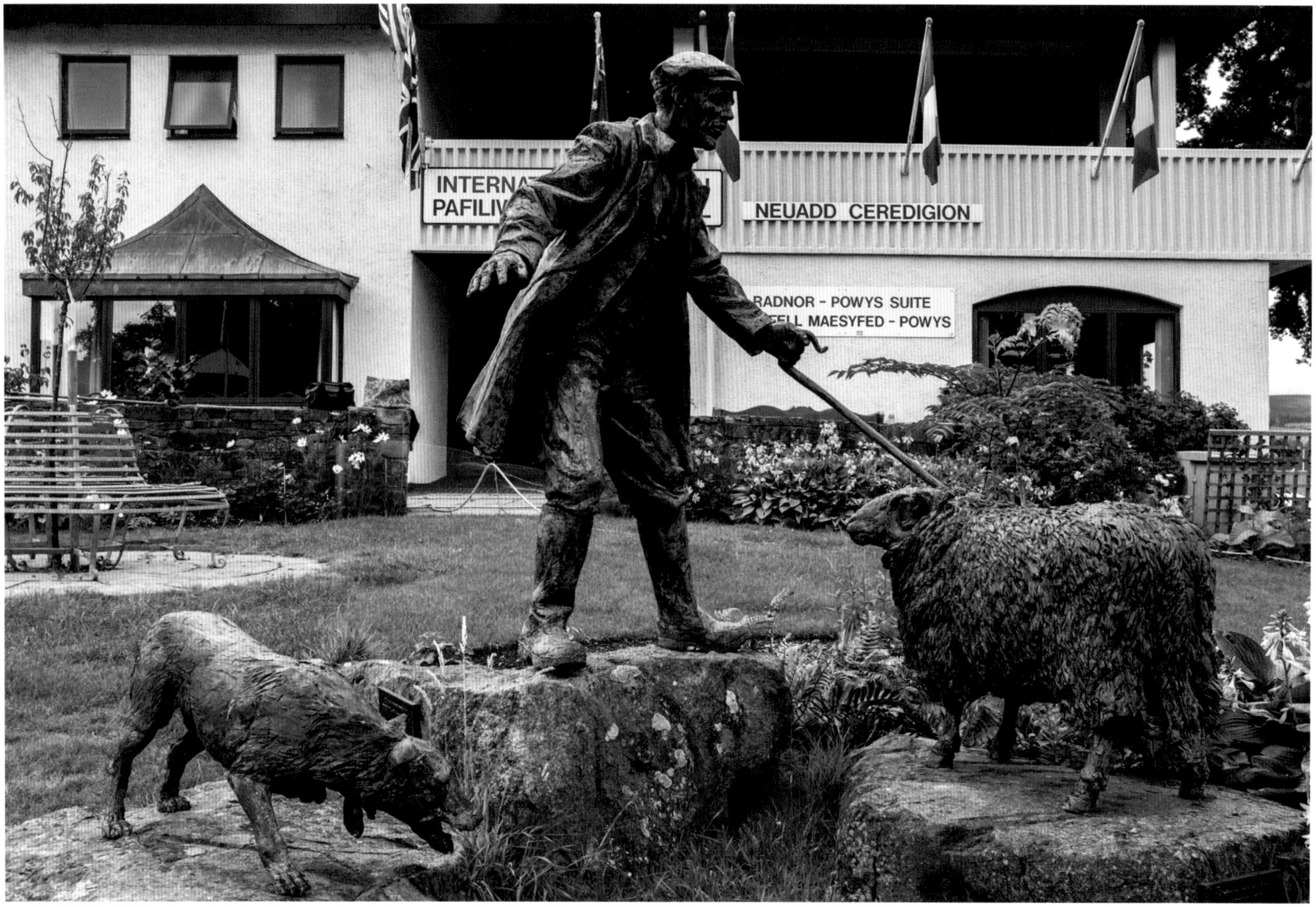
NEUADD CEREDIGION
RADNOR - POWYS SUITE

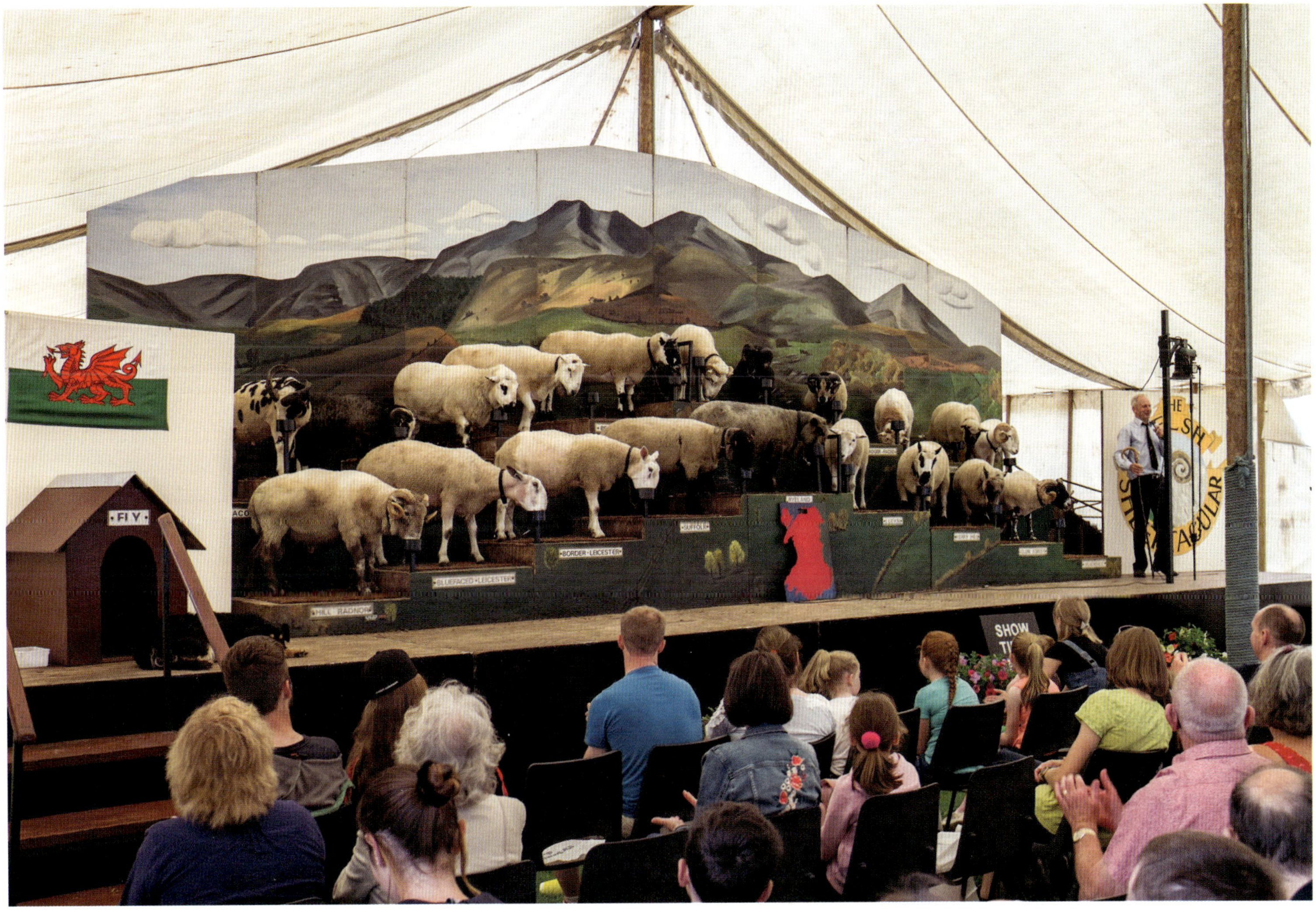
FIY
BORDER LEICESTER
BLUEFACED LEICESTER
HILL RADNOR
SUFFOLK
RYELAND
SHOW

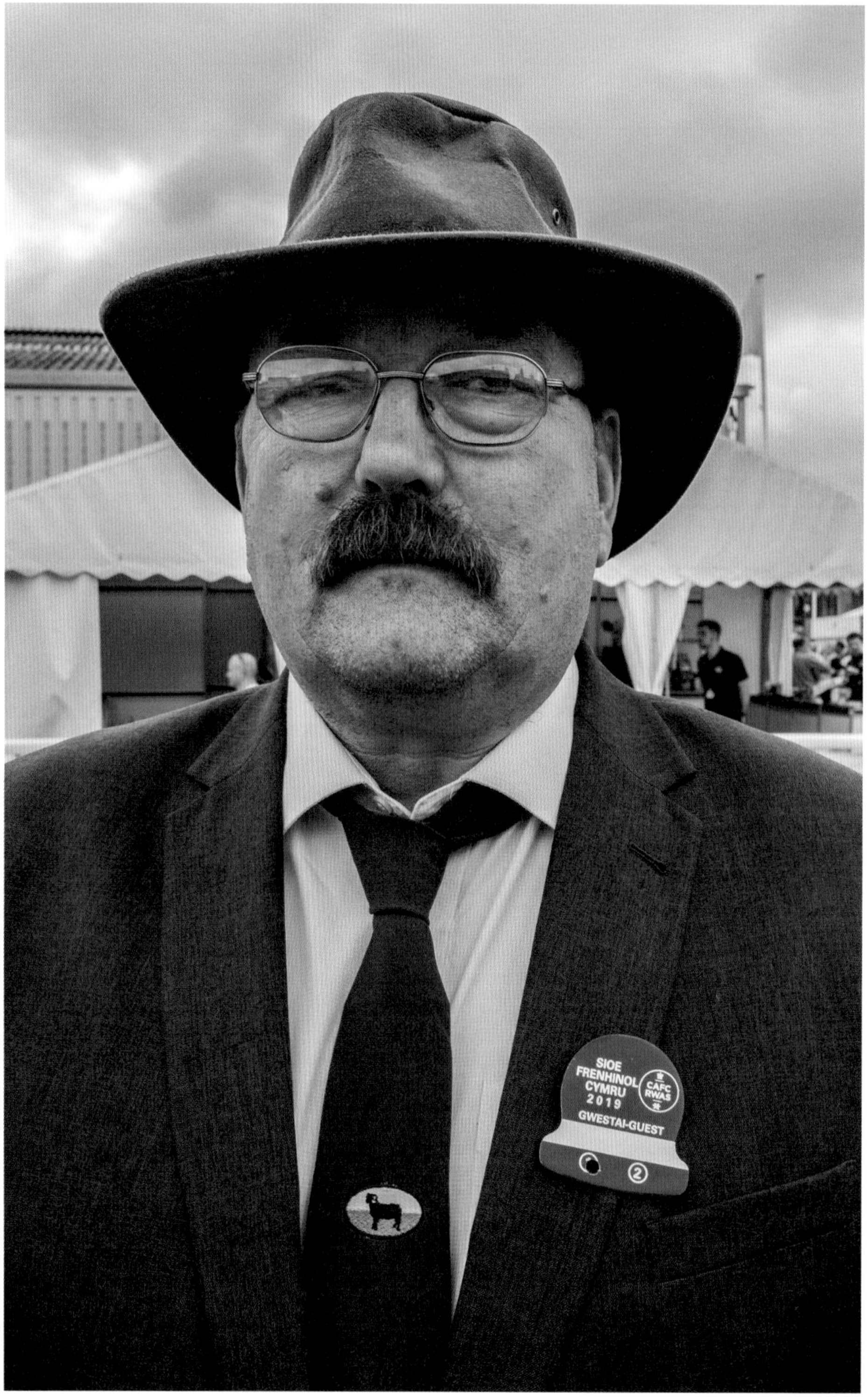
SIOE
FRENHINOL
CYMRU
2019
CAFC
RWAS
GWESTAI-GUEST
2

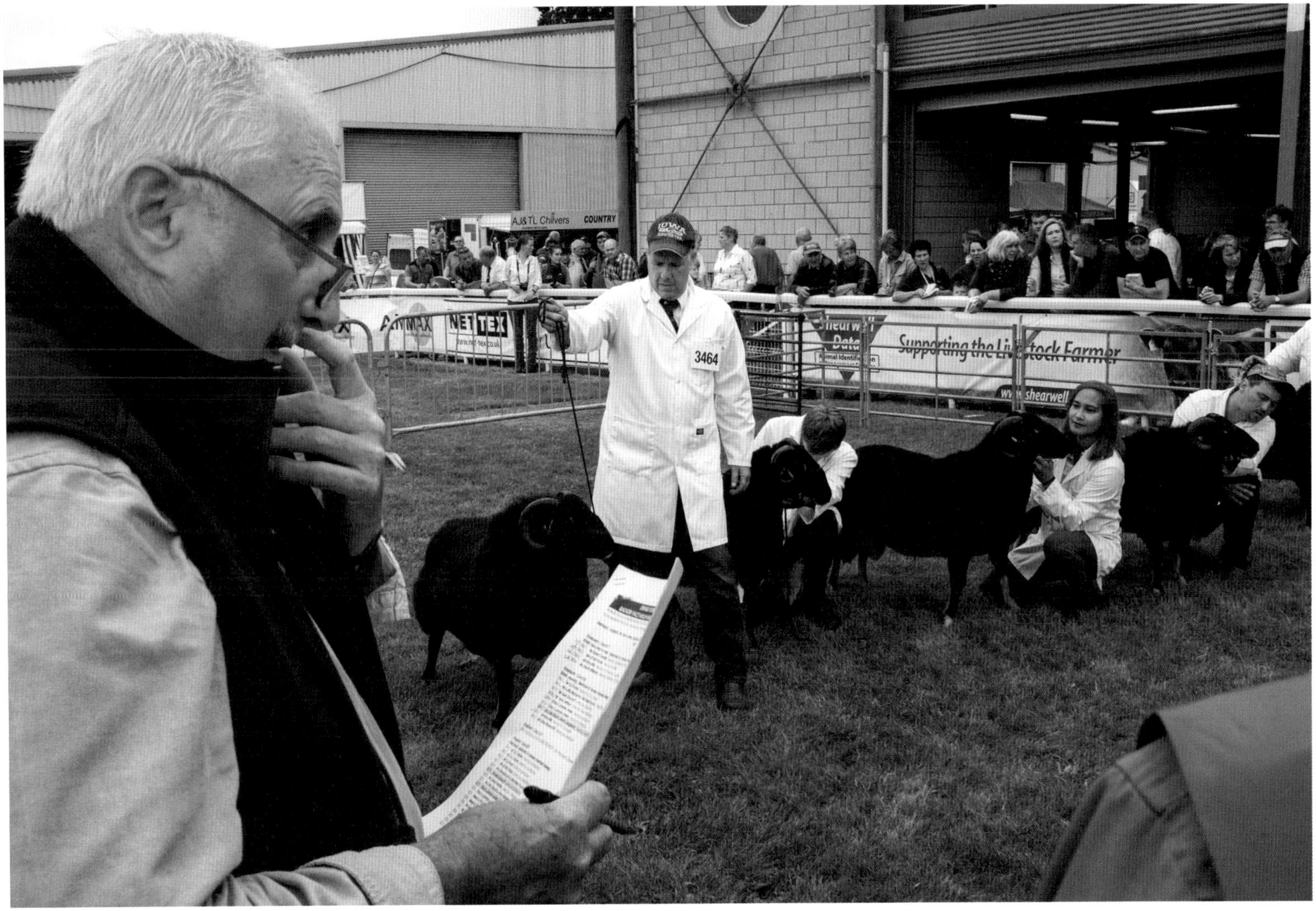
AJ&TL Chilvers
COUNTRY
NET TEX
3464

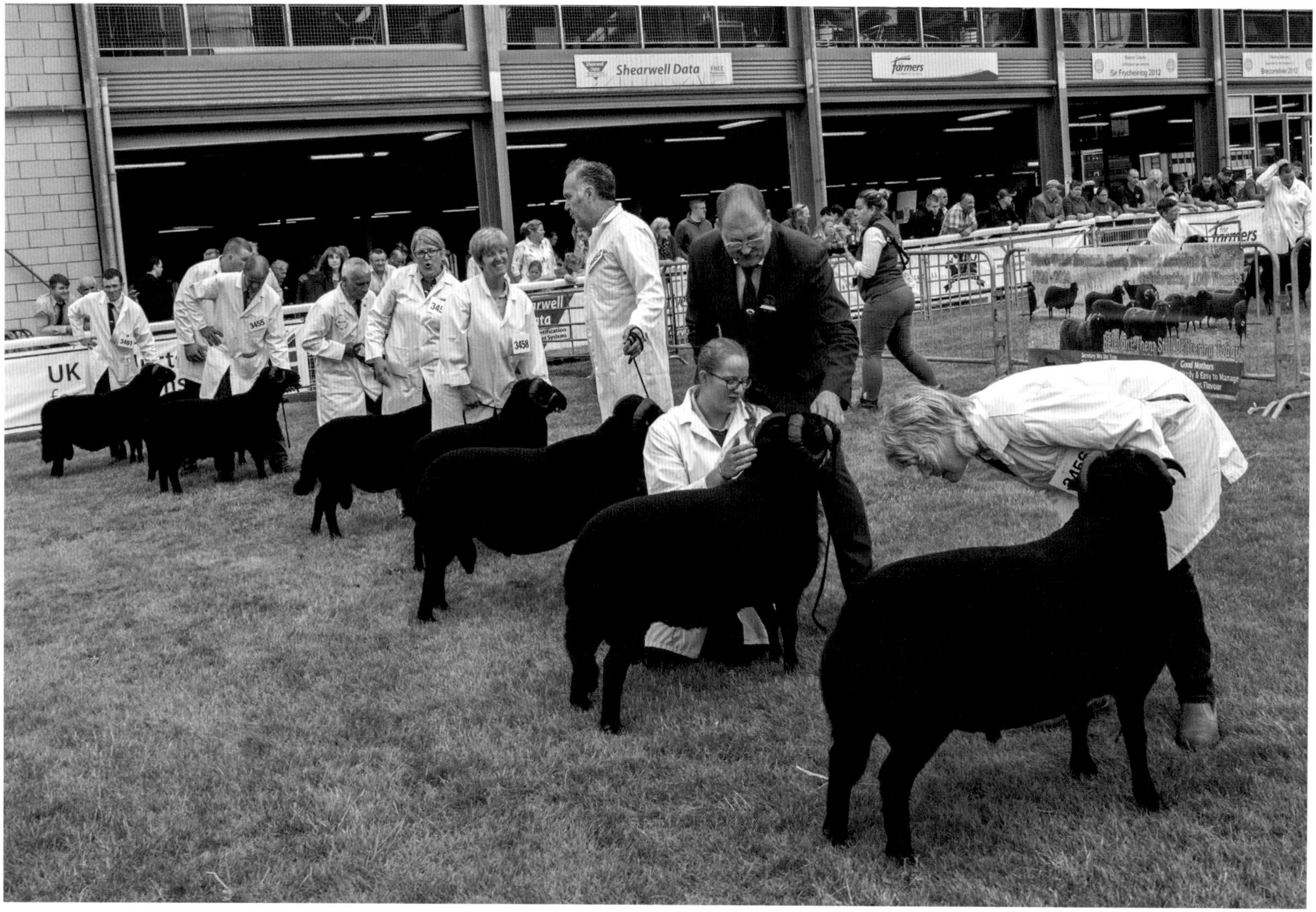
Shearwell Data
Farmers
3455
3458
UK

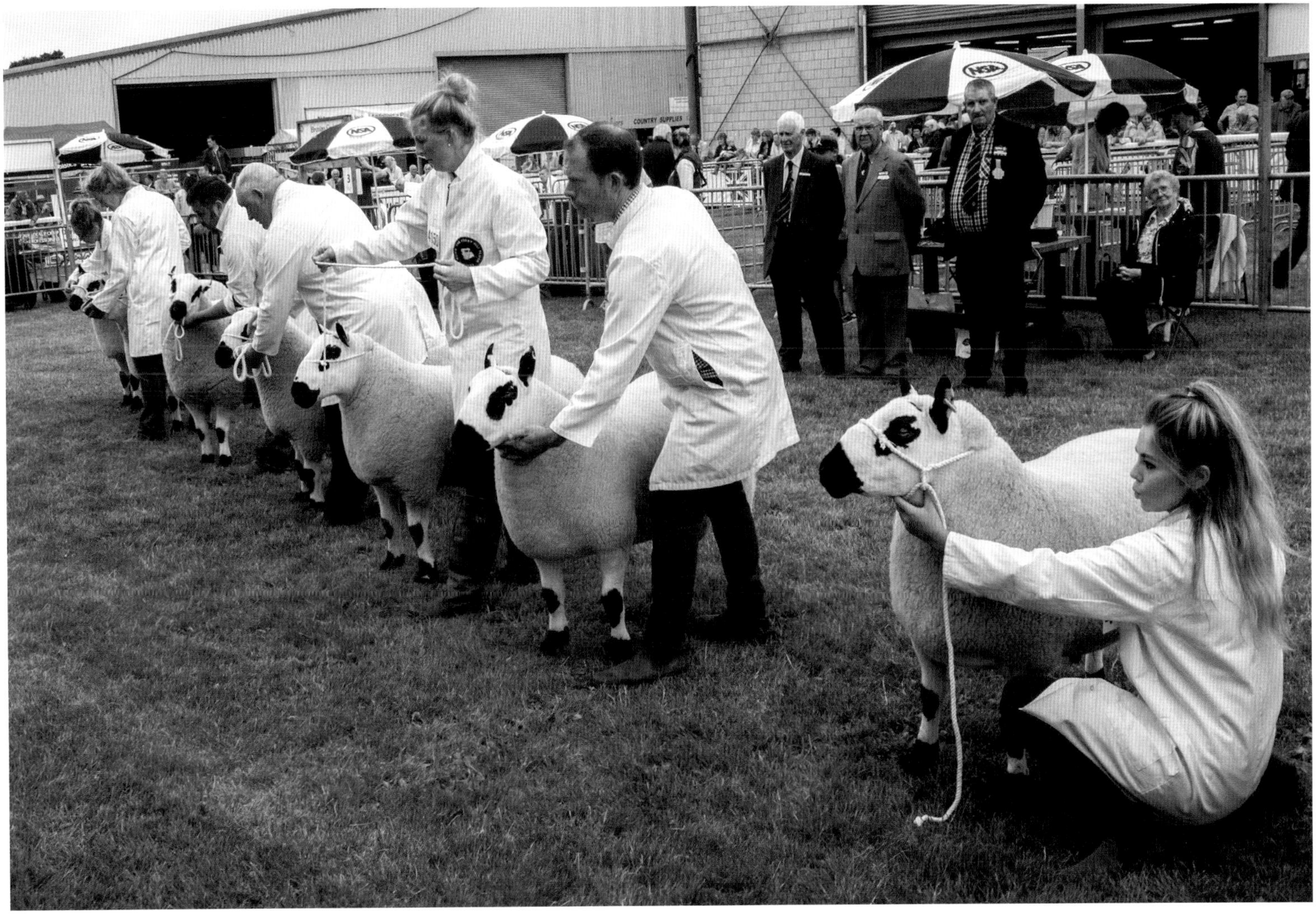
COUNTRY SUPPLIES

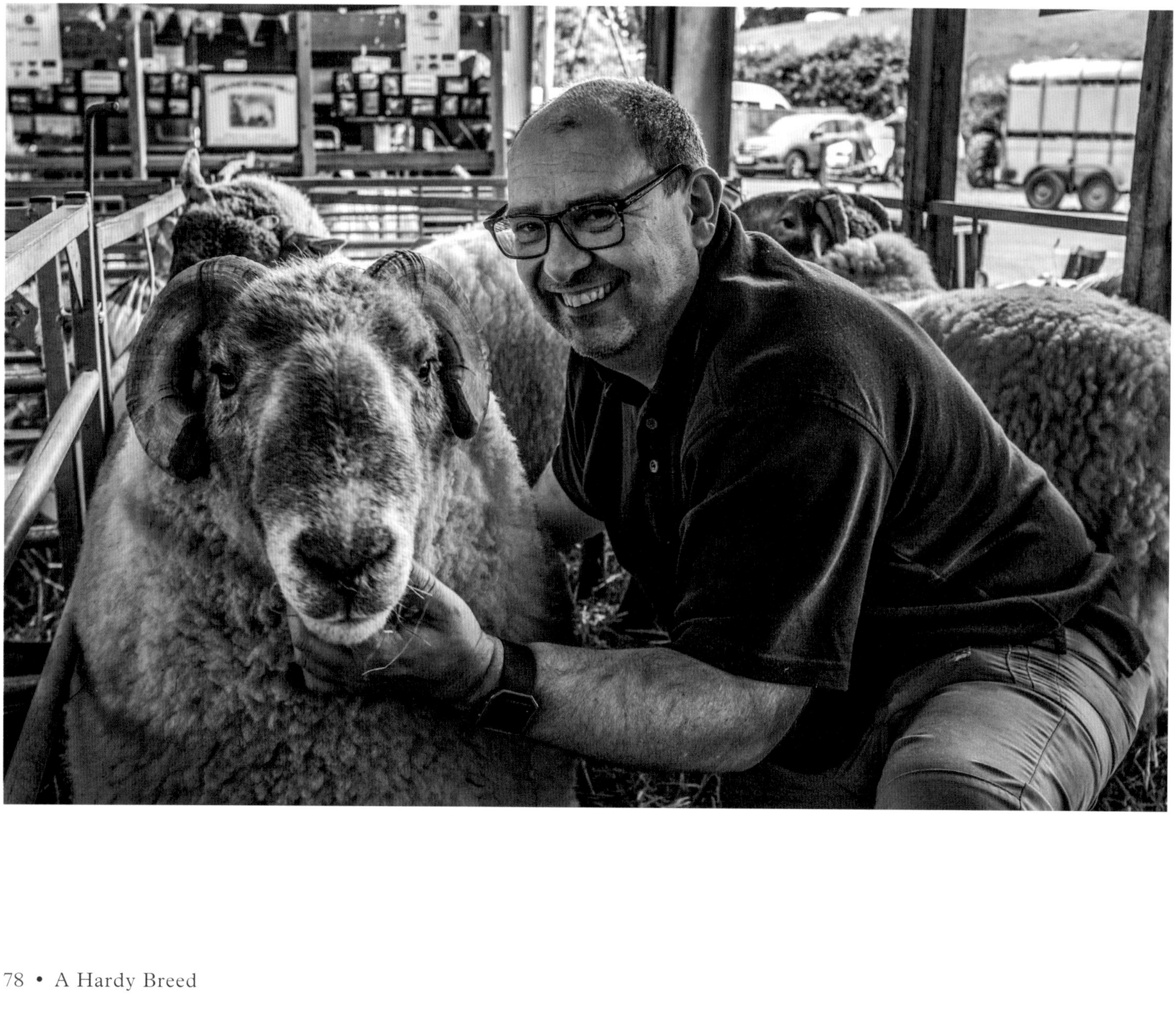

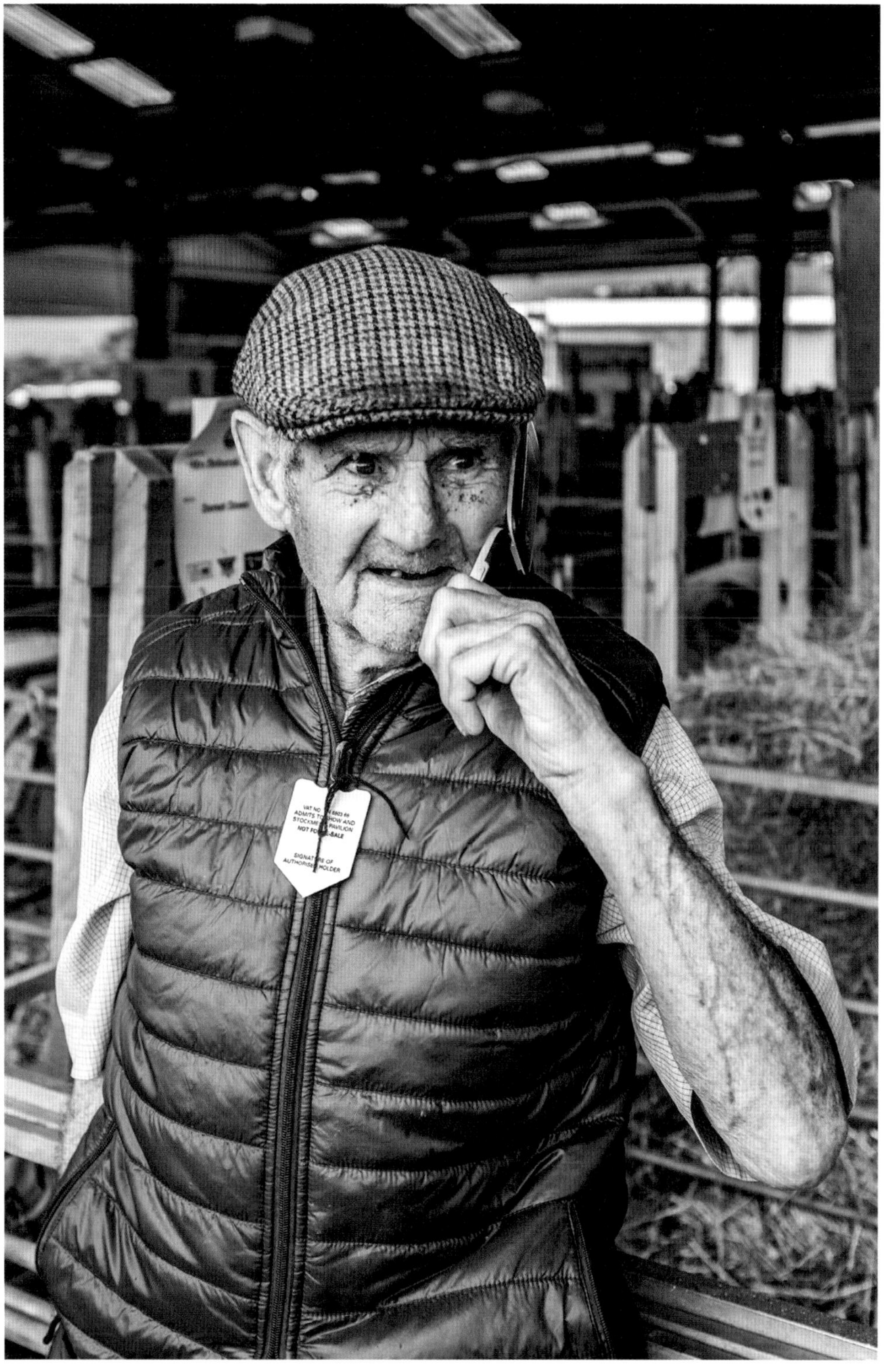
VAT NO
ADMITS
SHOW AND
PAVILION
NOT
SIGNAT
OF
HOLDER

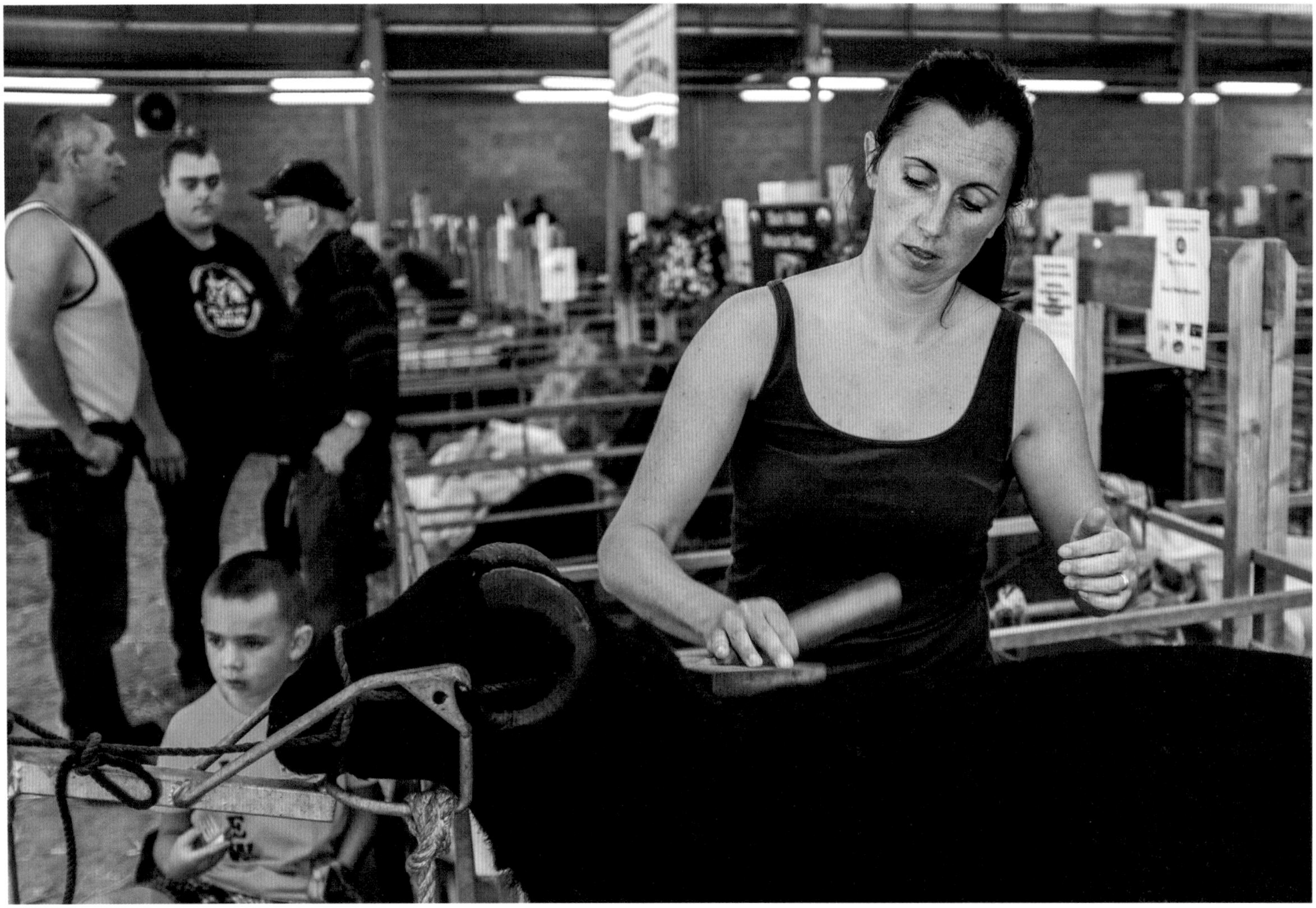

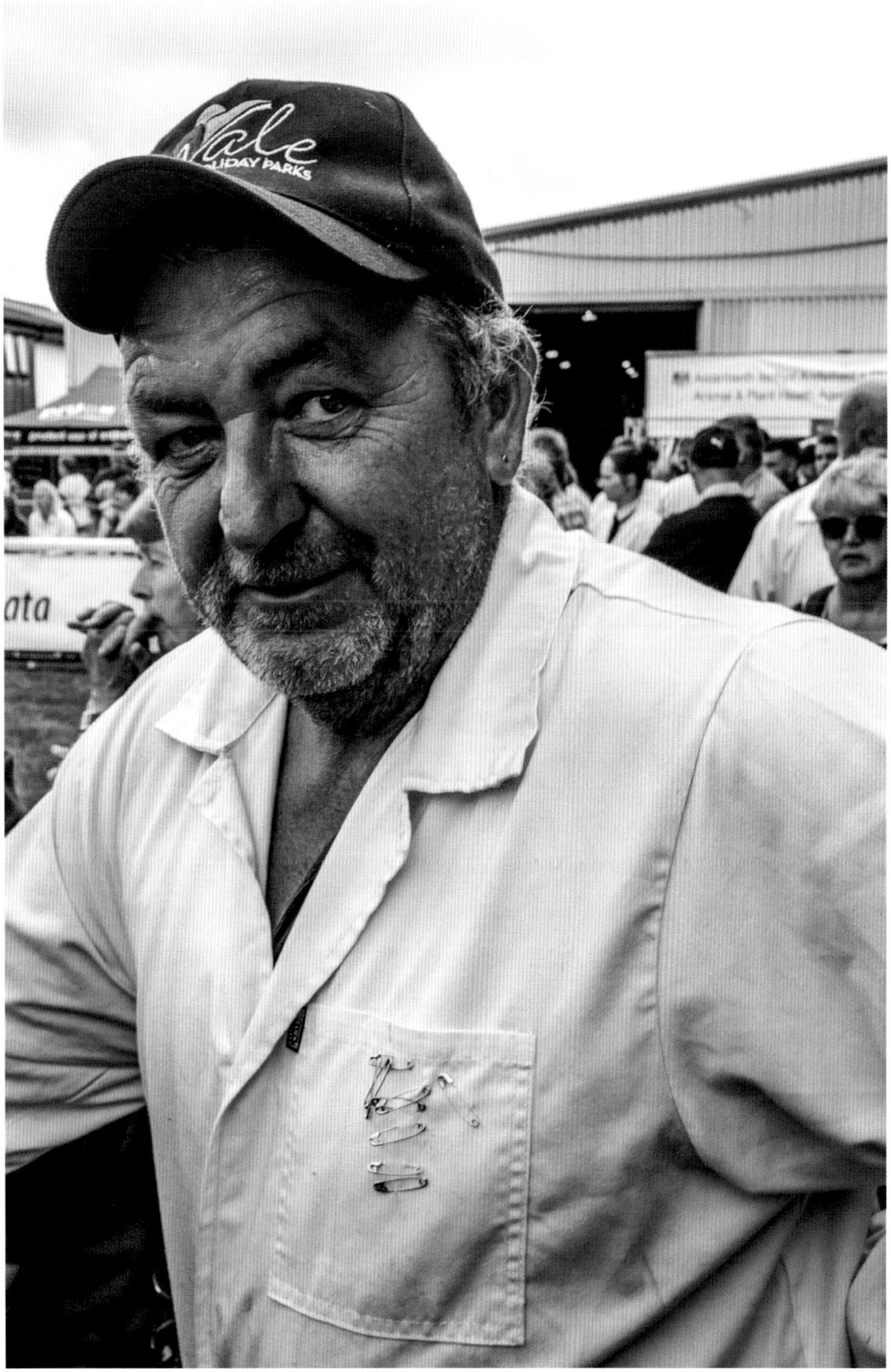
Vale

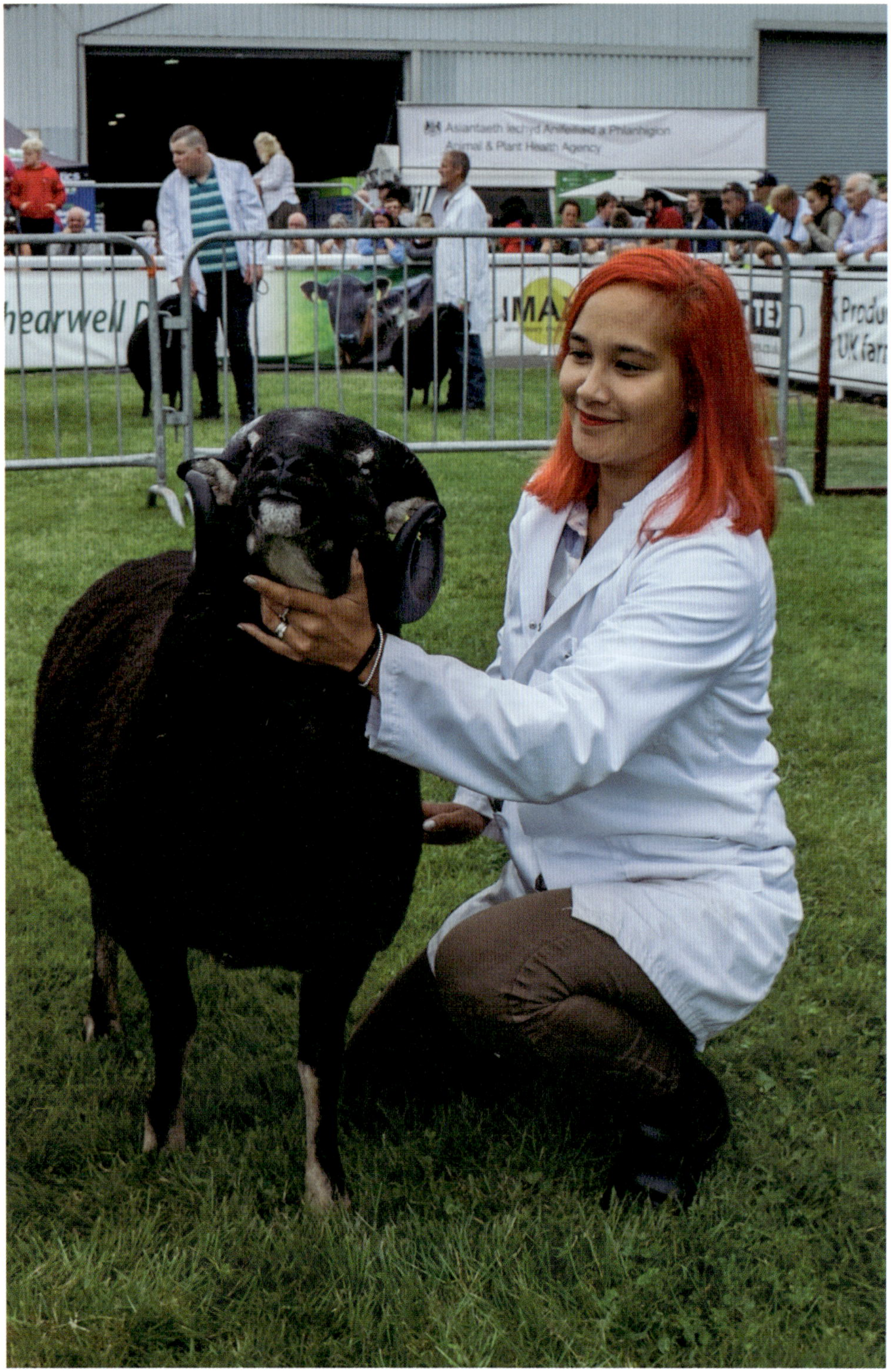
Asiantaeth Iechyd Anifeiliaid a Phlanhigion
Animal & Plant Health Agency

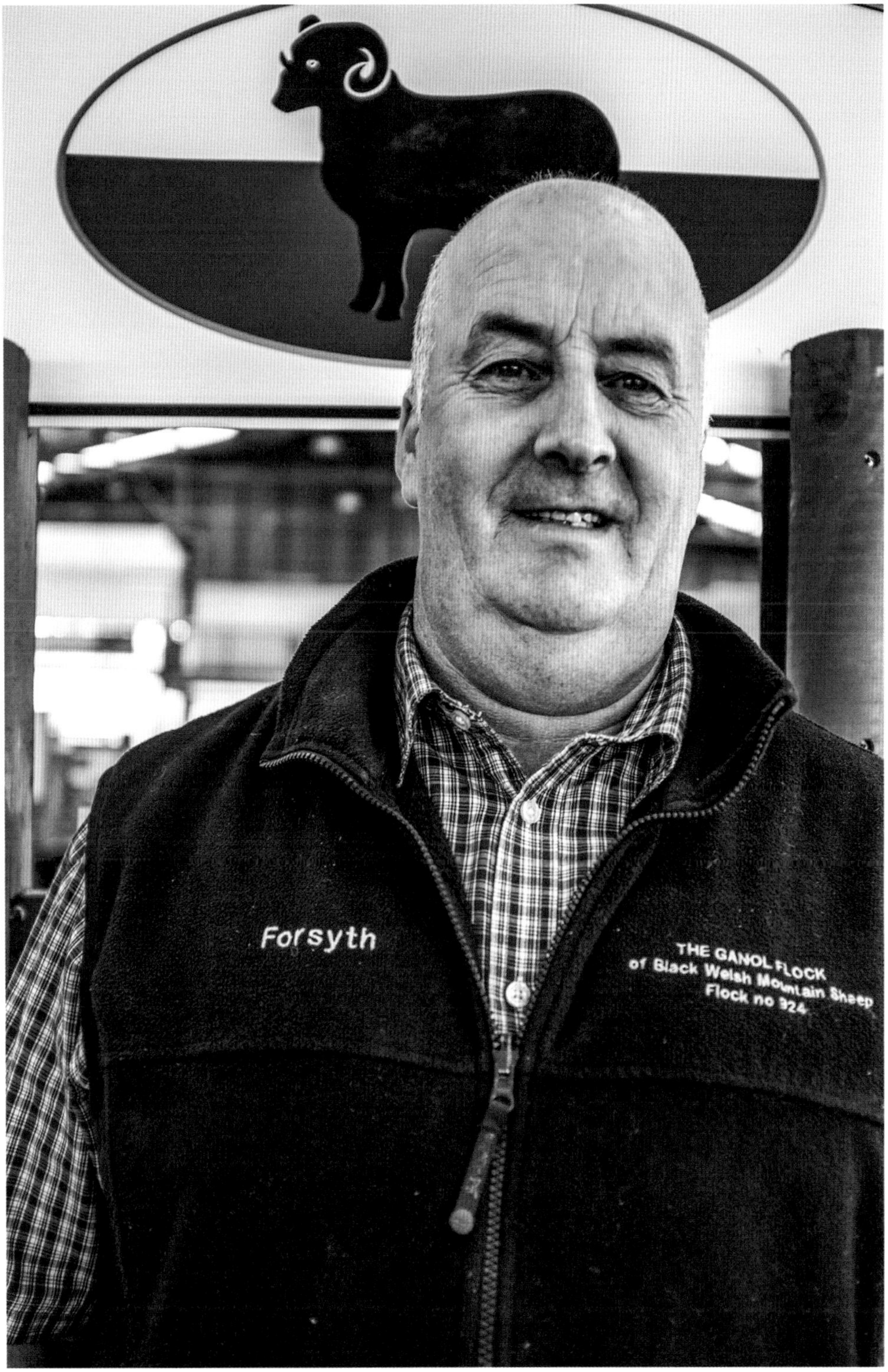
Forsyth
THE GANOL FLOCK
of Black Welsh Mountain Sheep
Flock no 324

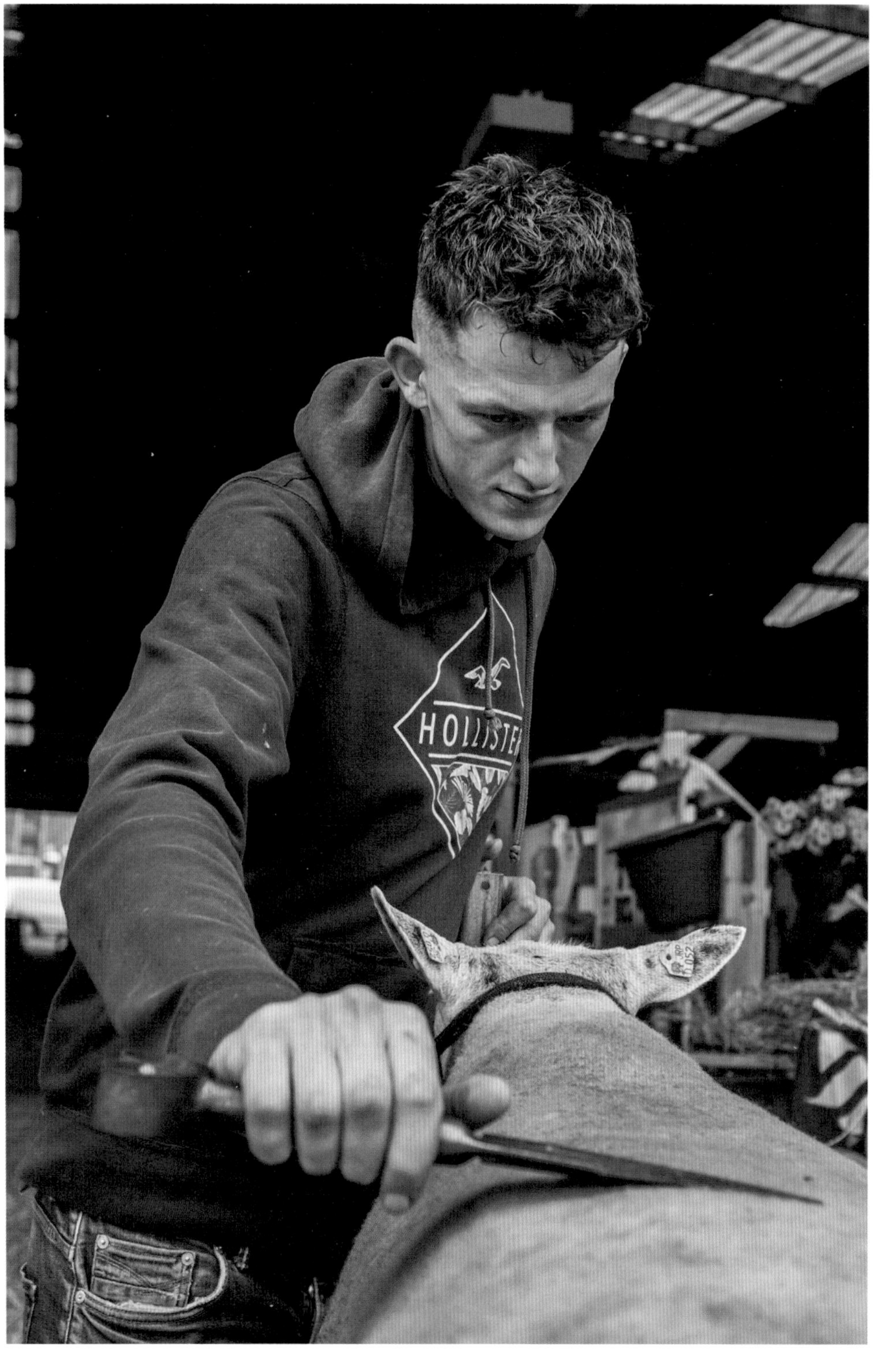
HOLLISTER

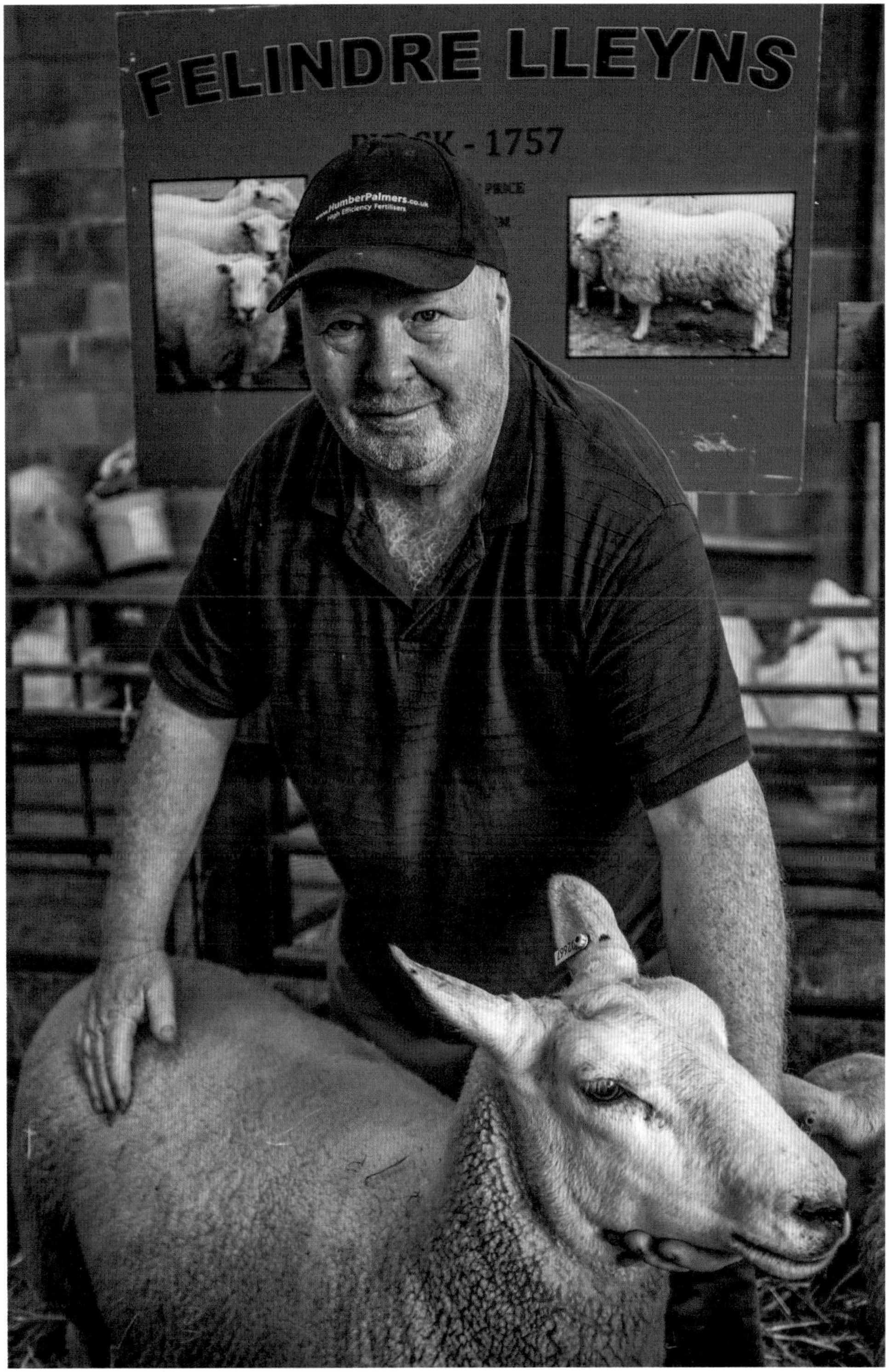
FELINDRE LLEYNS

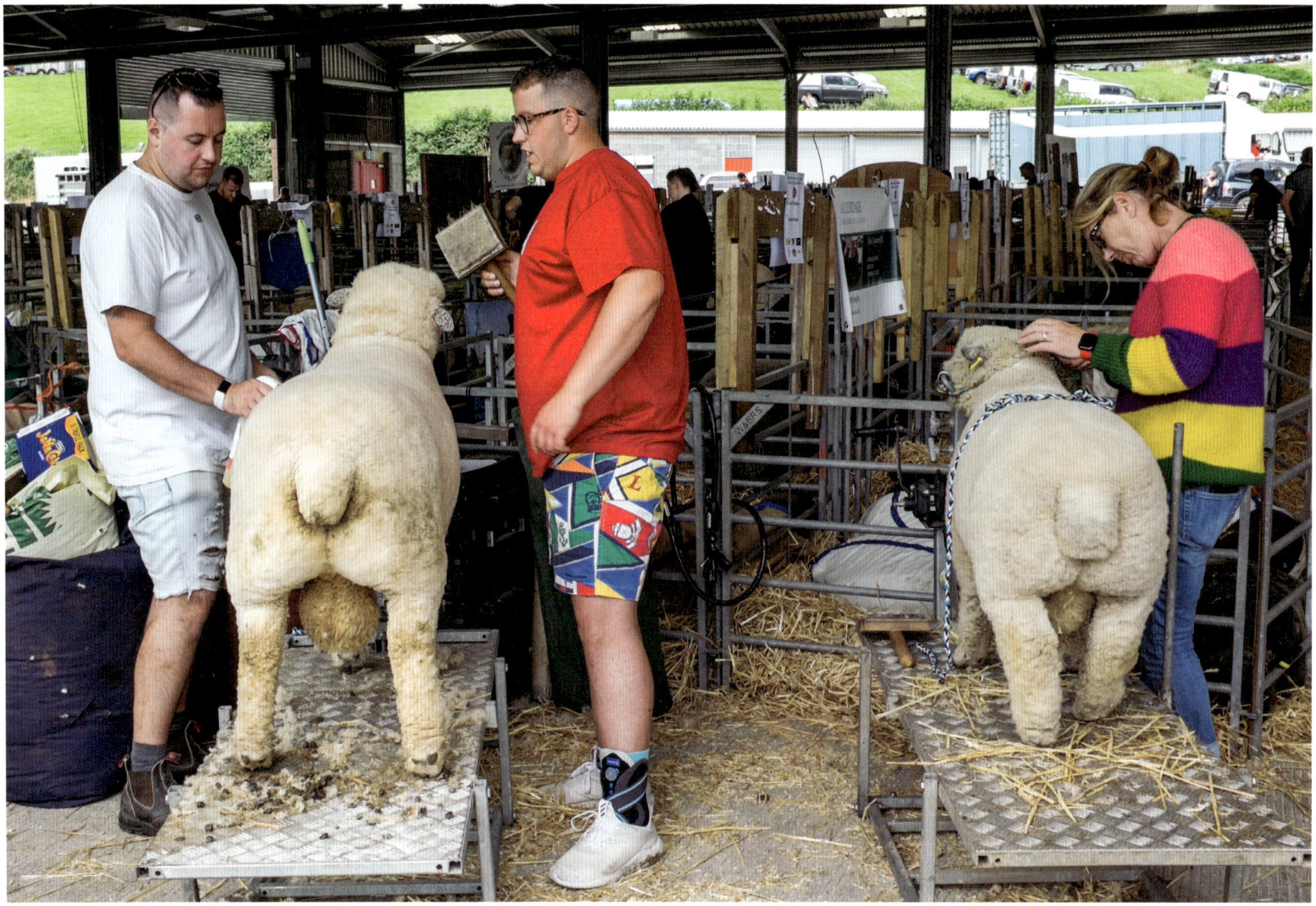

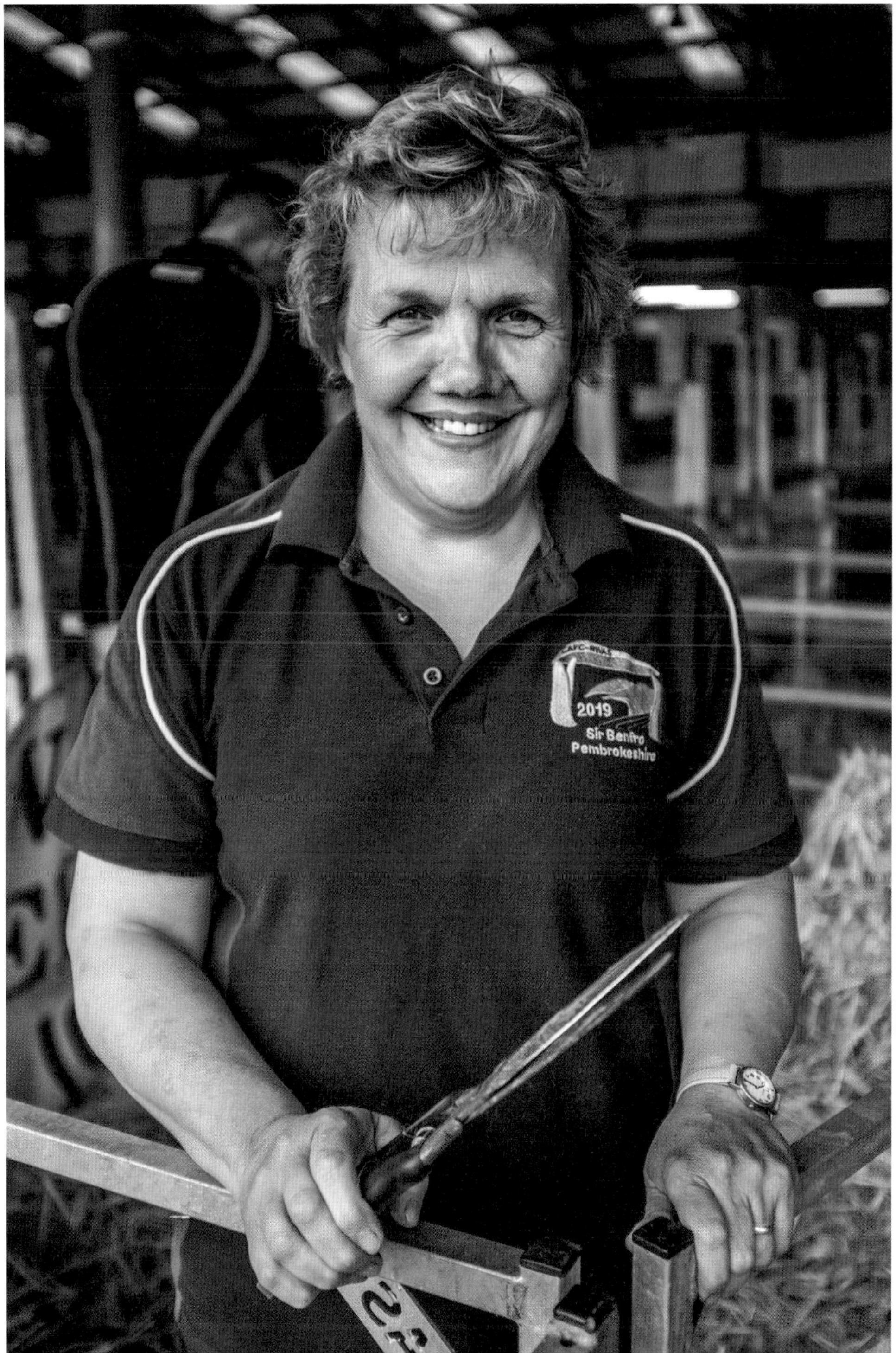
2019
Sir Benfro
Pembrokeshire

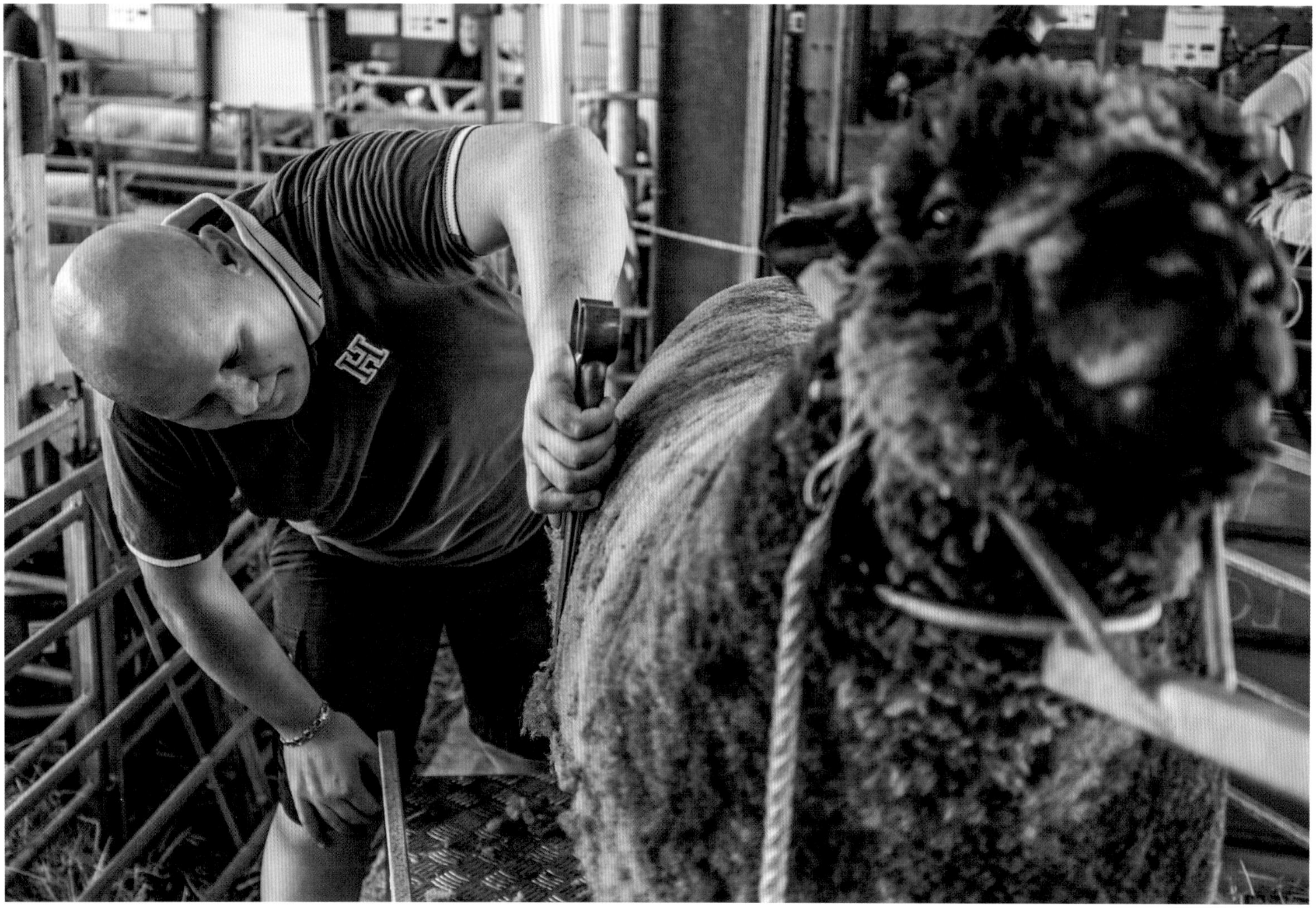

MARKET

A trip to market is more than an economic transaction when you live miles from your nearest neighbour. It is also a social occasion, a chance to exchange news and gossip with friends as well as to keep abreast of developments in the farming world.

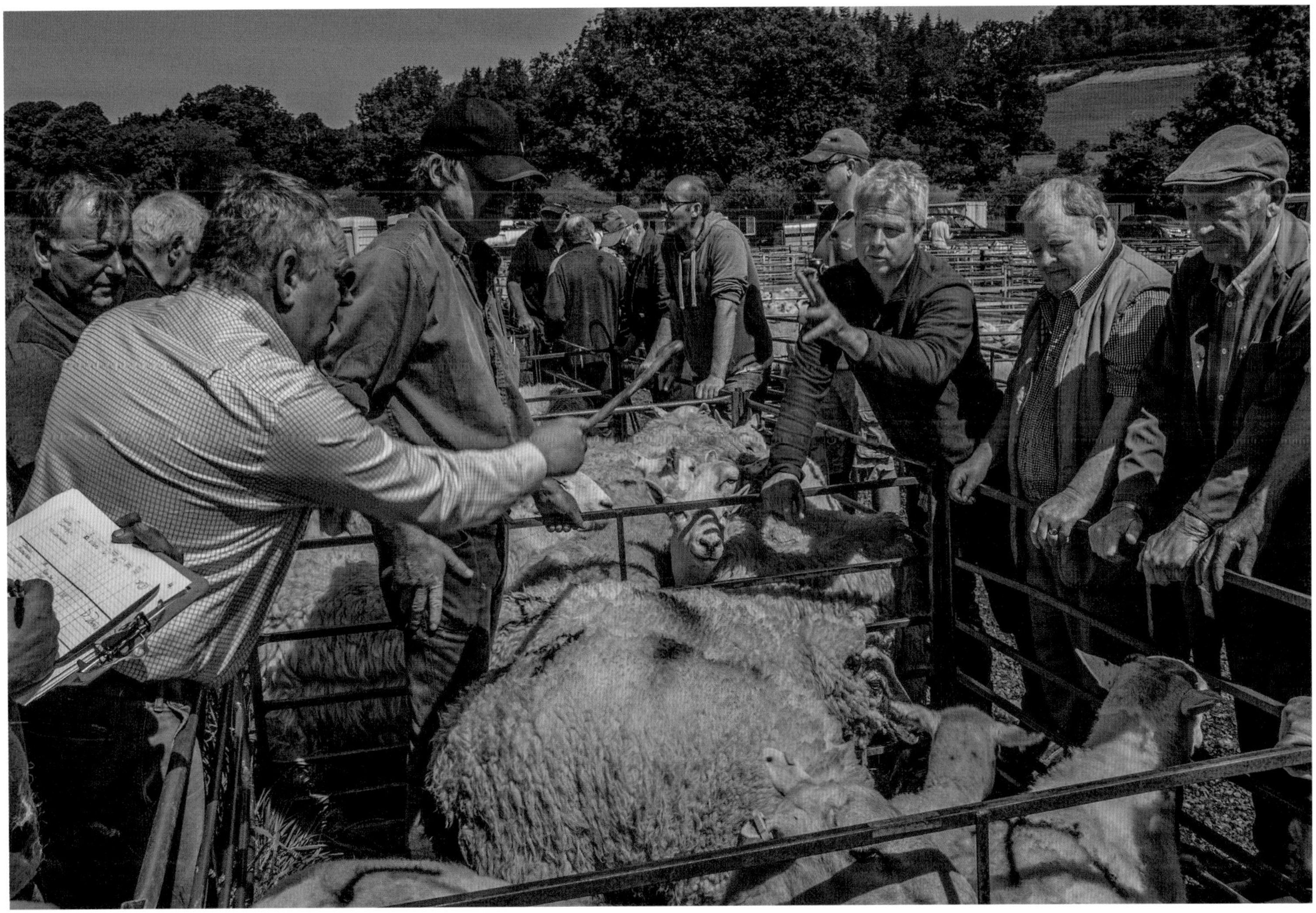

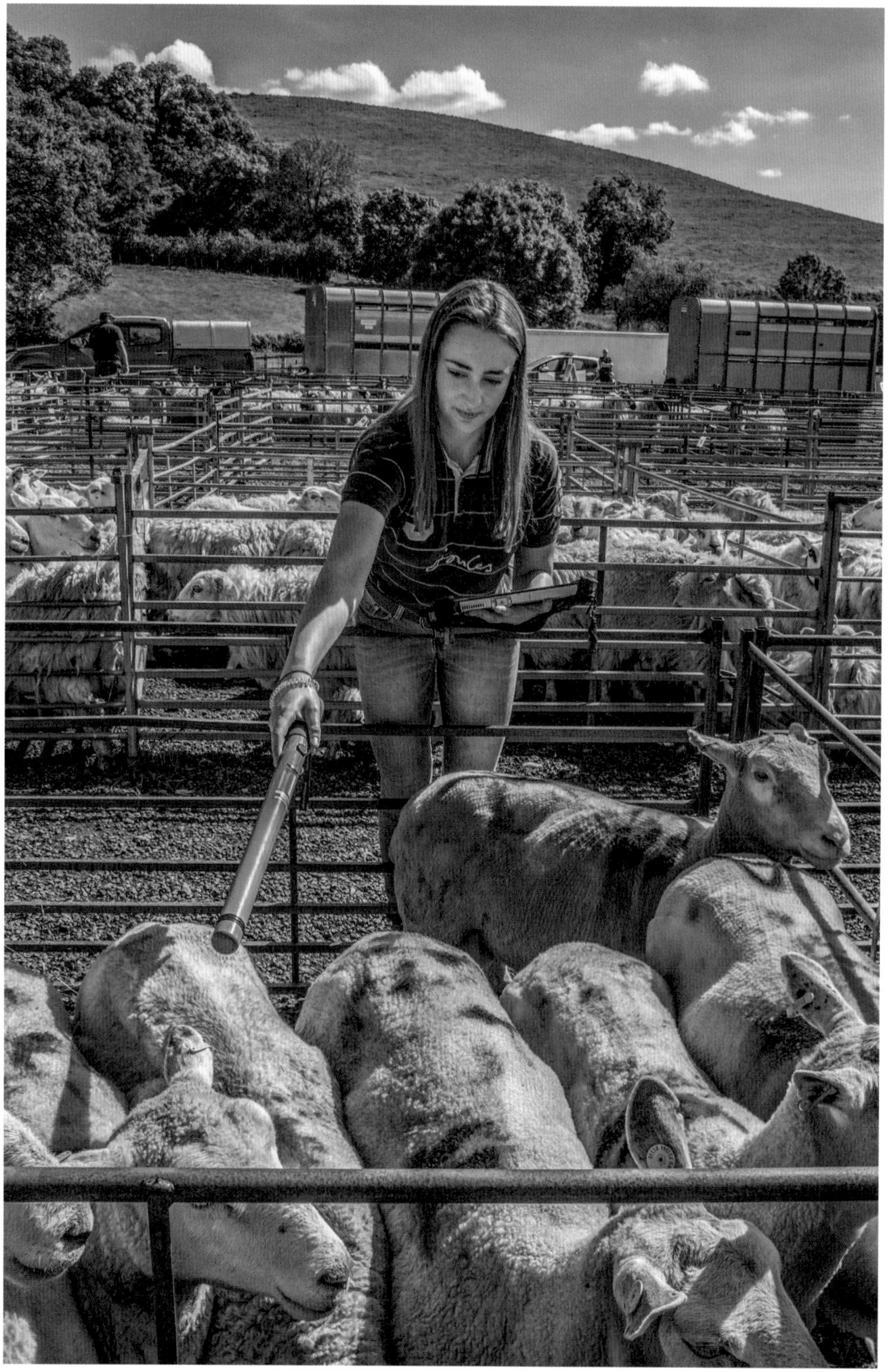

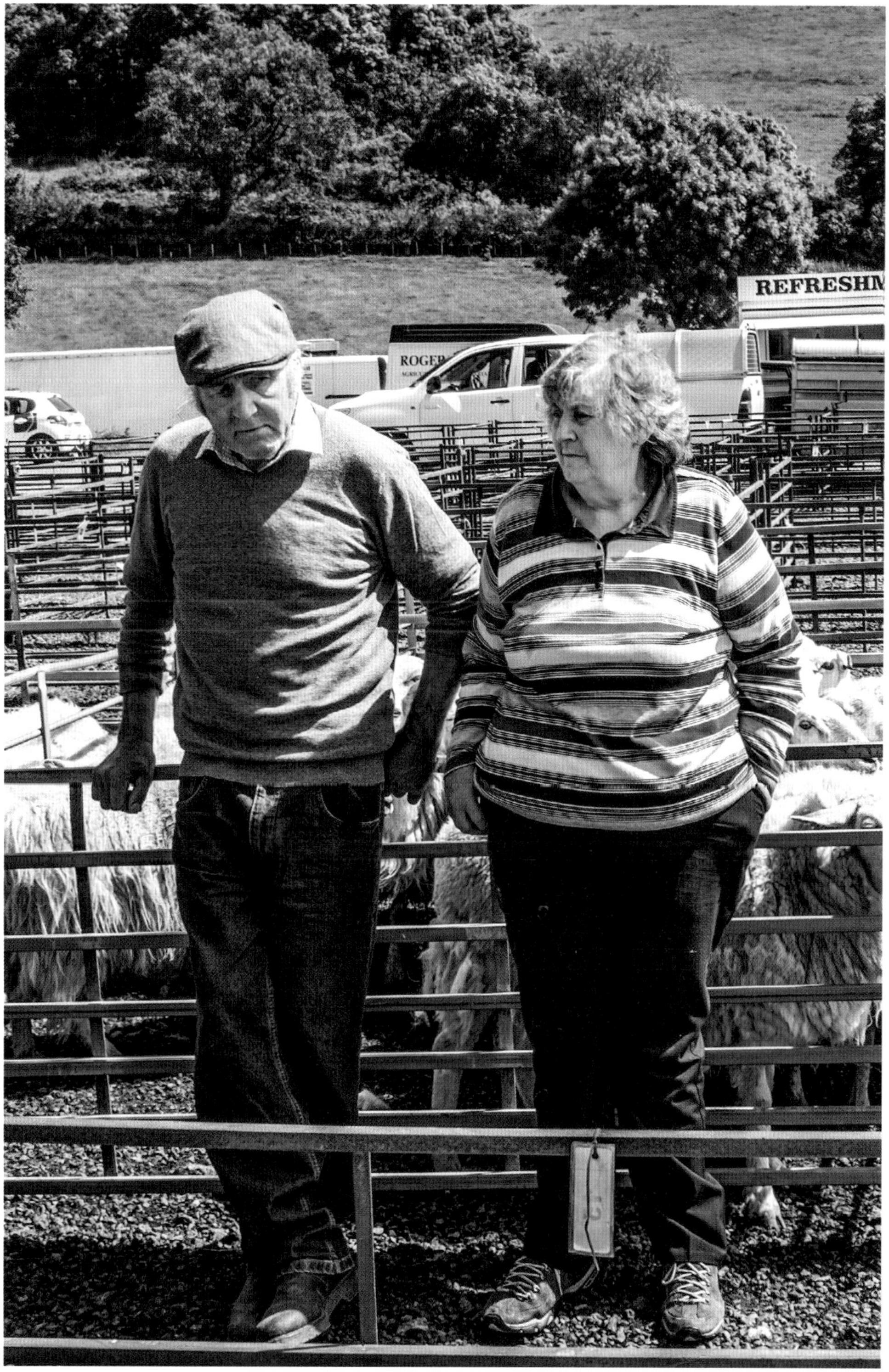

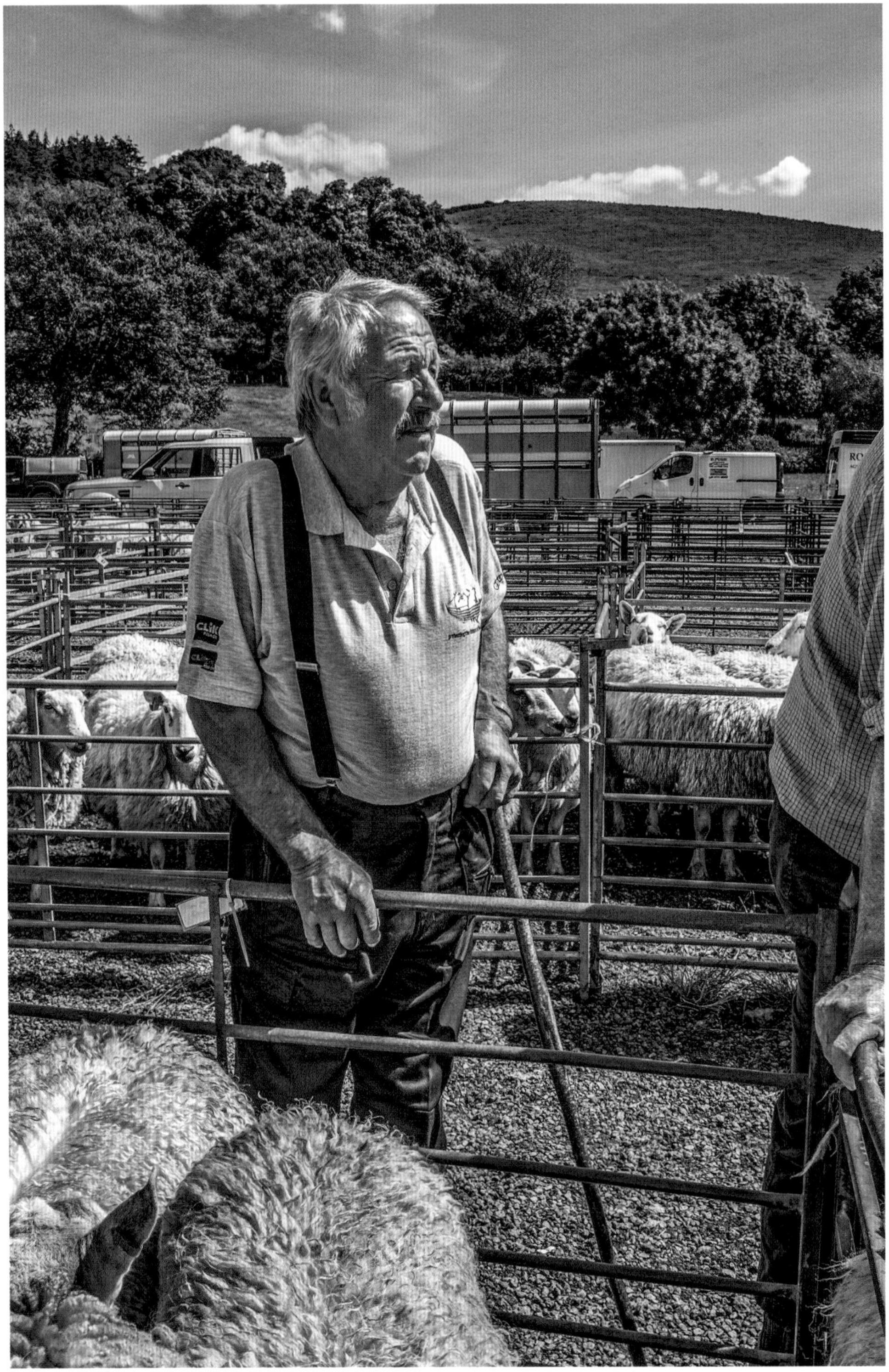

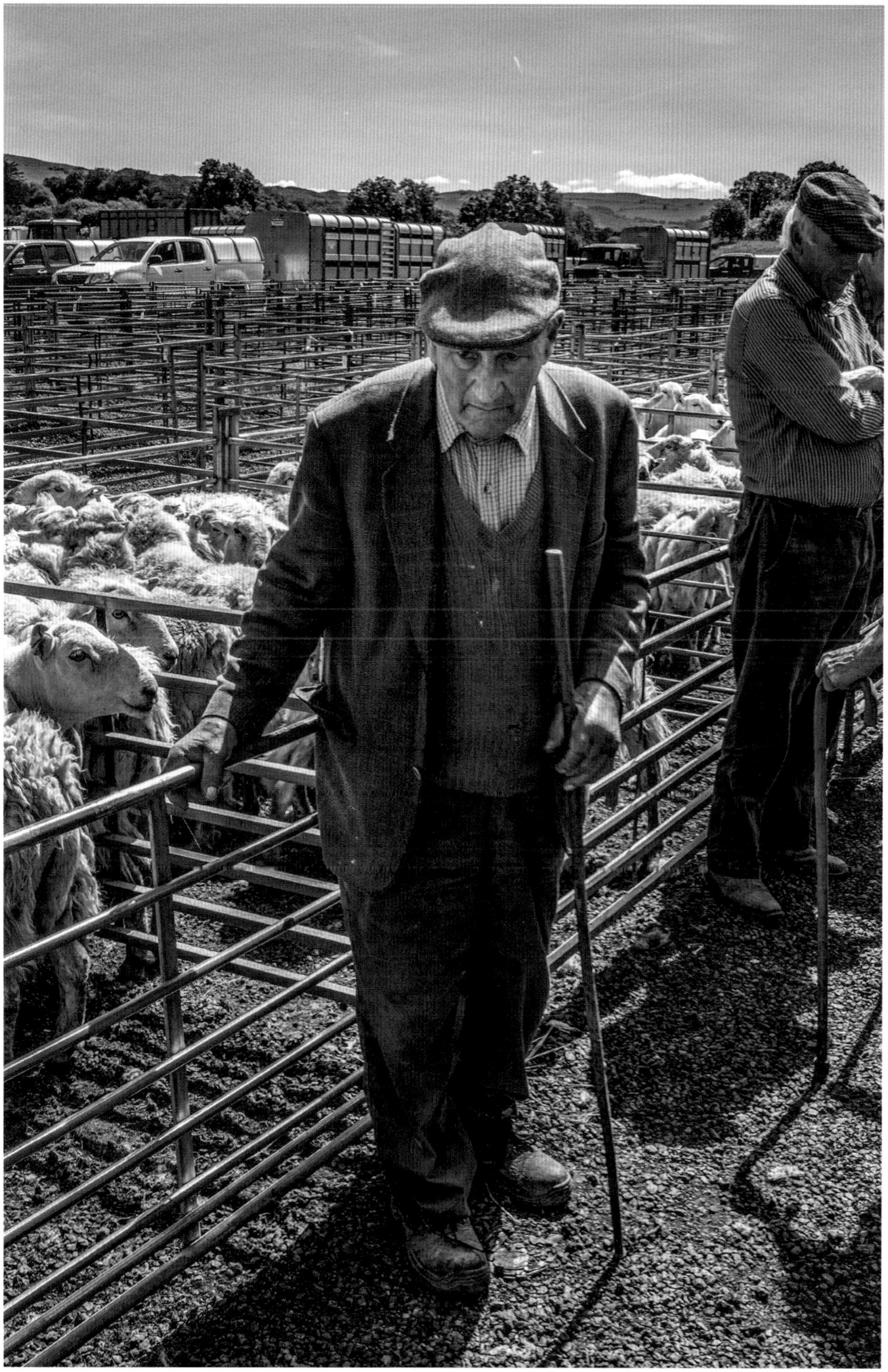

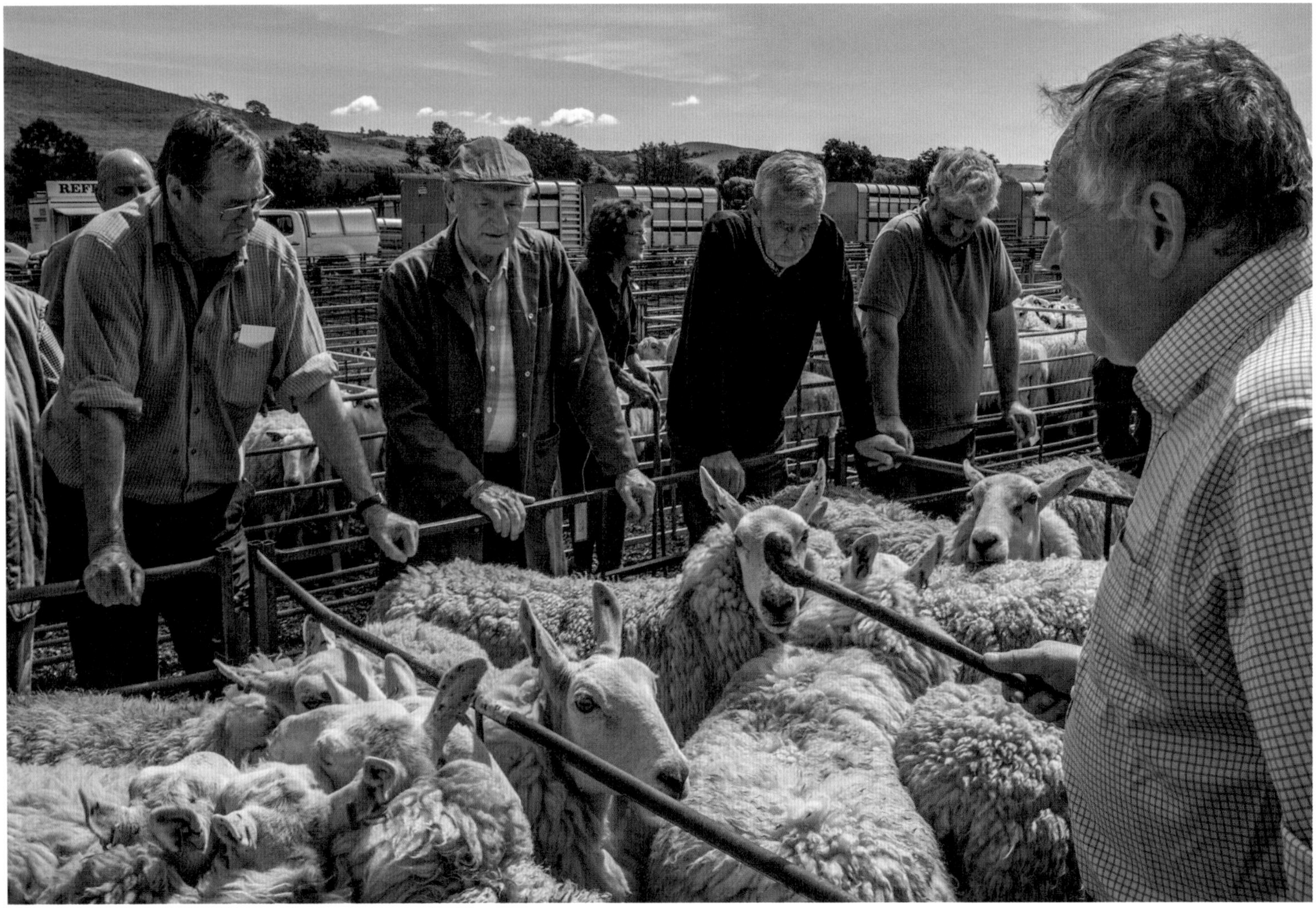

Diversification

Anwen Roberts

Agriculture and the Arts have long been intertwined in Anwen Roberts' life.

"Of three sisters in our family," she says, "I was the one who was always helping my father on the farm. My Taid and Nain had a farm on Anglesey, and they had a shepherding neighbour called Iwan who helped them out when it was needed. I met him there through my grandparents, and then during the last year of my Fine Arts Degree in Staffordshire University we got married. Farming is the common thread between us."

Anwen and Iwan have about 150 ewes now at Bunwerth, near Trearddur Bay, substantially down from a higher number when their two boys were on the farm at home. Cai and Osian now have their own flock of 400 ewes, and feel very committed to a shepherding future. Iwan additionally has an outside full-time job, and they run a small caravan site on their land. As a talented and accomplished artist Anwen is also able to contribute to the family budget; her in-depth understanding of the rural world, combined with her artistic flair, creates powerful and engaging art works of country life.

Her father Brian is at his happiest now stone walling, as since the death of his wife he likes to keep occupied, and finds the work therapeutic.

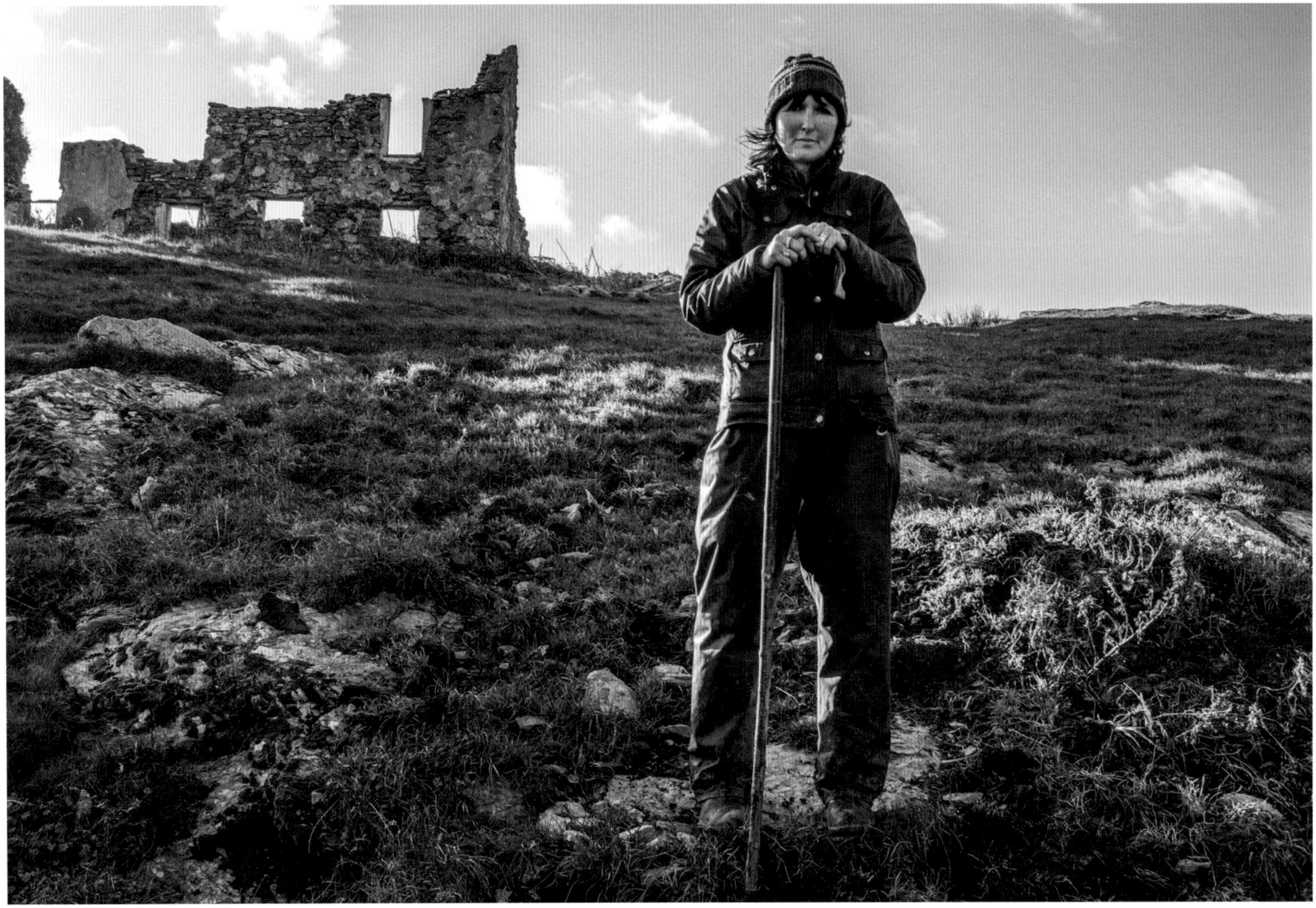

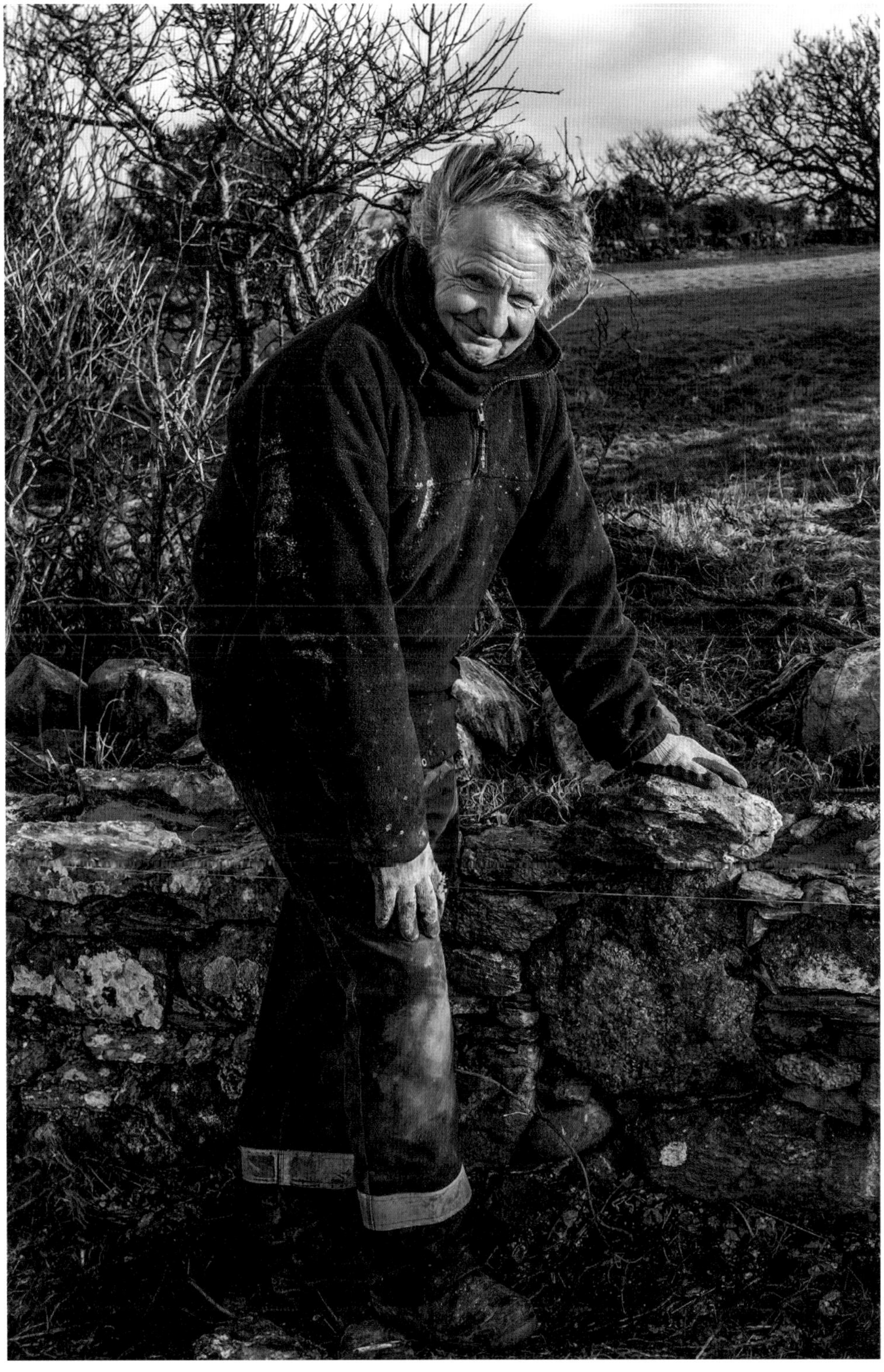

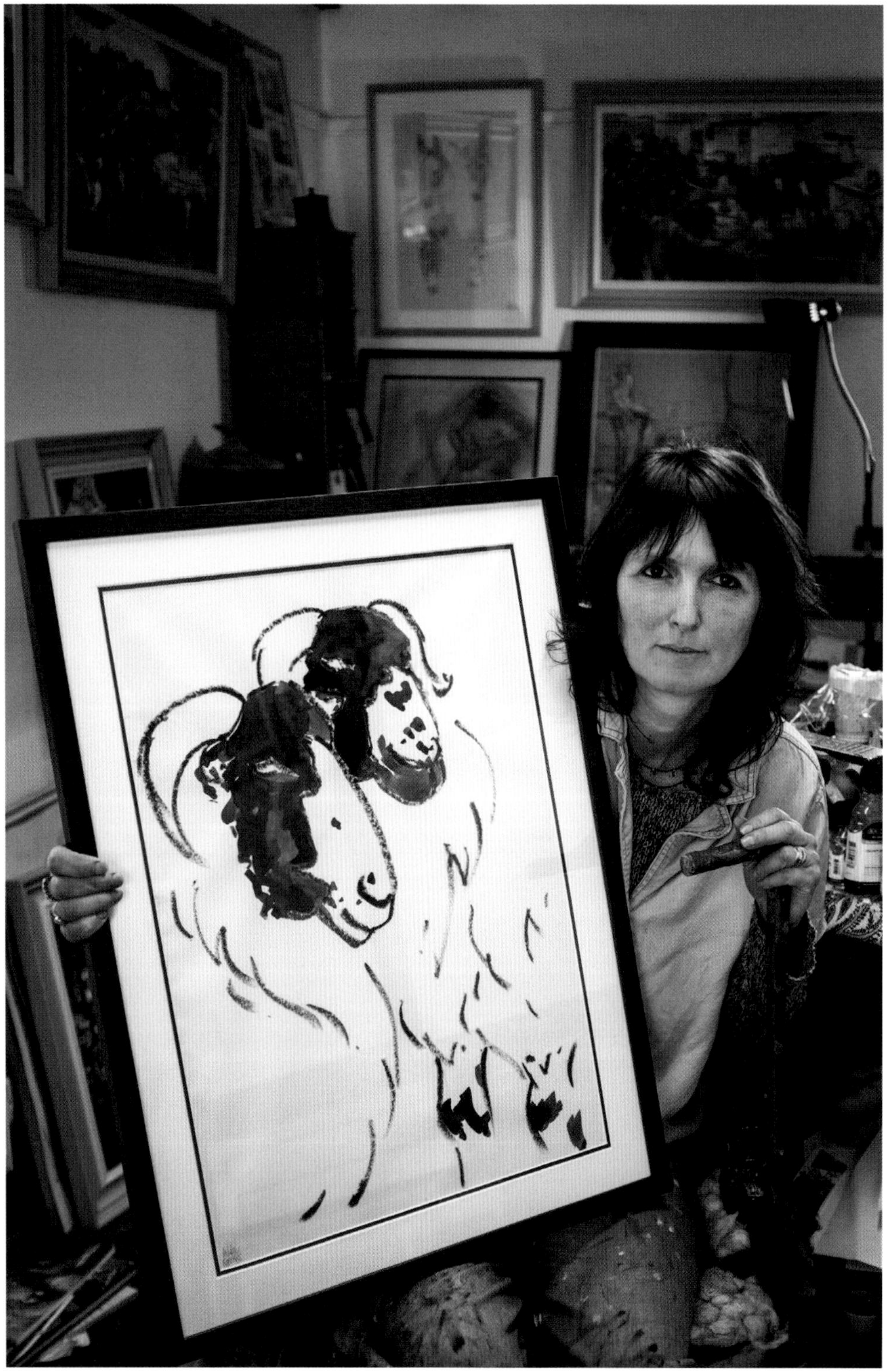

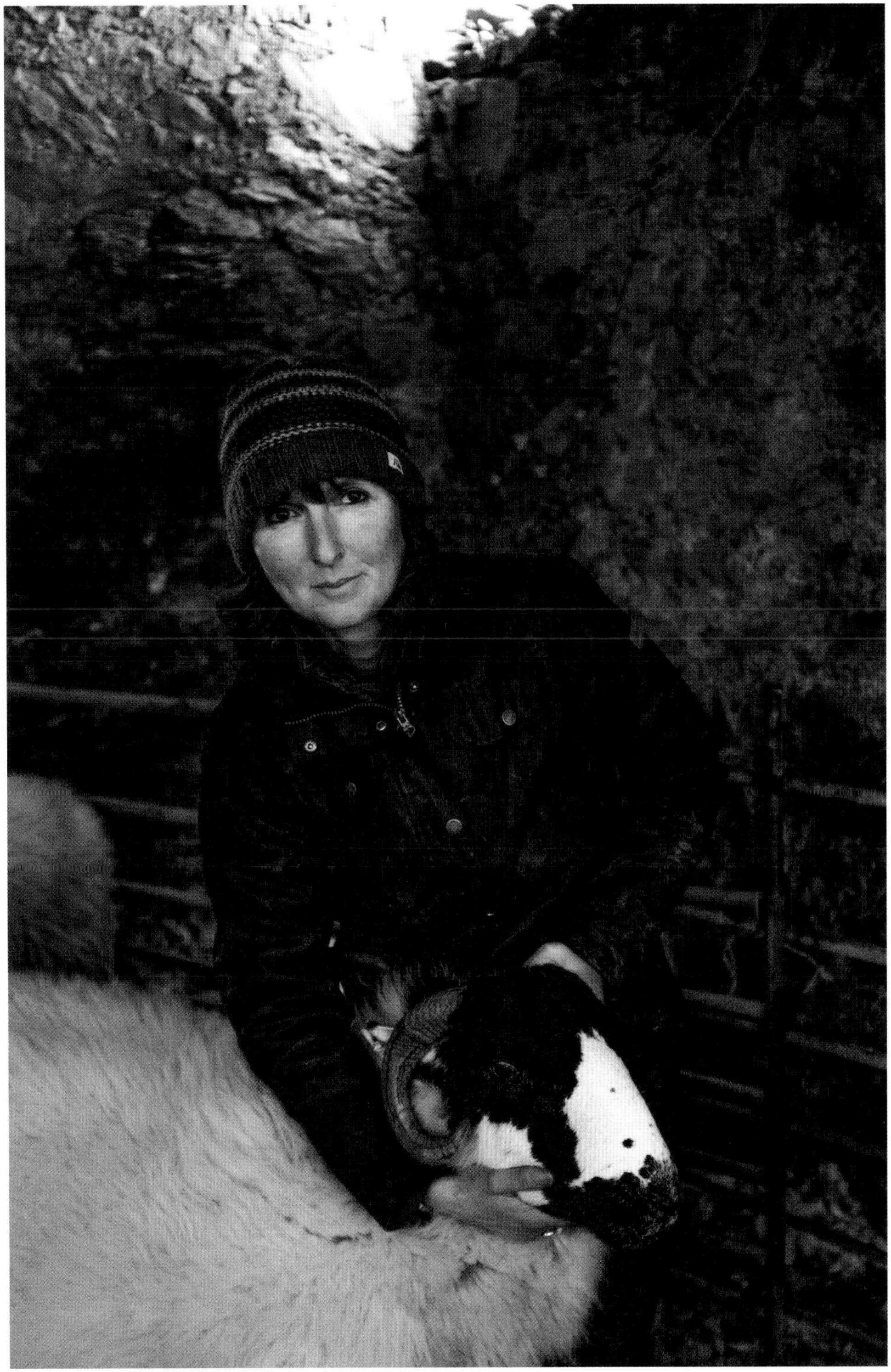

Gillian and John Williams

Gillian met John Williams in the Falklands Islands during 1999, when he went over for the shearing. Her family were then running a 6,000 strong flock producing fine merino-type wool for clothing. Gillian explains how John and she got together, "Before building our current home in Wales, we spent six months of the year working with the shearing gangs in the UK during the summer, and then the six winter months away in the Antipodes, working their shearing season."

They now live in that comfortable home in Wales, and run 250 Welsh Mountain cross Romney ewes on rented land, a downsize from the huge Falkland sheep numbers. "The cross gives us a bigger ewe which is still hardy, and we aim for the meat market with the rams."

Gillian started The Welsh Woolshed project in 2020, during the first Covid lockdown, as a spur of the moment idea to sell wool to crafters through Facebook. Three years later it has grown hugely, to the extent that she has given up her part-time job to concentrate on it. "Now the wool all leaves the farm as finished products, crafted by myself, mostly items of home décor such as fleece rugs."

As well as shepherding their flock, John takes on fencing, walling, shearing, and contract work to supplement the budget. Their youngest son, Gruff, would like to follow in his father's footsteps. "We don't try to second guess what might be happening in ten years time," Gillians reflects, "just get on with making the best of what is there on the day."

Given the successful outcomes of all their hard work, that seems to be a good plan.

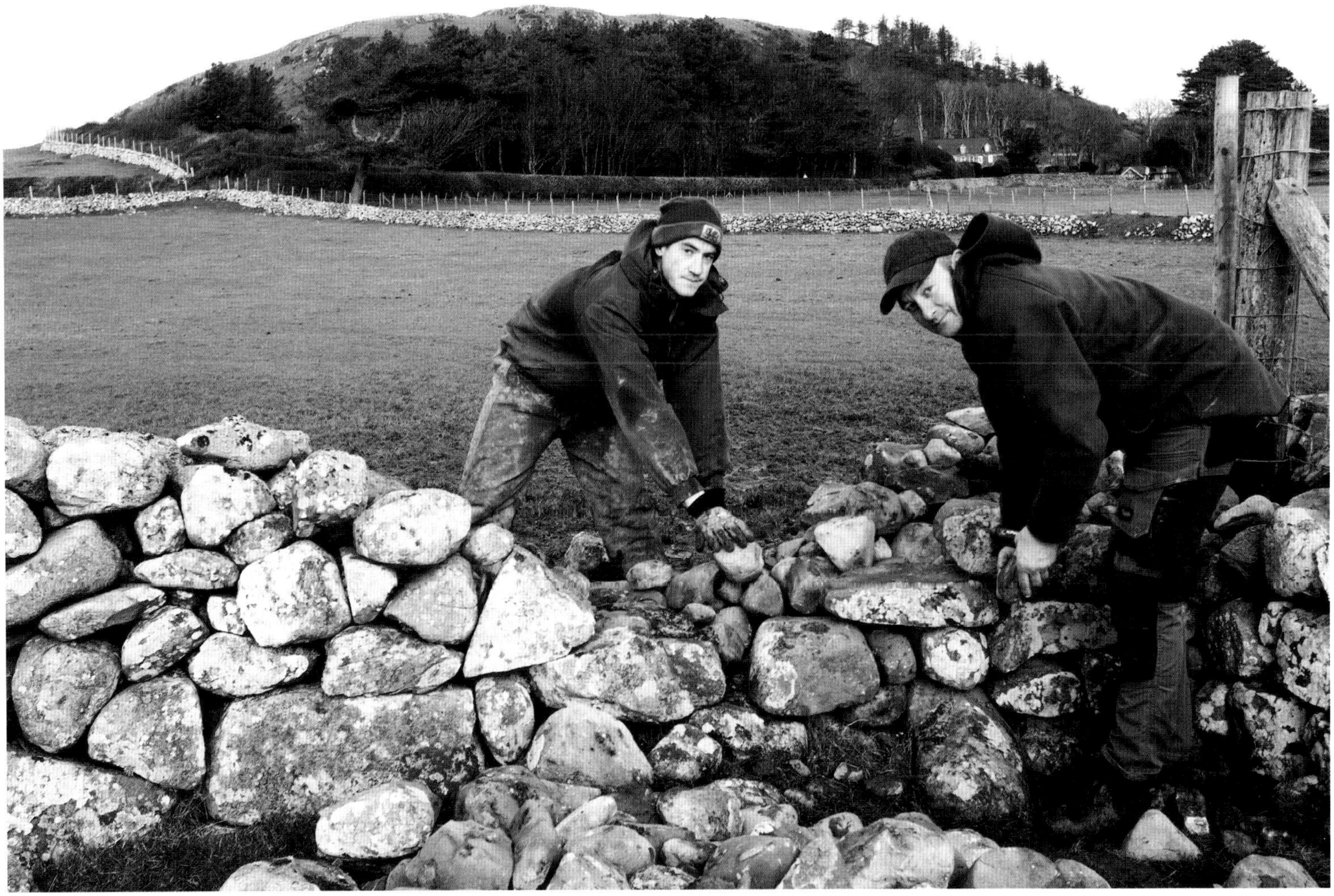

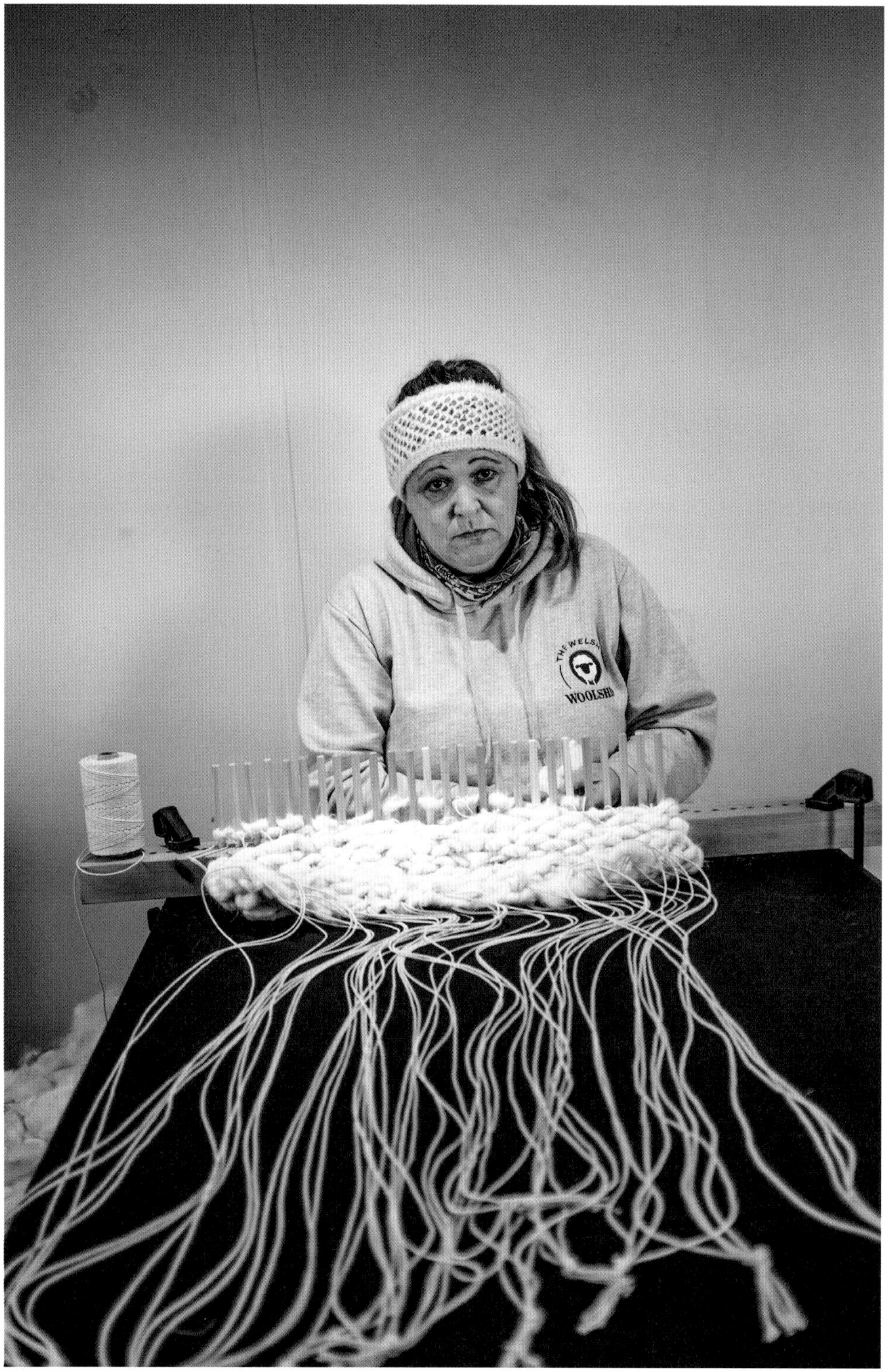

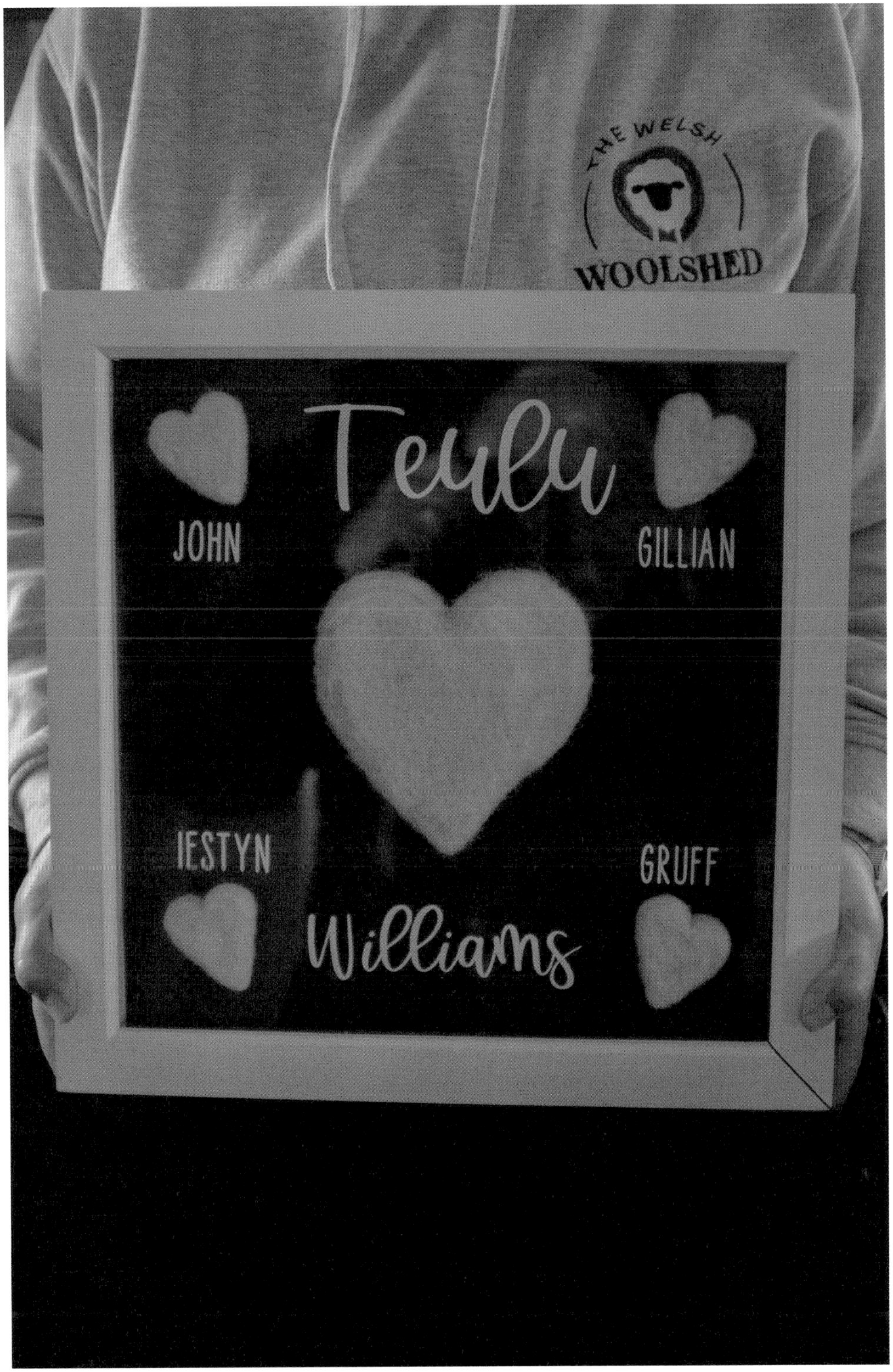
THE WELSH
WOOLSHED
Teulu
JOHN
GILLIAN
IESTYN
GRUFF
Williams

Nick and Wendy Holtham

From a career as staff in a stately home in England, to all Wales prizewinners for the best cheese in show during their subsequent retirement? If that sounds unlikely, then meet Nick and Wendy Holtham.

In the Royal Welsh Show of 2022, a cheese from their 120 strong flock of Friesland milking ewes won the President's Prize for the Best Cheese in Show, and they also picked up three Silver Medals and a Gold for their produce. Stellar success by any standard, but all the more remarkable because of their late entry into the business in 2013.

"We didn't have any background in cheese," Wendy explains, "when we moved from England to Wales in 1998 to try and realise our dream. I remember talking to a cheese maker in North Wales who told of how her Mother had been milking Lleyns, a native Welsh sheep, many years before and making cheese to sell to miners. We were starting from scratch."

Wendy also uses her own spinning wheel to produce wool from their flock for sale for additional income.

Nick nods his agreement, "Wales is a wonderful place to be, and if you don't mind long hours and the hard slog anything is possible here. You need to sort out your market, and accept that you won't make megabucks immediately, but if you are prepared to give it a good go it can make a valuable financial contribution to a sheep farming family."

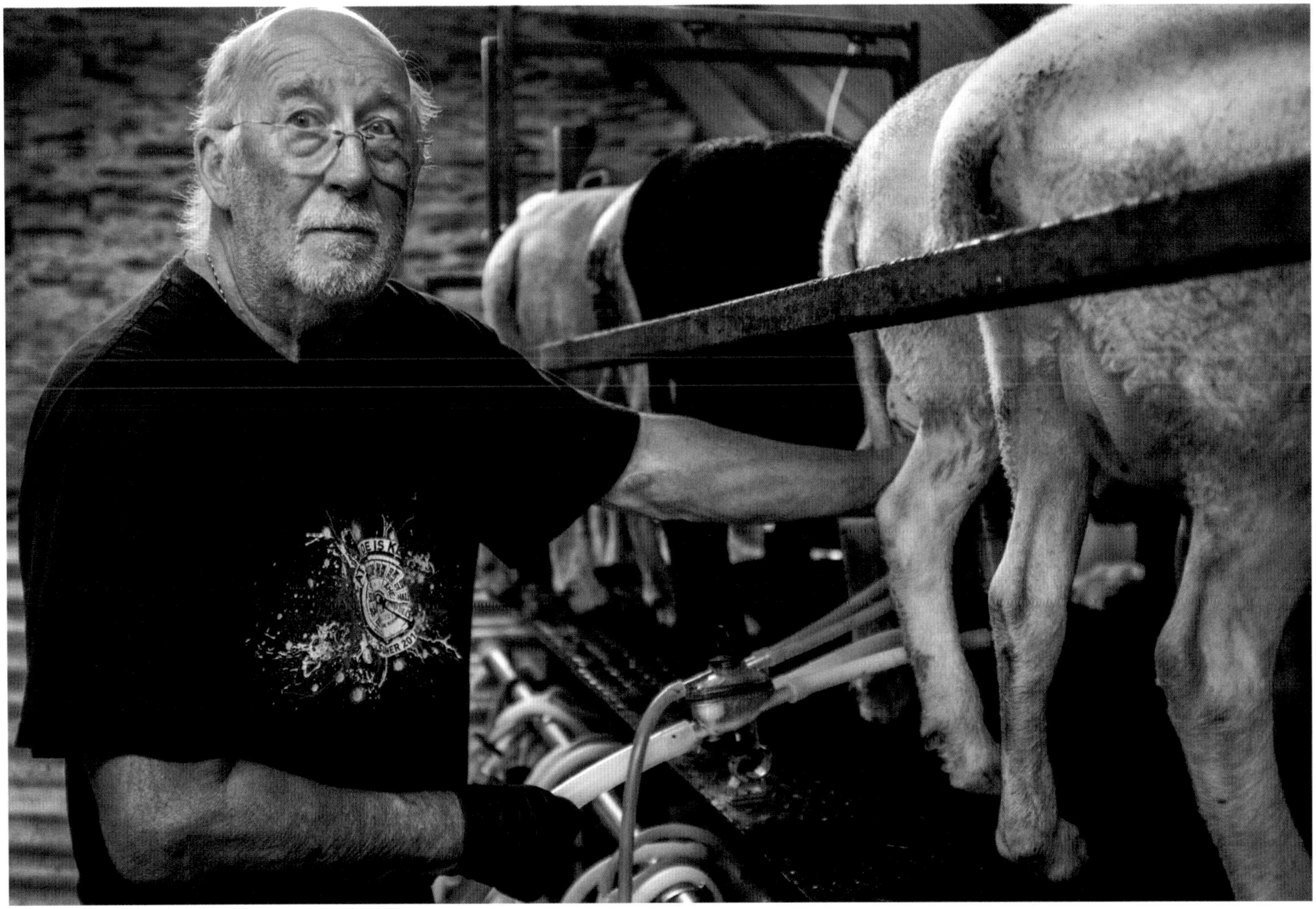

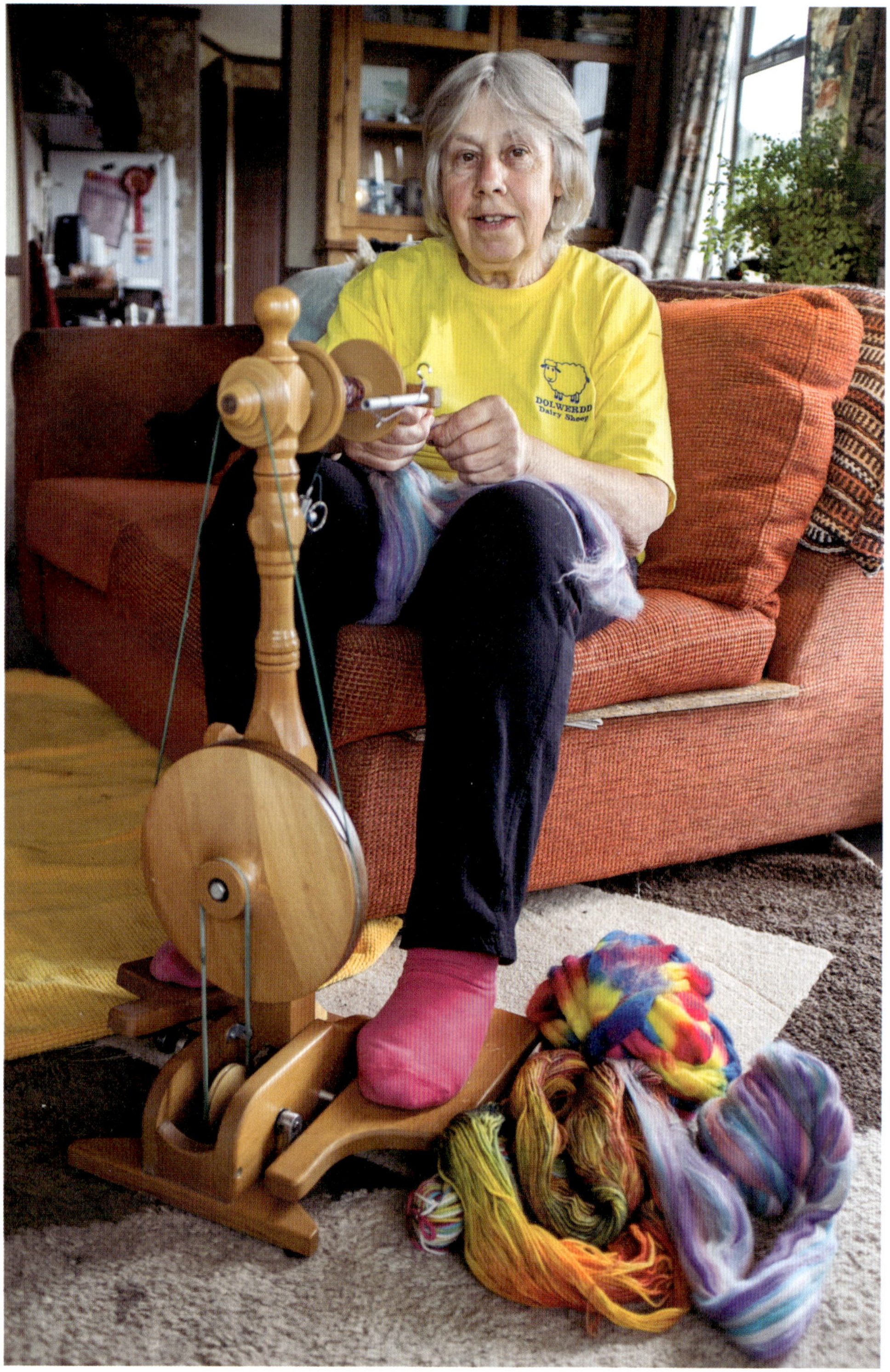
DOLWERDD
Dairy Sheep

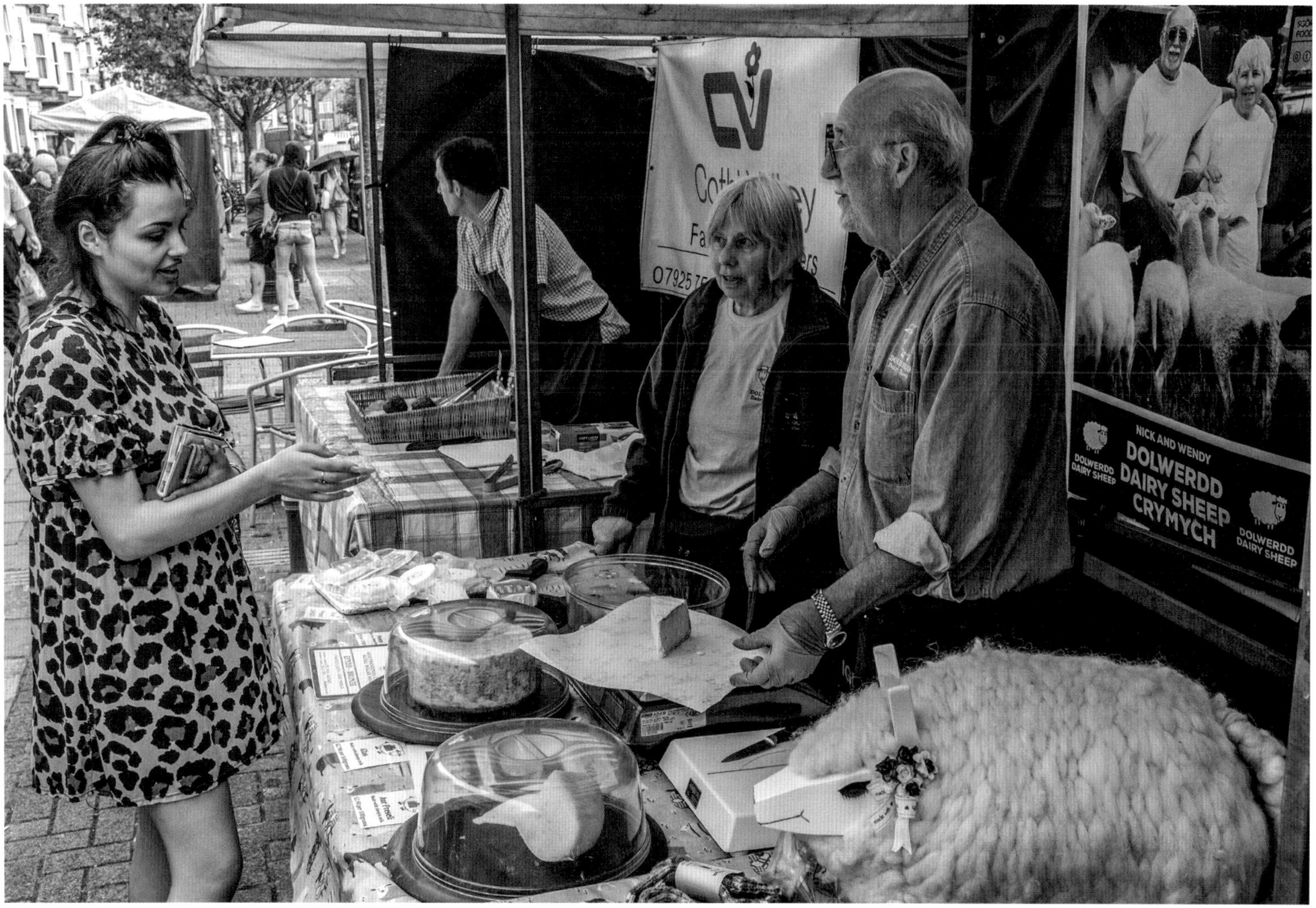
DOLWERDD
DAIRY SHEEP
NICK AND WENDY
DOLWERDD
DAIRY SHEEP
CRYMYCH
DOLWERDD
DAIRY SHEEP

Conservation

Arwyn Owen

Based at Hafod y Llan farm at the foot of Snowdon, Arwyn Owen is responsible for shepherding 600,000 acres of grazing in some of the most picturesque landscape of North Wales. Most of the holding is on Hafod y Llan itself, and on nearby Gelli Iago farm. Around 2,500 acres are located in other blocks around the Nant Gwynant area.

"The land was acquired for the nation by the National Trust in 1998-1999 after a public appeal raised the necessary finance," Arwyn explains, "and then I came on board in 2007. Our key missions here are to maintain the traditions and regimes that have made the area what it is, and also to improve the habitats that support the nature conservation interests. To achieve these results the numbers of sheep have been halved, and the Welsh Black cattle herd increased, creating a more mixed pattern of grazing that favours greater plant diversity. It is," he reflects, "a real challenge to make money out of sheep and beef today, but agriculture is the backbone of Wales, not just economically but also socially and culturally. Take the language, for instance, at least ninety per cent of life and work here is in Cymraeg."

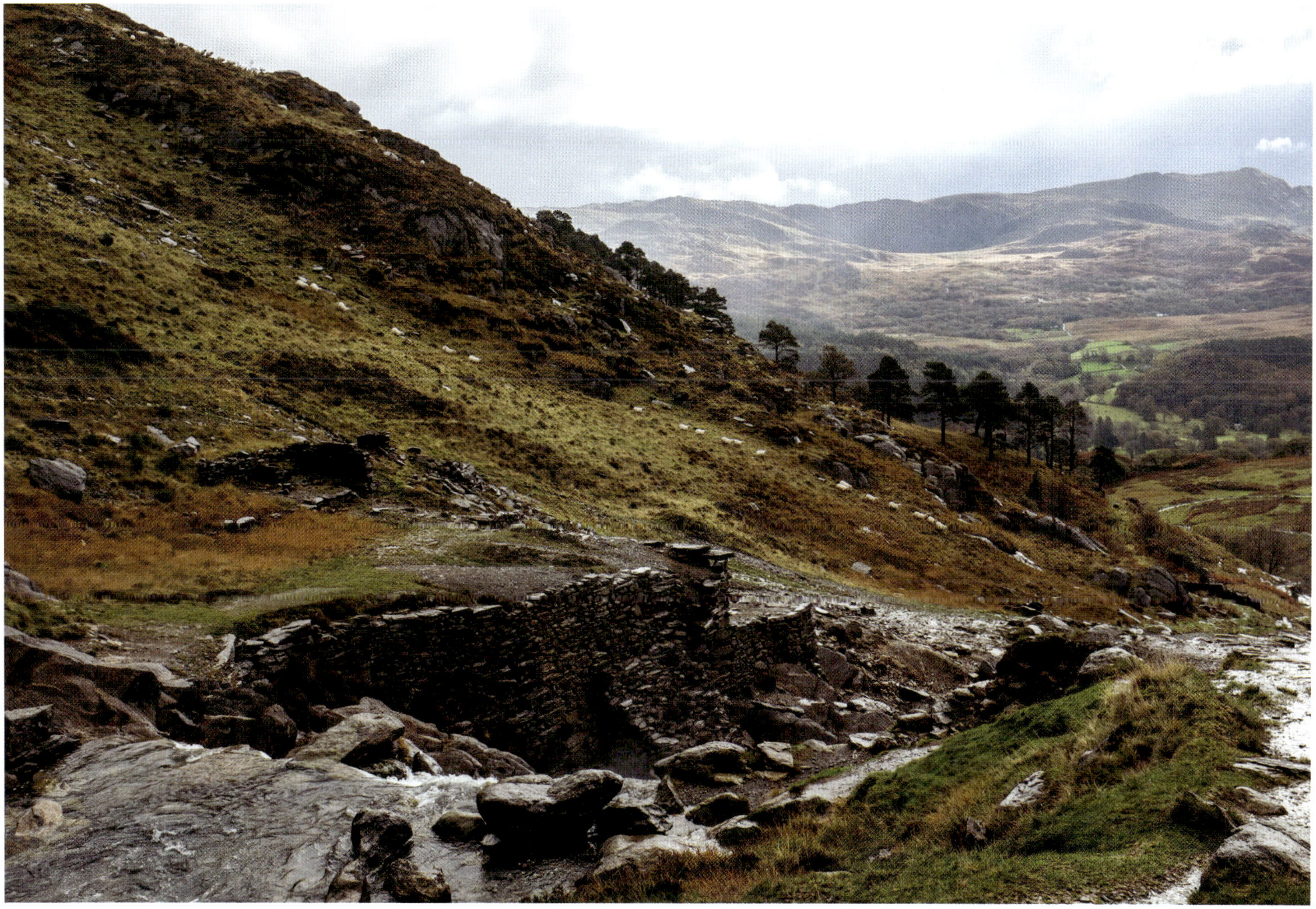

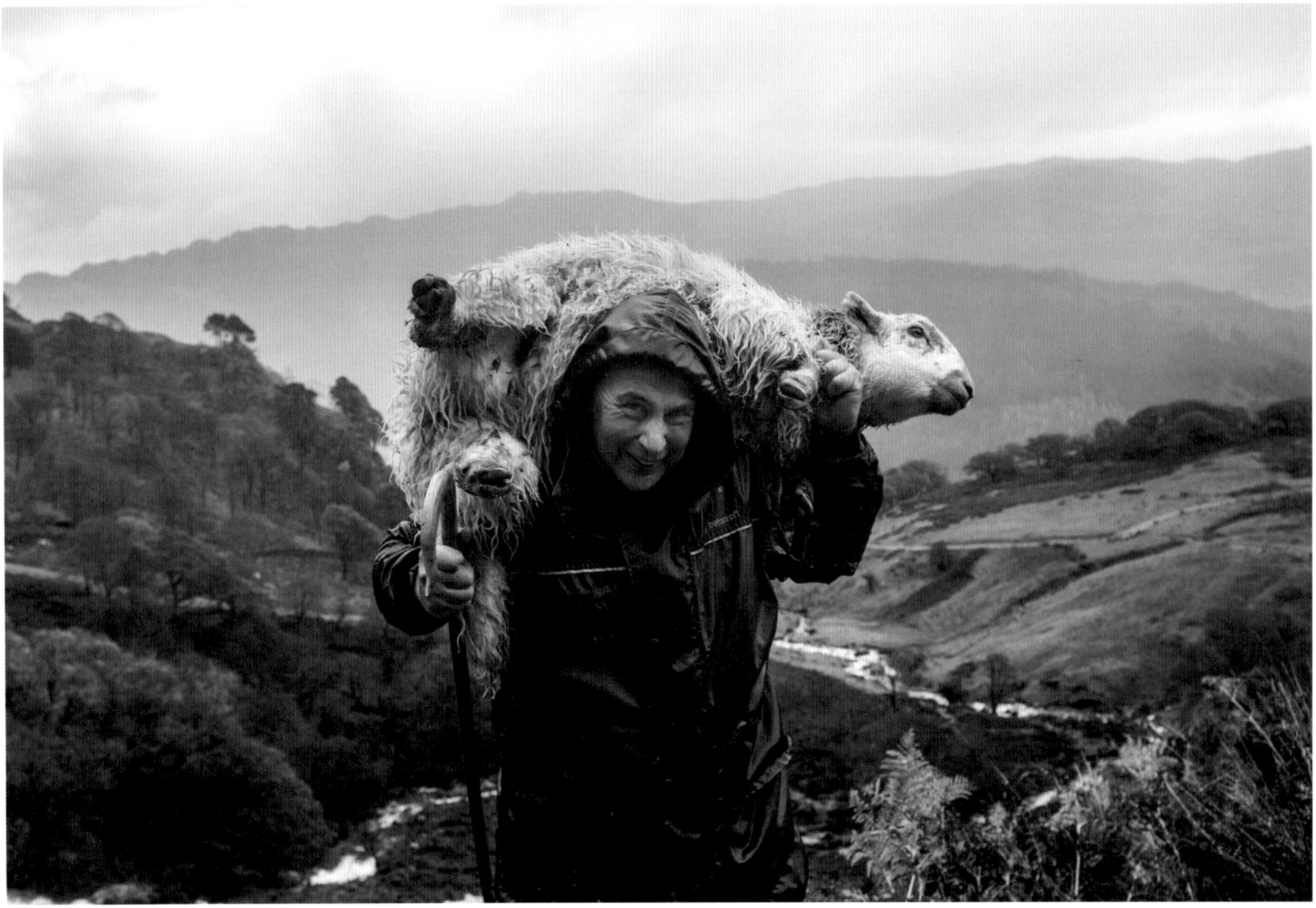

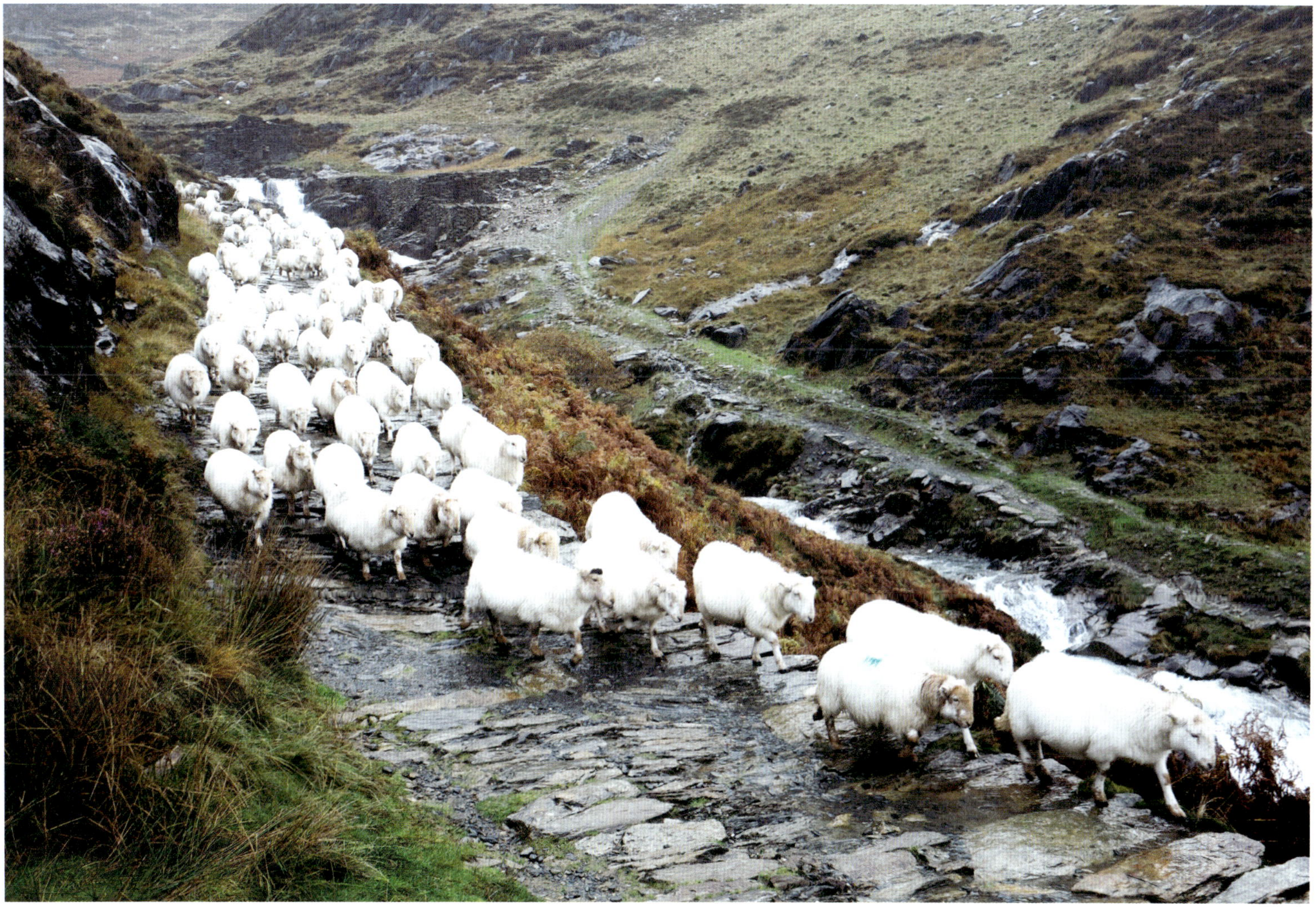

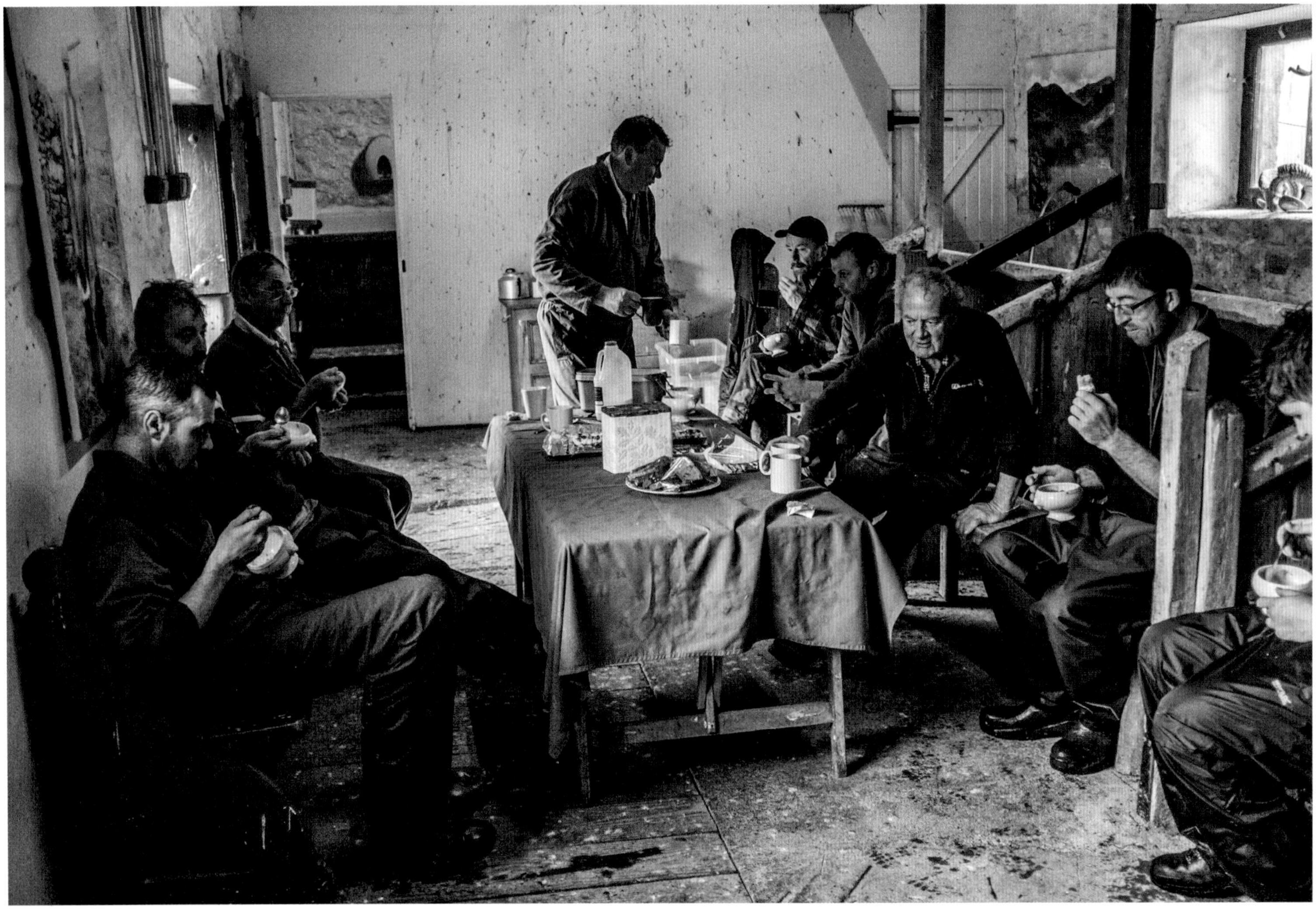

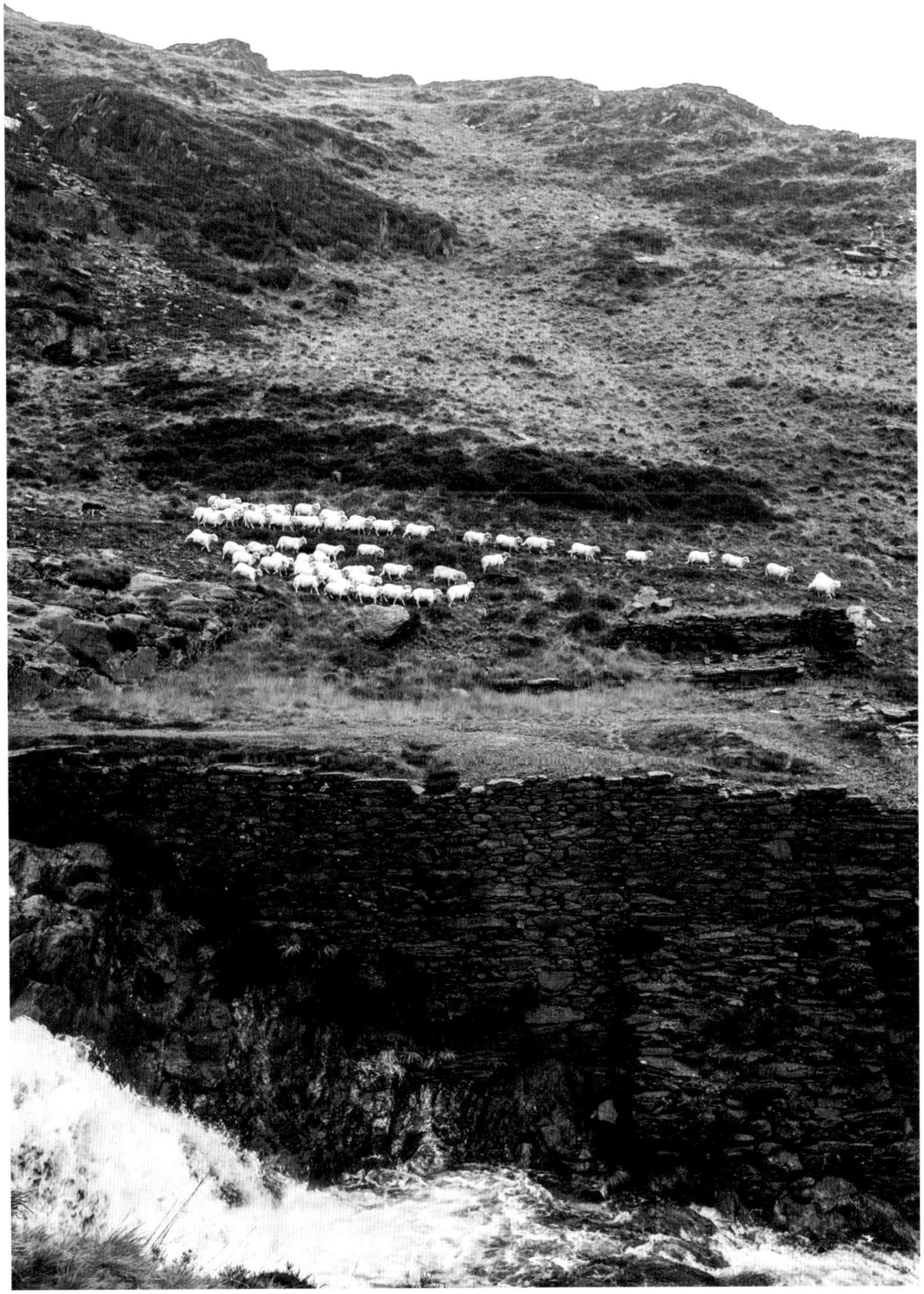

Pete Godfrey

Pete Godfrey, together with his dogs, manages a close shepherding regime for the RSPB. At the reserve on South Stack, Anglesey, they are using historically ancient hardy breeds of sheep to create very specific habitat for rare or threatened species of birds. There is very tricky balance between conservation and public access to be maintained here, as the high numbers of visitors with pet dogs can cause real problems for the sheep in this precipitous landscape. Pete and the dogs literally have to be on the case throughout all public visiting times.

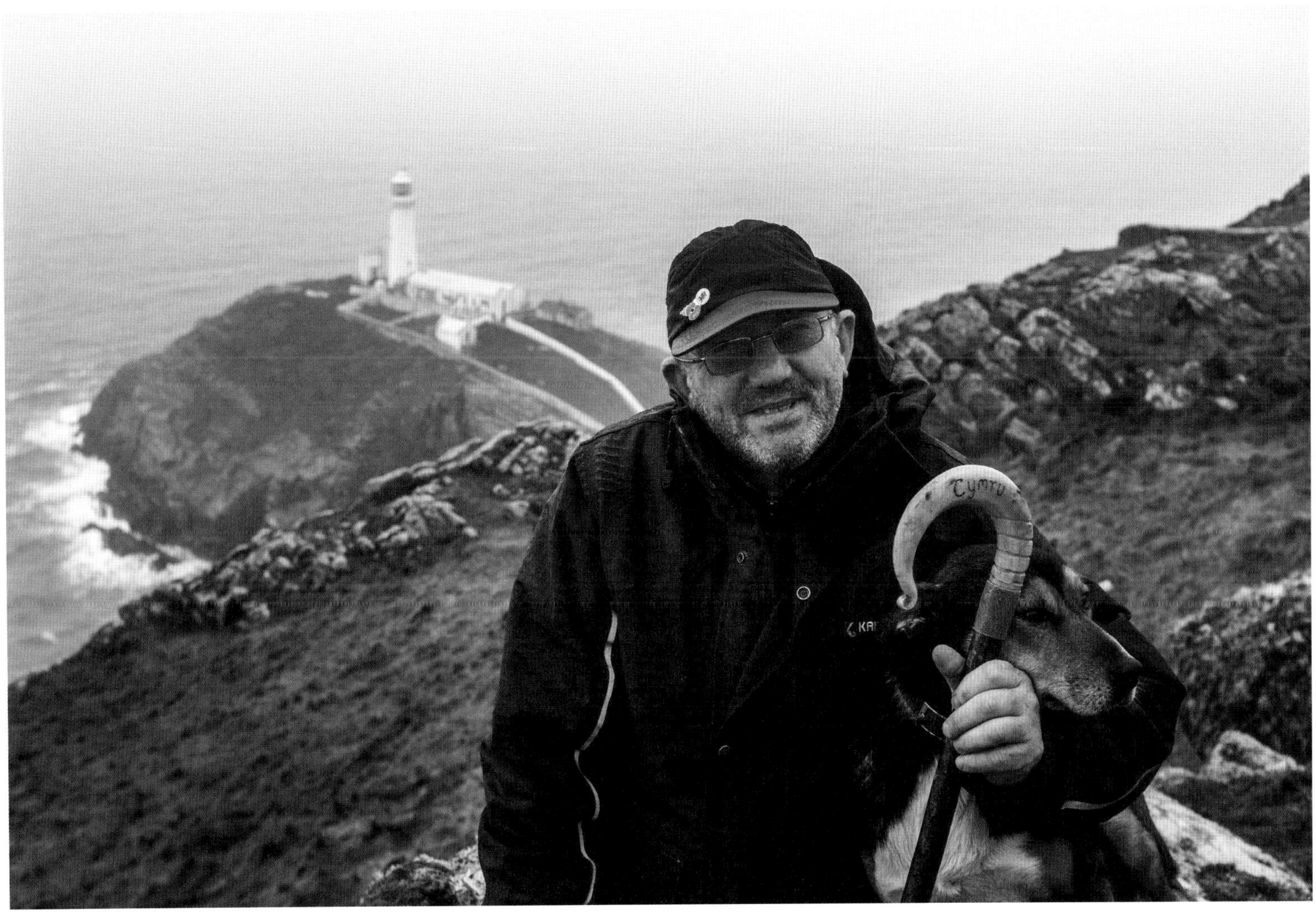
Cymru

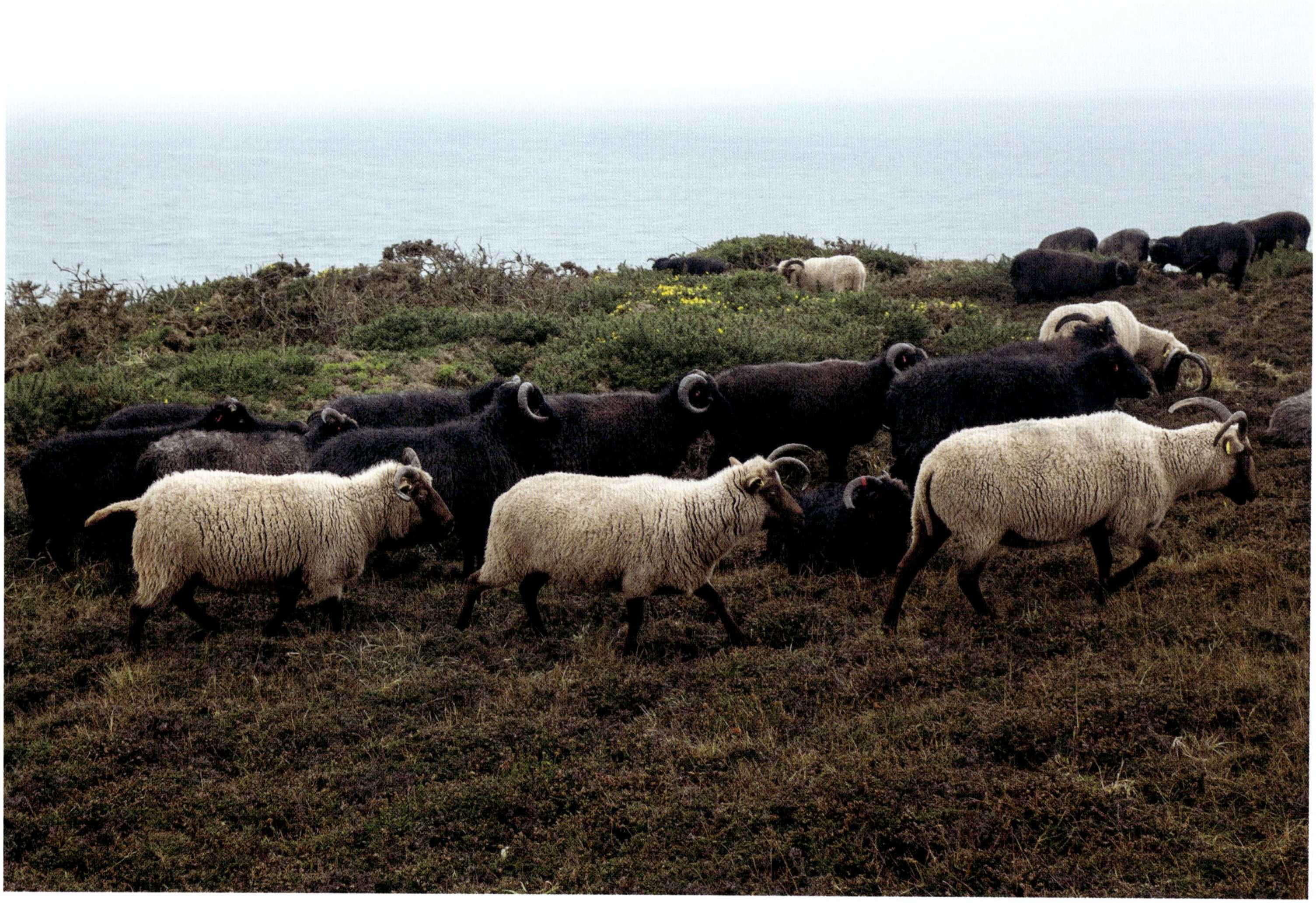

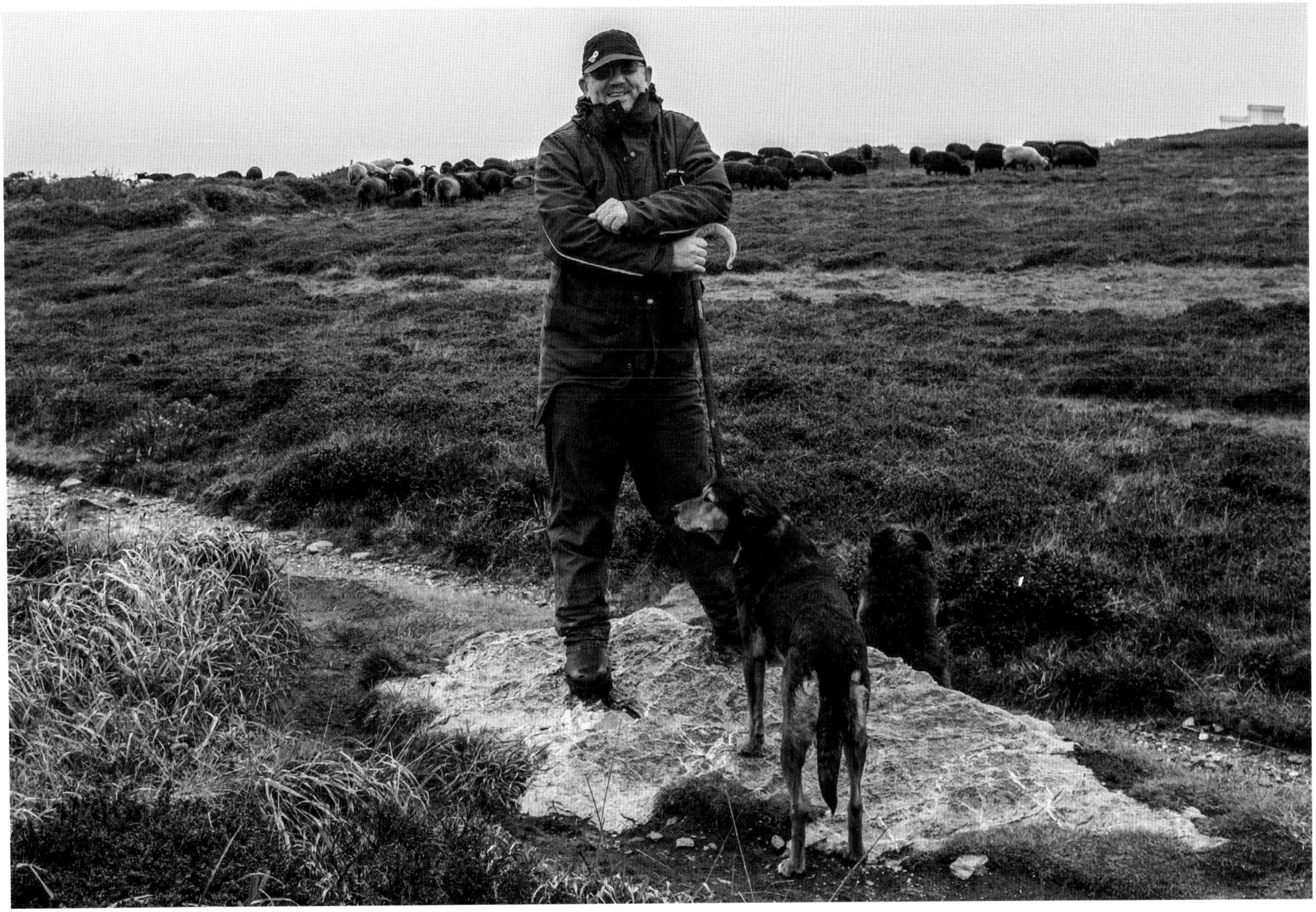

Terry and Josephe Mills and Gethin Evans, Cruglas

Since 1995 Terry and Josephe Mills have been farming a 300 hectare holding at Cruglas. Through a combination of their lifetime of business experience, and the specialised local knowledge of the area which previous owners John and Jean Thomas had acquired over 40 years they have transformed the landscape. From a virtually sterile prairie of agricultural land, Cruglas has blossomed into a showpiece of the possible co-existence between agriculture, landscape conservation, biodiversity, and tourism.

"Our aim was to show that farming can be done entirely in harmony with nature, without the need to intensively exploit every single square yard of land," Terry explains. "We looked for a location with some existing wood and water, where we could create a mosaic of nature in addition to pasture for the animals."

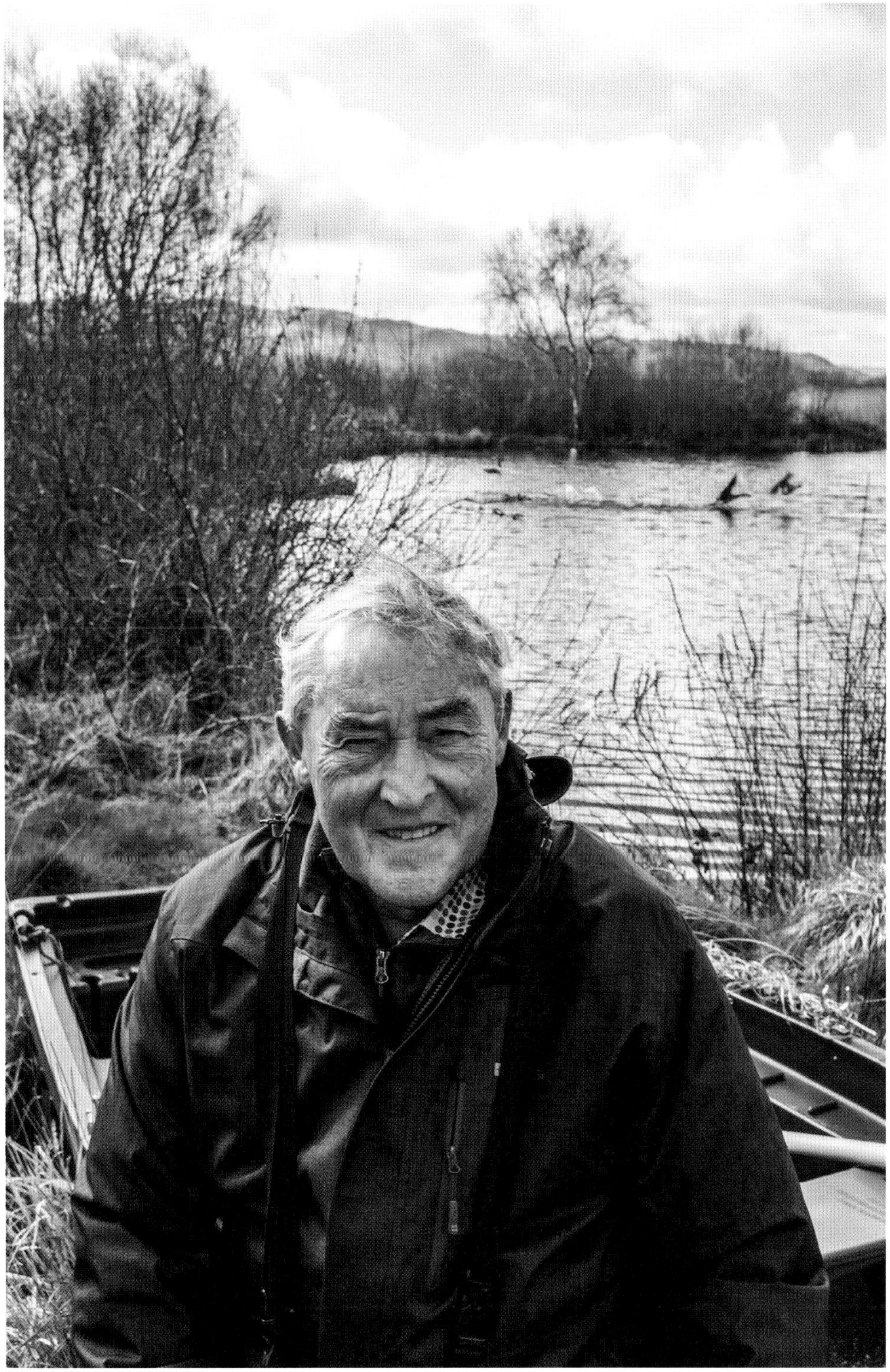

From a stocking rate of 800 breeding ewes, they gradually reduced to the current level of 400-500. The process of creating wetlands, planting small mixed woodlands, and creating wildlife corridors of species rich hedgerows was supported financially by some grant aid, but was also supplemented by Terry and Josephe from their own private resources. Terry had enjoyed a successful business career, but he acknowledges that "not everyone will be in a position to do the same. It could still have been done without my financial input," he says, "but it would have taken fifteen years to achieve the environmental reward that we now enjoy, instead of the seven years in which we managed to achieve them."

He is passionate about how future agricultural support must work, in order to avoid the unproductive scattergun approaches of the past. "They must keep the schemes flexible and specifically targeted," he says, "the one size fits all prescription is wasteful and inefficient, as there is a wide spectrum of farm types in Wales. There are different soils, different altitudes, different carrying capacities, and importantly differing hydrologies. Water is a key element in creating biodiversity. The devil is in the detail, and the recognition of it in planning. For instance, hedgerows can grow almost anywhere, and sequester carbon at a much better rate than planted woodland. Because they are planted more densely together, and because early growth spurts are repeatedly restarted by cutting back, hedgerows remove a lot more carbon from the atmosphere over time. We should also be careful that indiscriminate woodland planting doesn't compromise other scarce natural habitats, such as species rich grassland."

As well as supporting 144 different observed species of birds, including 80 species which breed there, and an extensive list of other indigenous wildlife, Cruglas is an important employer of local labour, and buyer of local goods. "If the public wonder what the country gets in return for agricultural financial support," Terry points out, "here at Cruglas we provide work for digger drivers, building and fencing contractors, a shepherd, gardeners and maintainance staff for the holiday cottages, as well as many others. That is besides producing food, enhancing biodiversity, reducing the carbon responsible for climate change, and managing the much admired Welsh country landscape."

Responsible for shepherding at Cruglas is Gethin Evans, who lives on the farm with his wife Charlotte and their three children. He was born on the family farm at Brynperffaith, near Devil's Bridge in Ceredigion, and was "brought up with sheep and beef from day one." The flock at Cruglas is almost exclusively Welsh Mountain, because "there are so many good different bloodlines available here, which avoids inbreeding."

He gained a Diploma in Agriculture from Gelli Aur College, and plied the shepherd's trade in thirteen different countries around the world, incuding two and a half years at Denmark's biggest sheep farm with 1,300 ewes. "You get to see so many different systems and situations," he says, "and it is a wonderful way to learn and see the world." The island of Sardinia made a particular impression on him. "Having learned the very efficient shearing techniques in New Zealand, I was able to shear up to 250 ewes in a day, and that without stressing them and affecting their milk yields. The owners treated me like a king because I was saving then so much money... beer from first thing in the morning and then all day, and seven course meals." He did suffer a lot of teasing about his weight on returning to Wales, in spite of the long hard work days he had been putting in.

Gethin does have some misgivings about the current state of farming in Wales. "Its like gambling today, because the prices of buying in and selling are fluctuating wildly, even over one year. Also the open market cost of renting land is making it unviable, and a lot of young lads are just breaking even. Their parents are advising them to find other career paths. I think the average age of farmers in Wales now is about seventy years. My parents tried to tell me to take another way, but I have always loved shepherding and farming, and never wanted to do anything else."

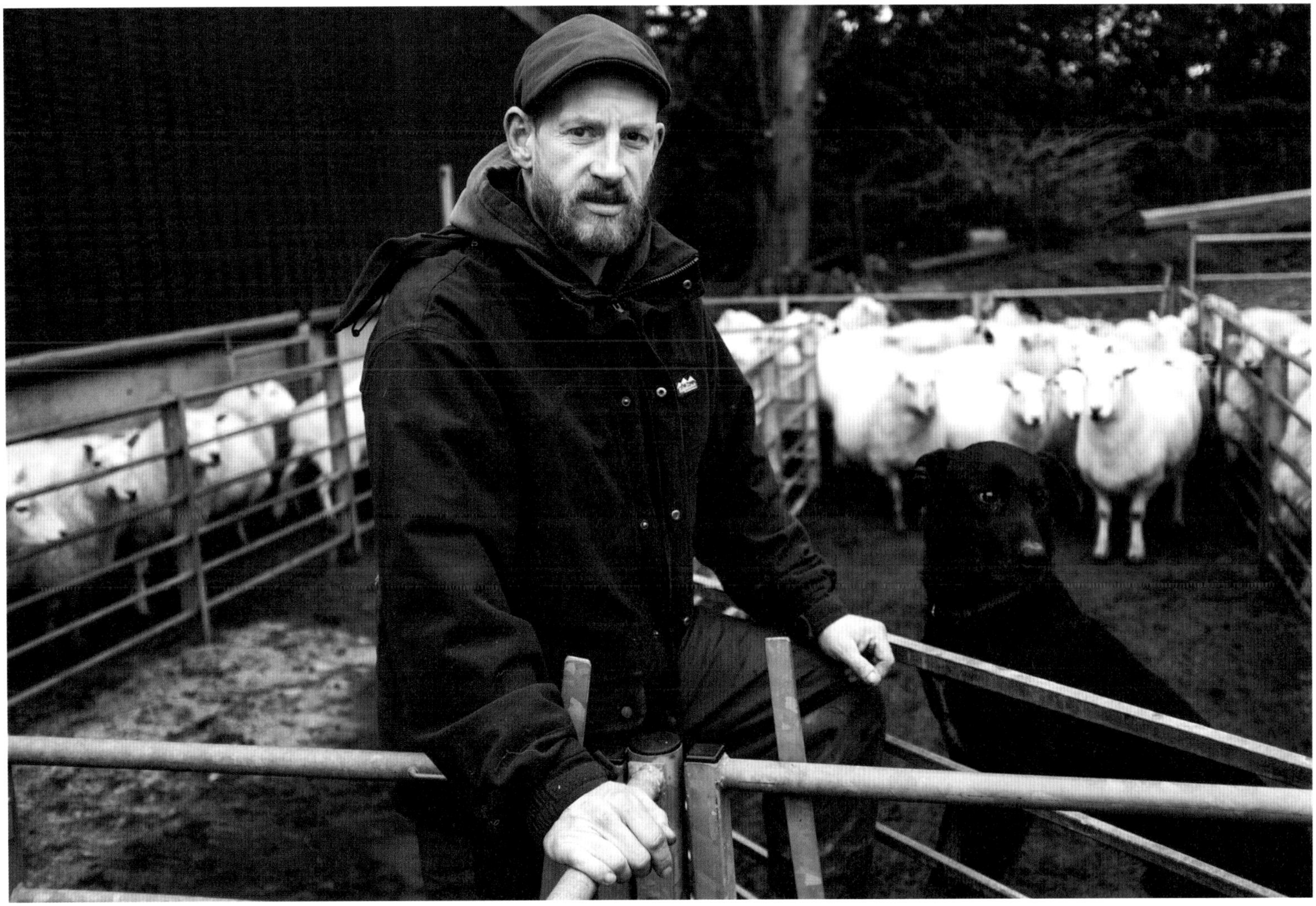

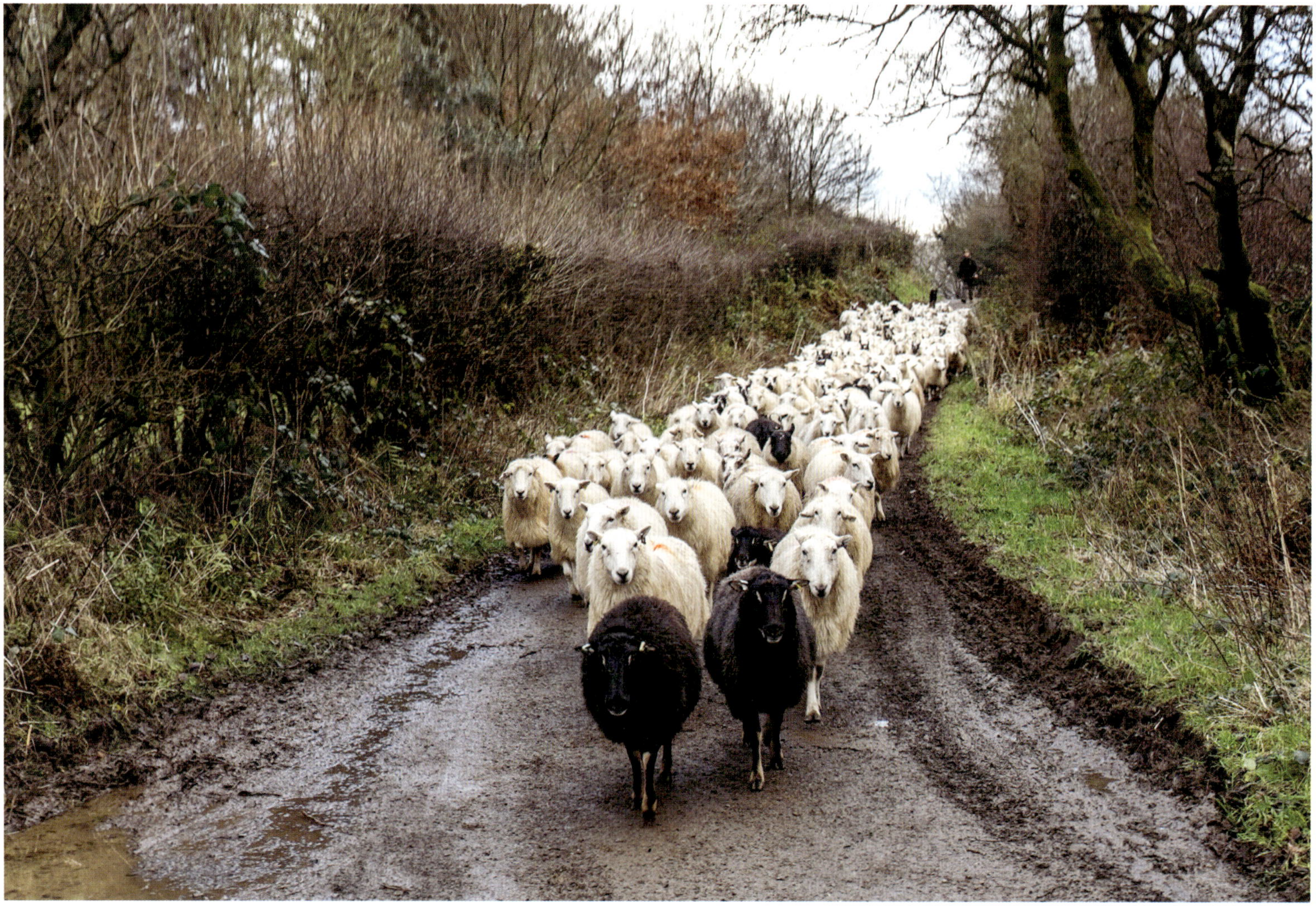

Shepherds of the past

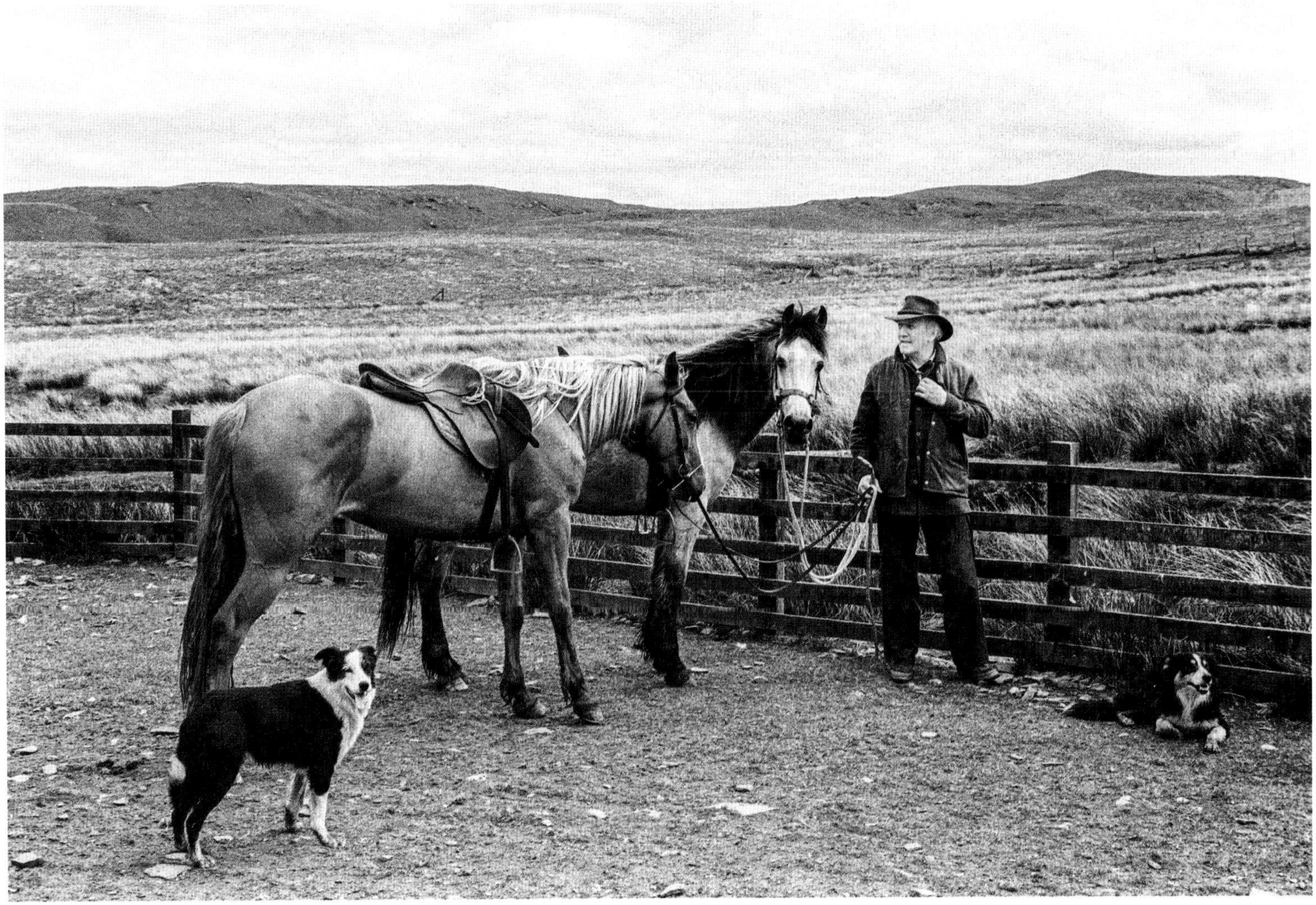

Dai Owen, Tynddol. 1944-2022

Dan Jones, Bryn Bras. 1923-2001

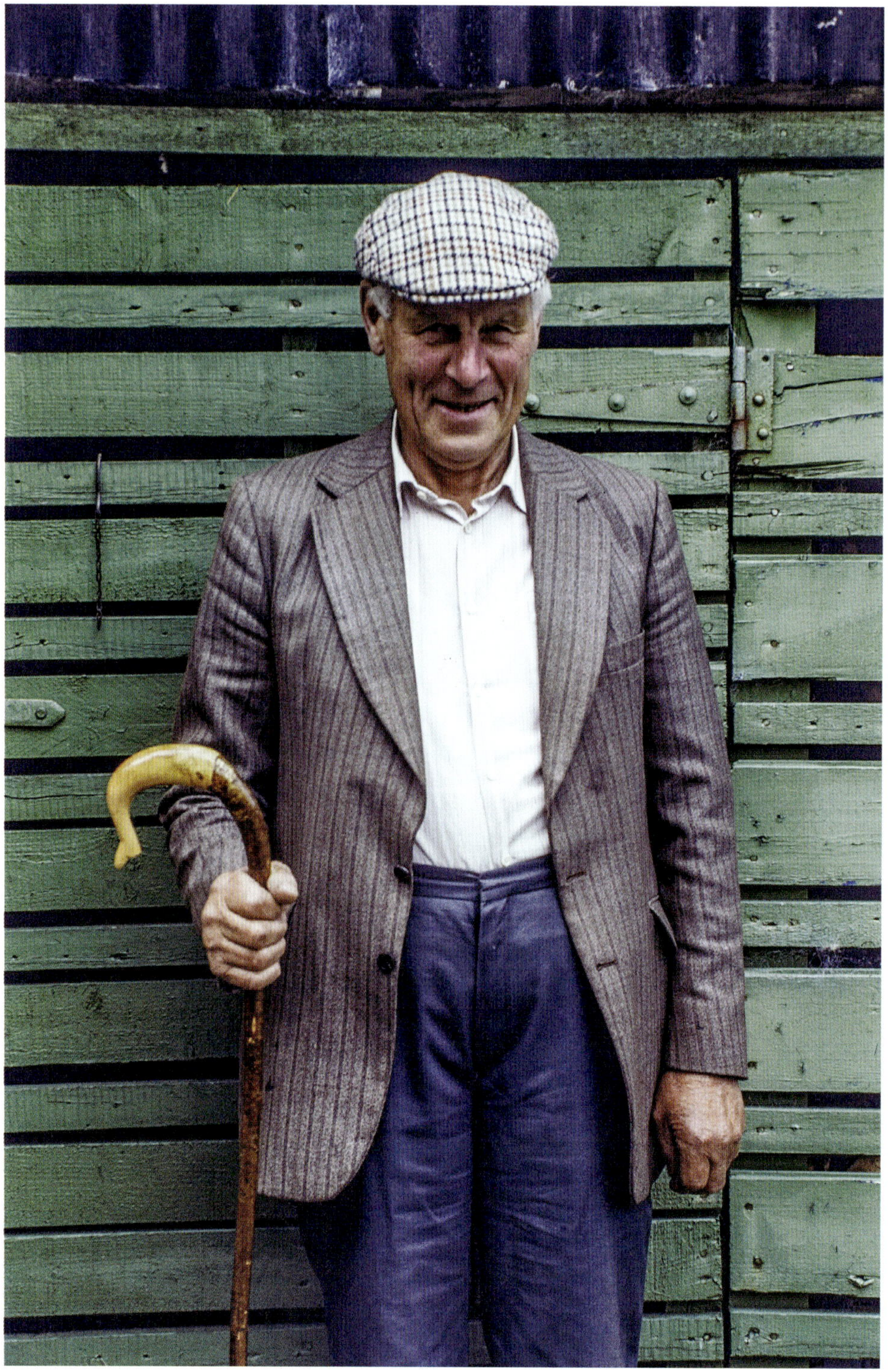

SHEPHERDS OF TODAY

Teleri Fielden

When Teleri was four years old, she told her Mother, "I want to be a lady farmer." By the time she was expecting a baby of her own she had realised that ambition, in a slightly atypical manner.

In her twenties she followed a boyfriend to a ski resort in the Rhône-Alpes, but she hated it, and soon relocated herself to some of the high mountain farms in the area. Having previously helped out with lambing around the Welshpool area she soon took to the work, and loved the locations. The determination to make a life like this for herself was born, and on returning to Wales she set about making it a reality.

She then won a scholarship with The National Trust at Llyndy Isaf near the foot of Yr Wyddfa/ Snowdon, working there for three years to learn the craft of shepherding, living on the job. "It was both tough and enjoyable," she recalls, "and you felt that you had a long way to go. The estate shepherds were very supportive, though, and very much my mentors. I love farming for the links it gives to food, culture, the environment, and the people around you. The characters that you meet are wonderful, and it feels like such a meaningful job."

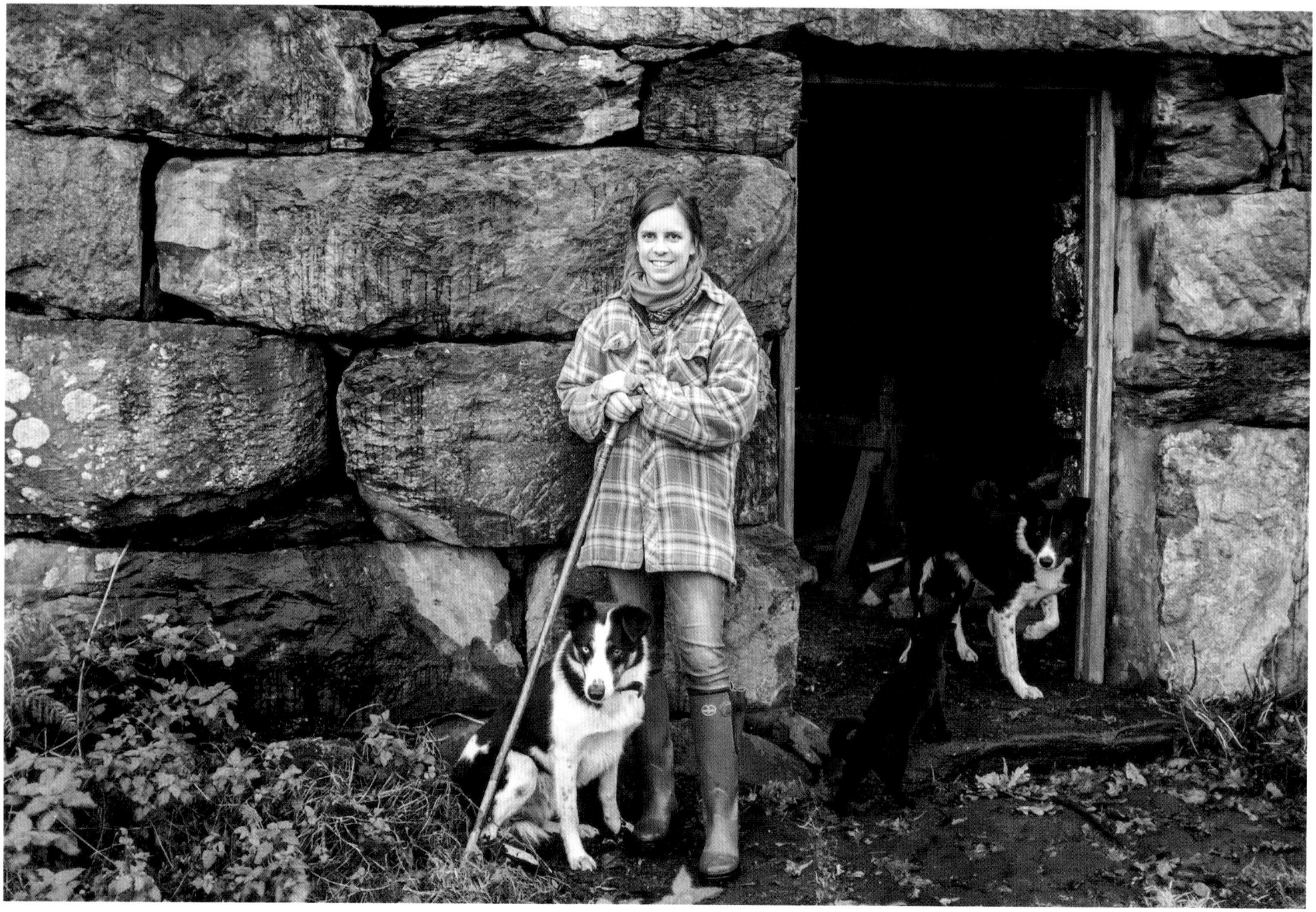

Teleri now has her own farm tenancy from the National Trust on the old Porthmadog Estuary. She has been at Hafod y Llyn Isaf for two and a half years now, with a reduced number of ewes at 100, but also 25 native breed cattle. "They complement each other, with their different grazing patterns," says Teleri. She and her partner Ned both also hold down full-time jobs, and they have diversified by selling meat boxes direct, undertaking conservation grazing for environmental charities, and holding educational events and tours.

Teleri, who has spoken Welsh from the age of five, is concerned about the direction of some incoming agricultural policies, "We need policies which reward active farm management that enhances biodiversity, so that the land can deliver on multiple objectives. If the most lucrative option is planting trees to offset carbon for other industries, we will lose a lot of the regular economic activity that farming brings, and the resulting local spend of income that is the lifeblood of the community. If the communities then die away we will be left with a countryside that is culturally sterile, and lose the skills and experience to work the land.

We must keep the people linked to the land."

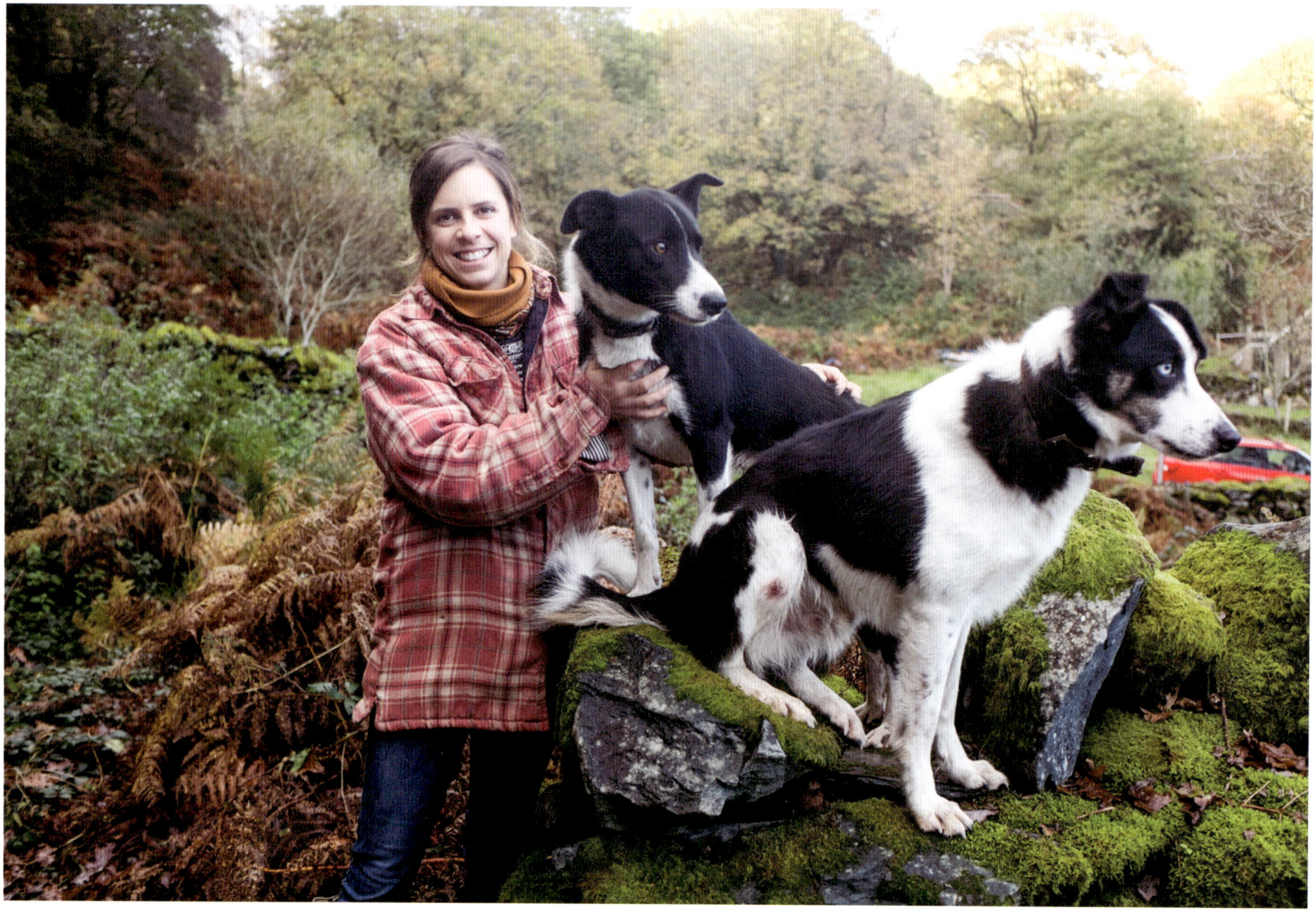

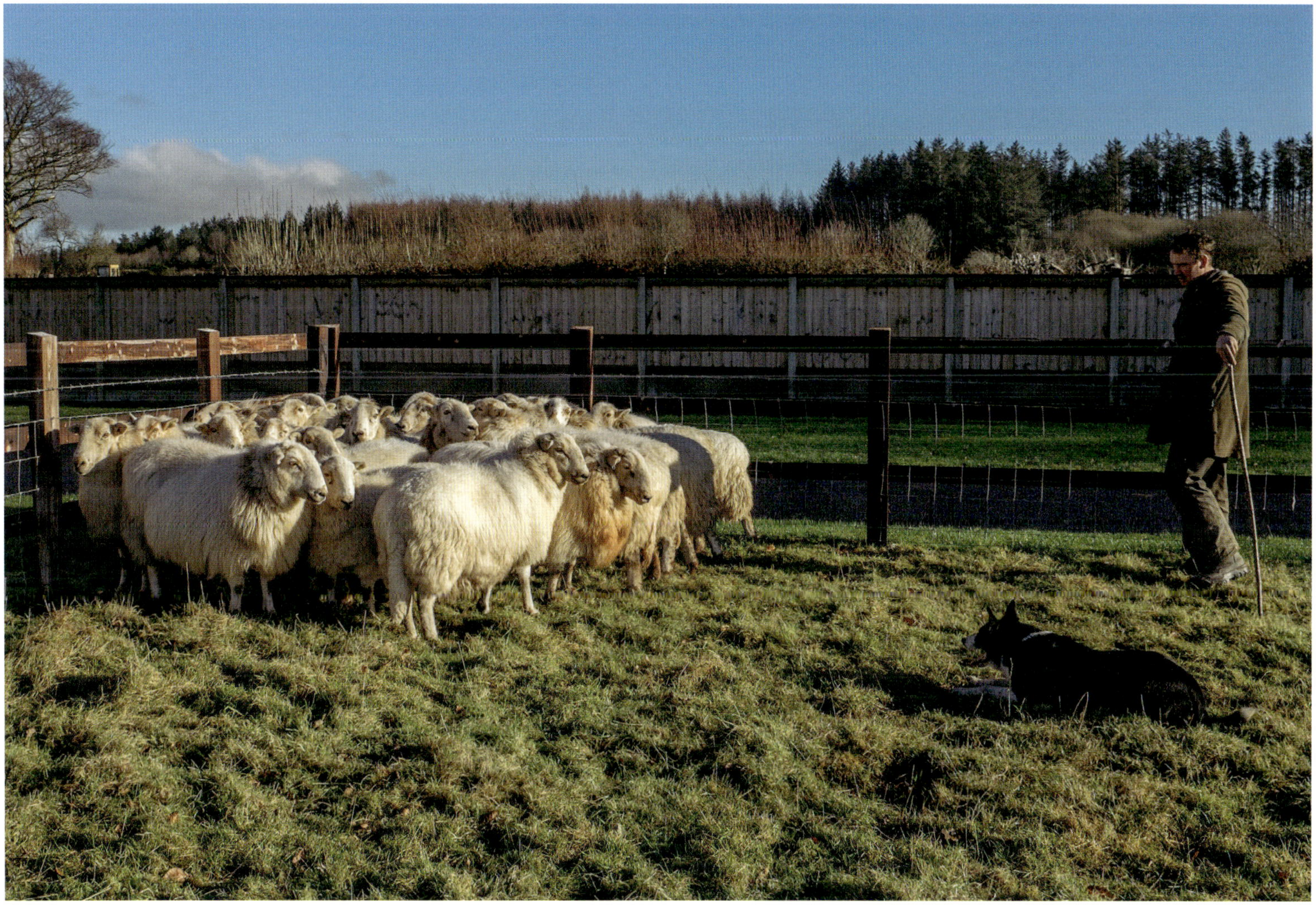

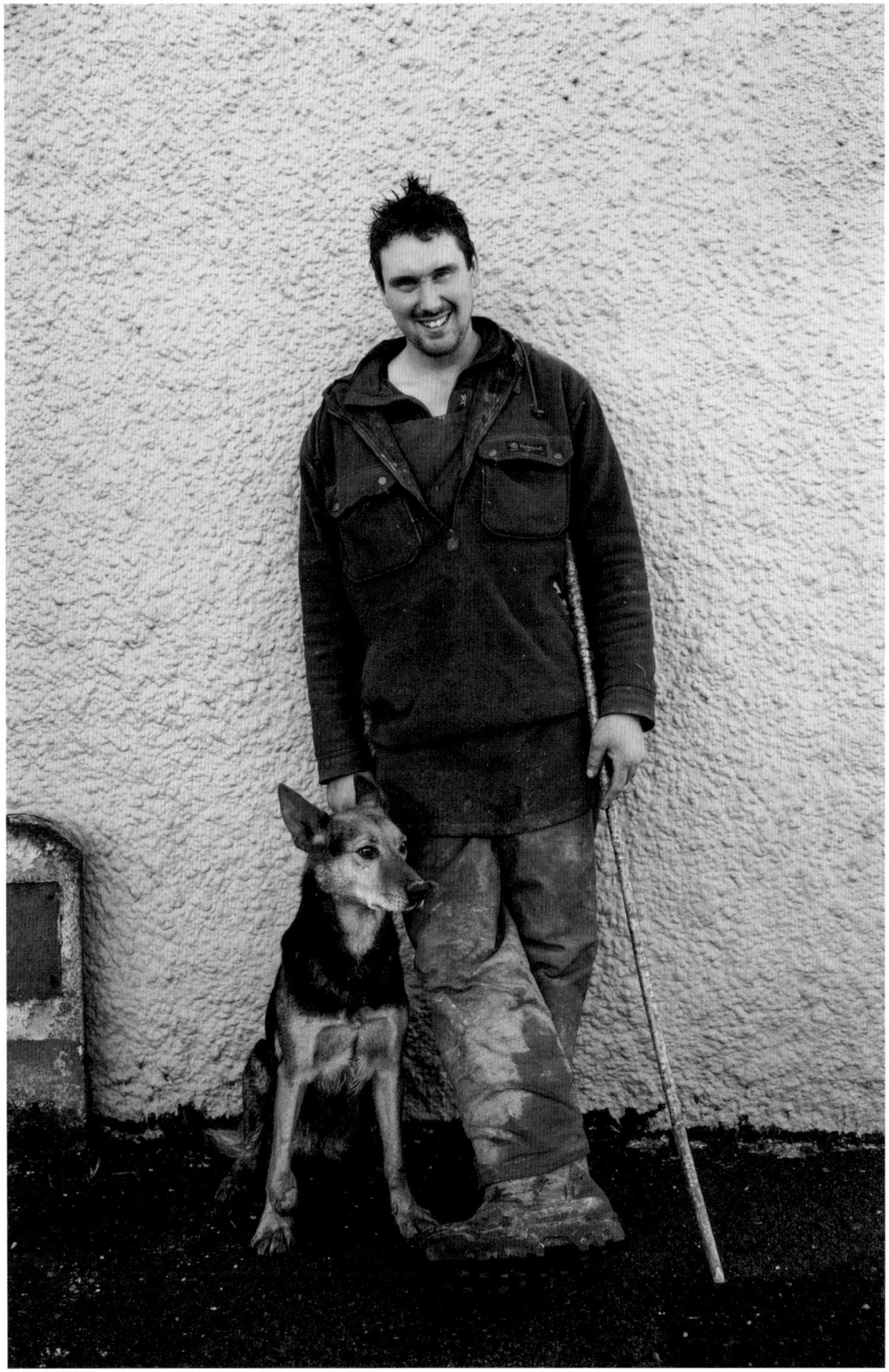

Shepherds of tomorrow

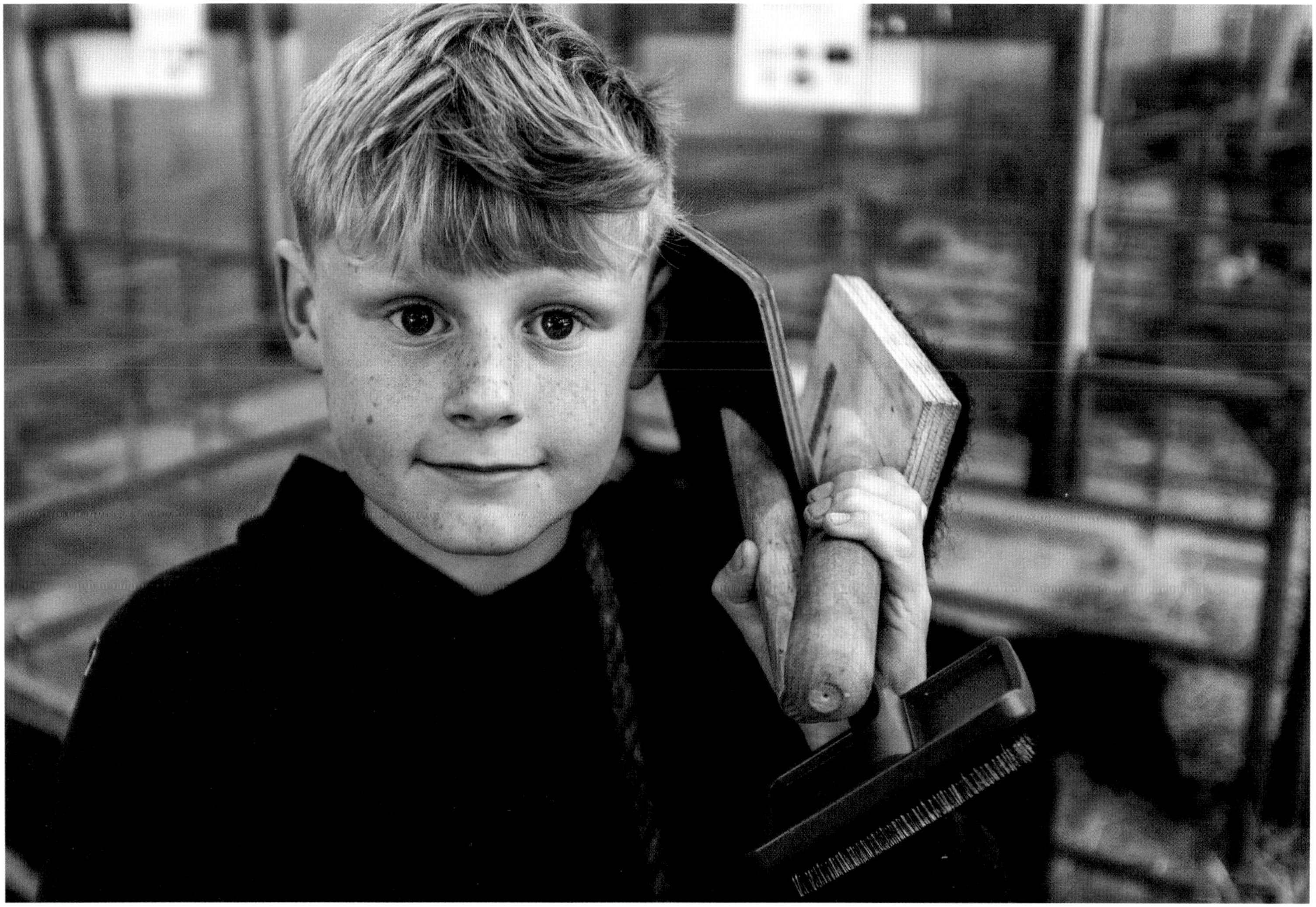

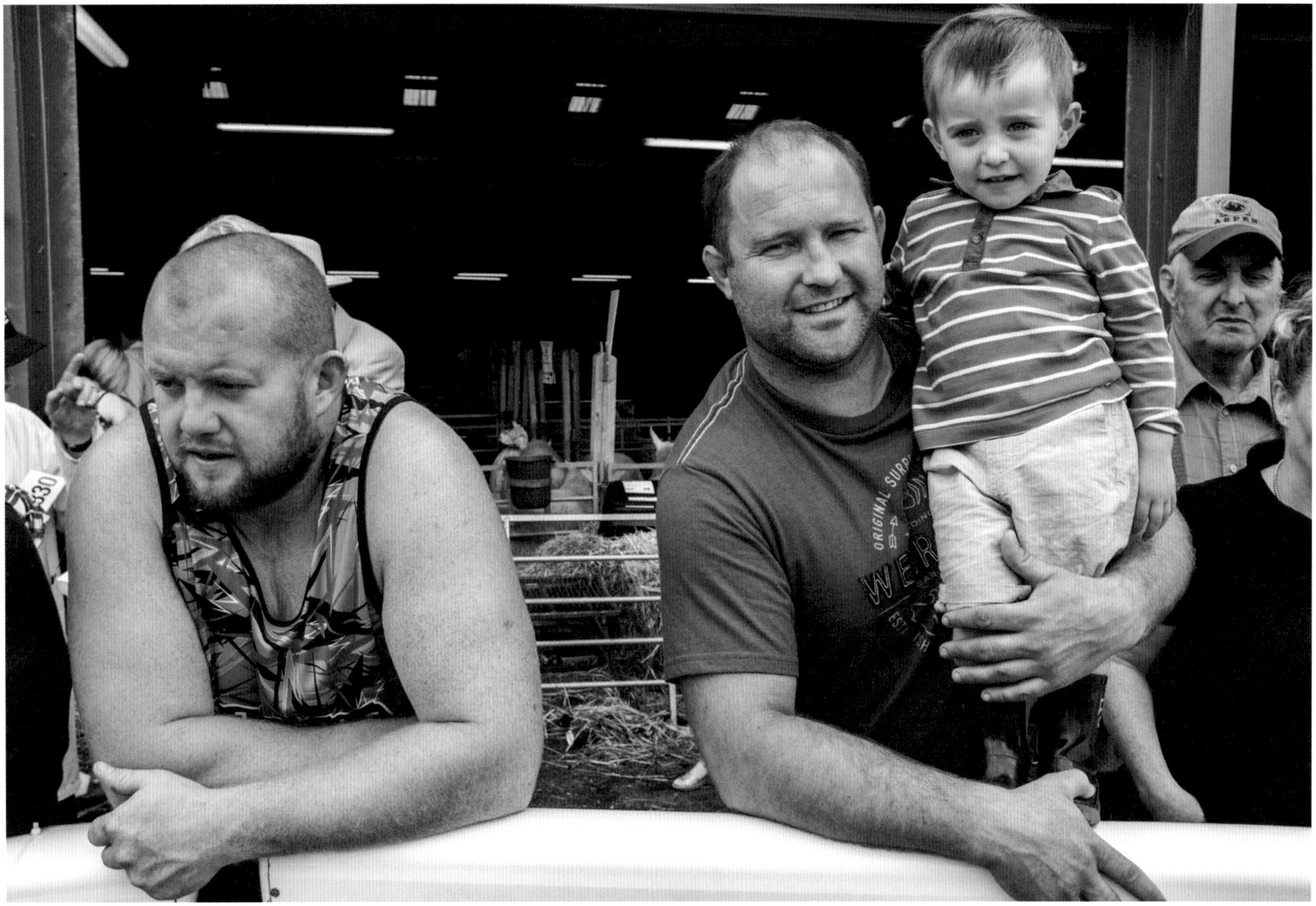

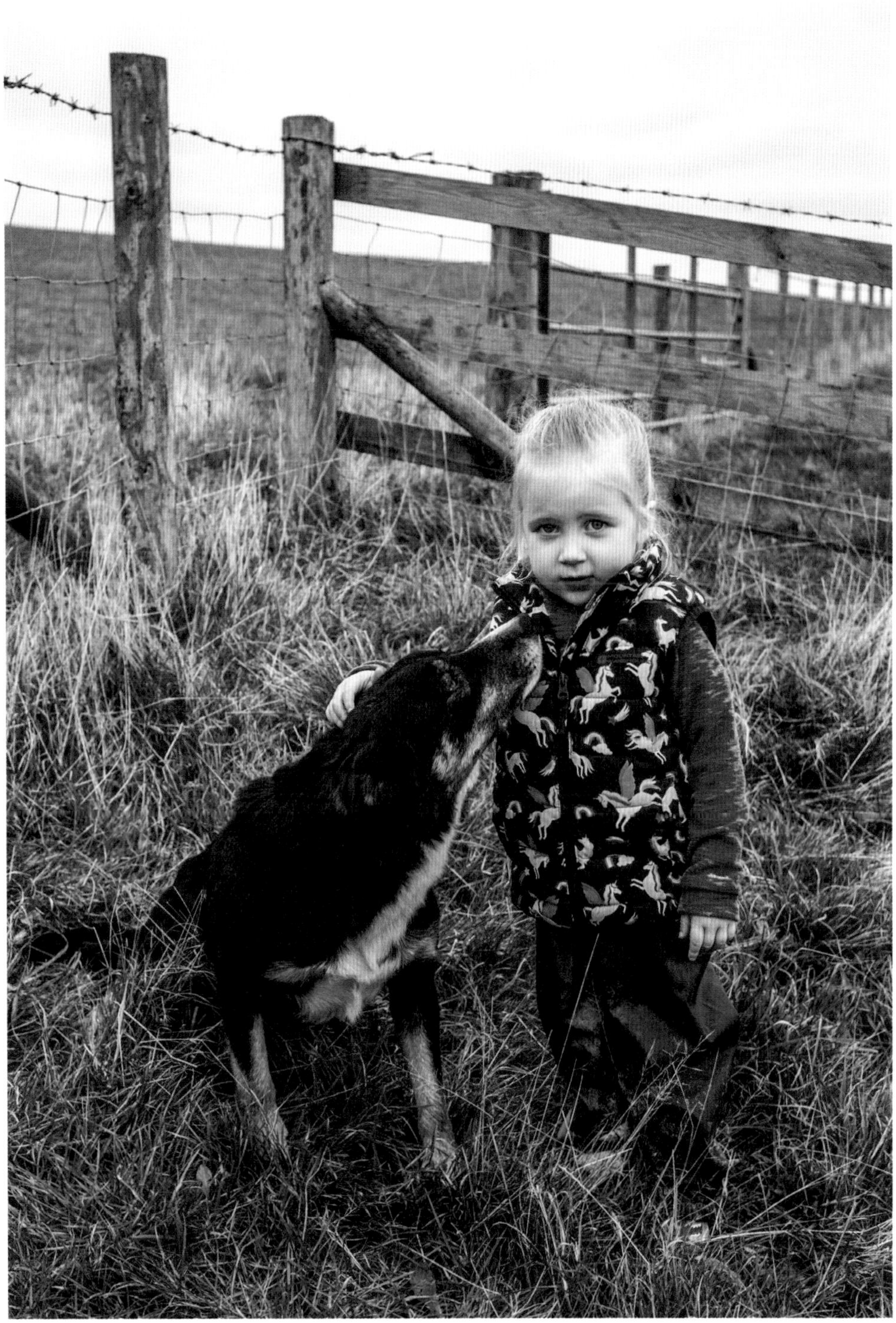

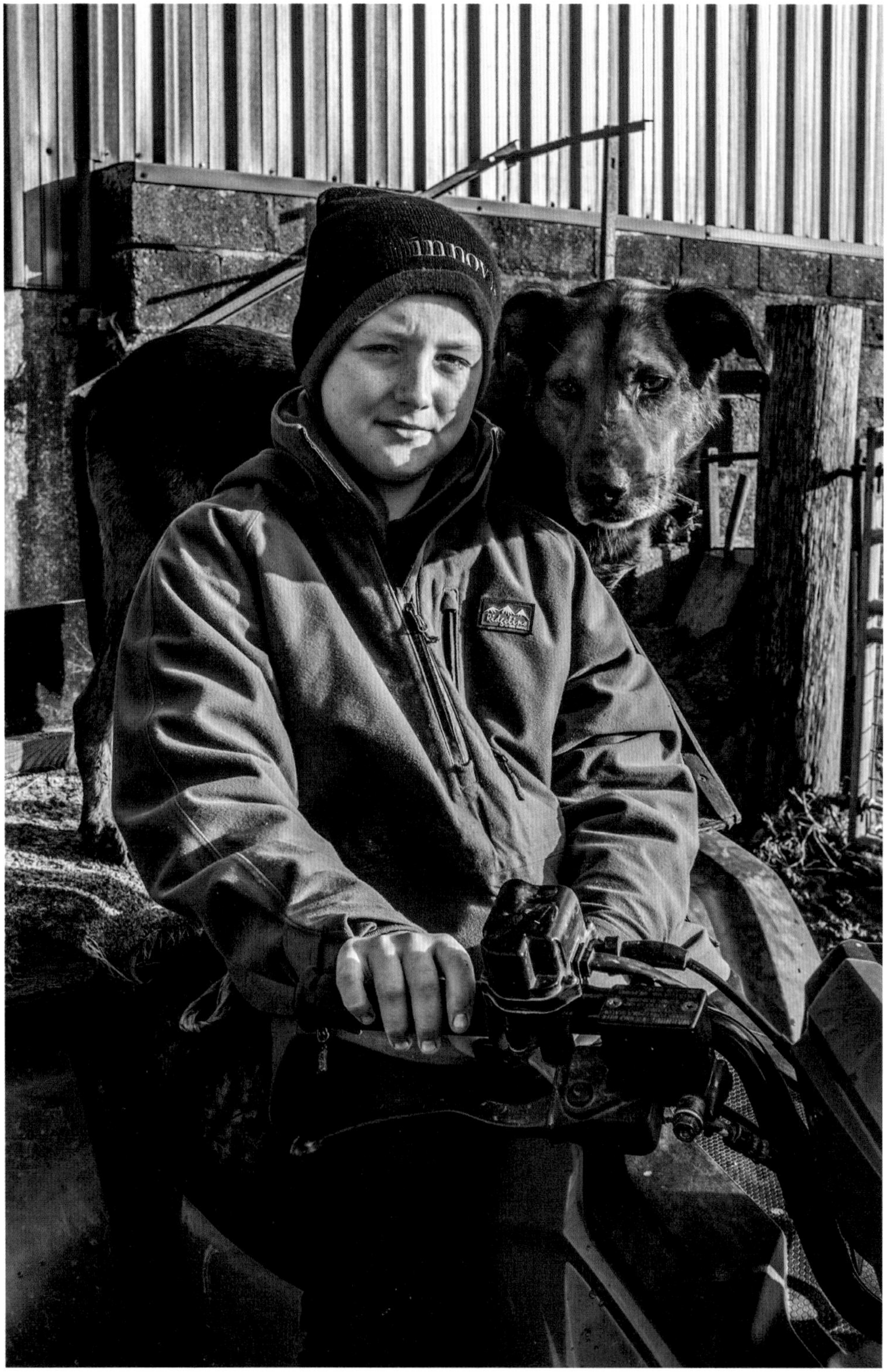

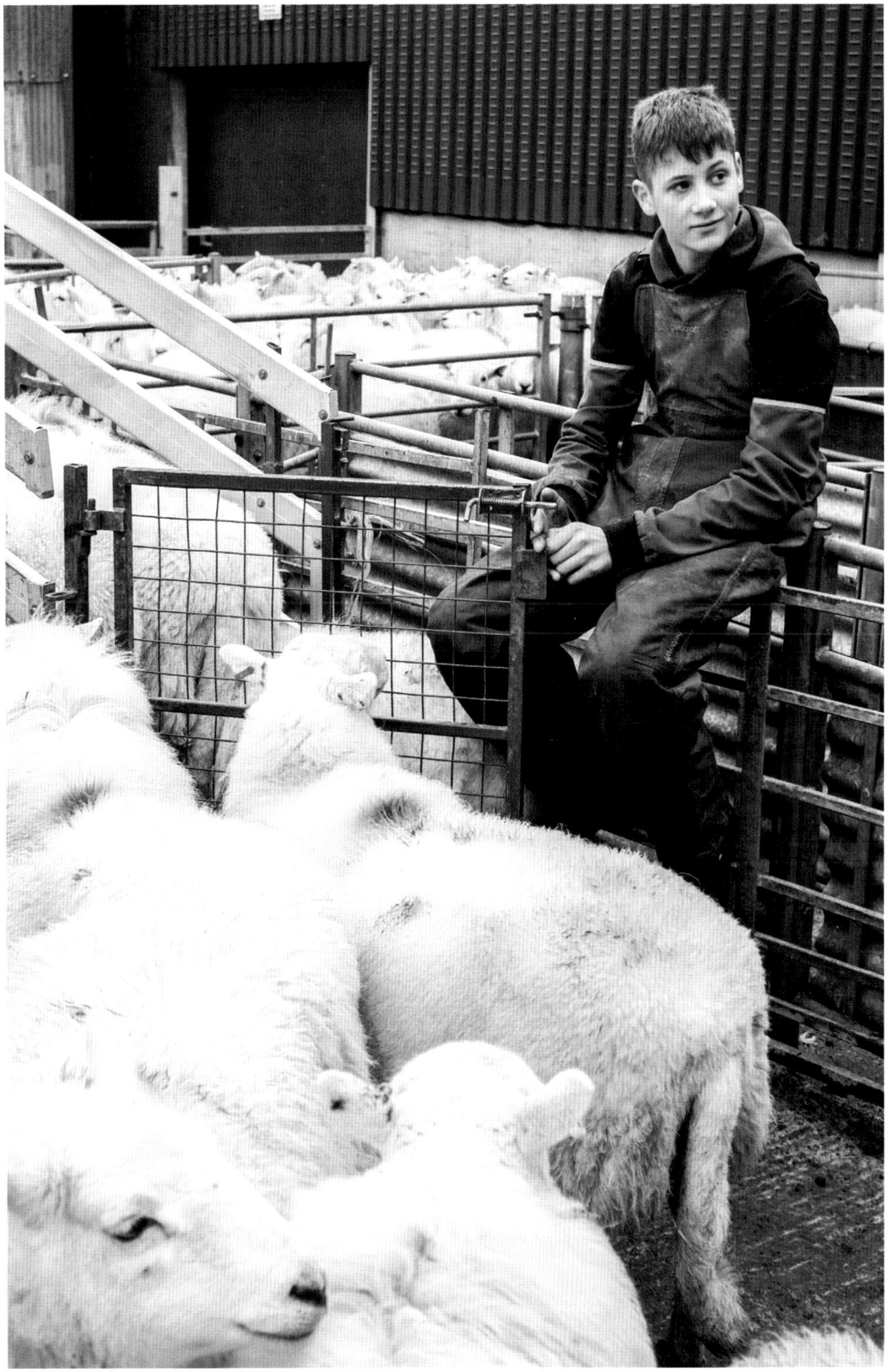

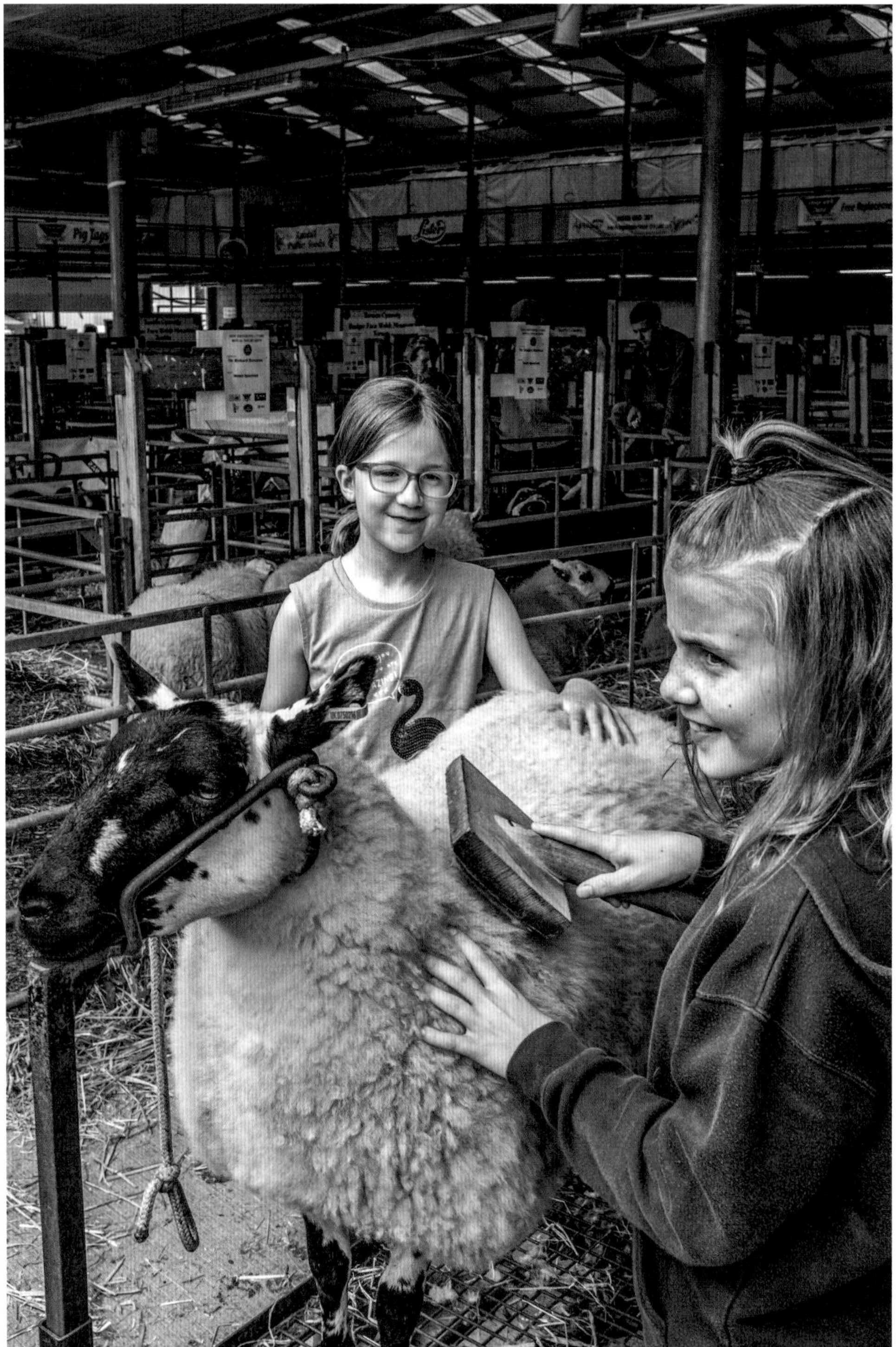

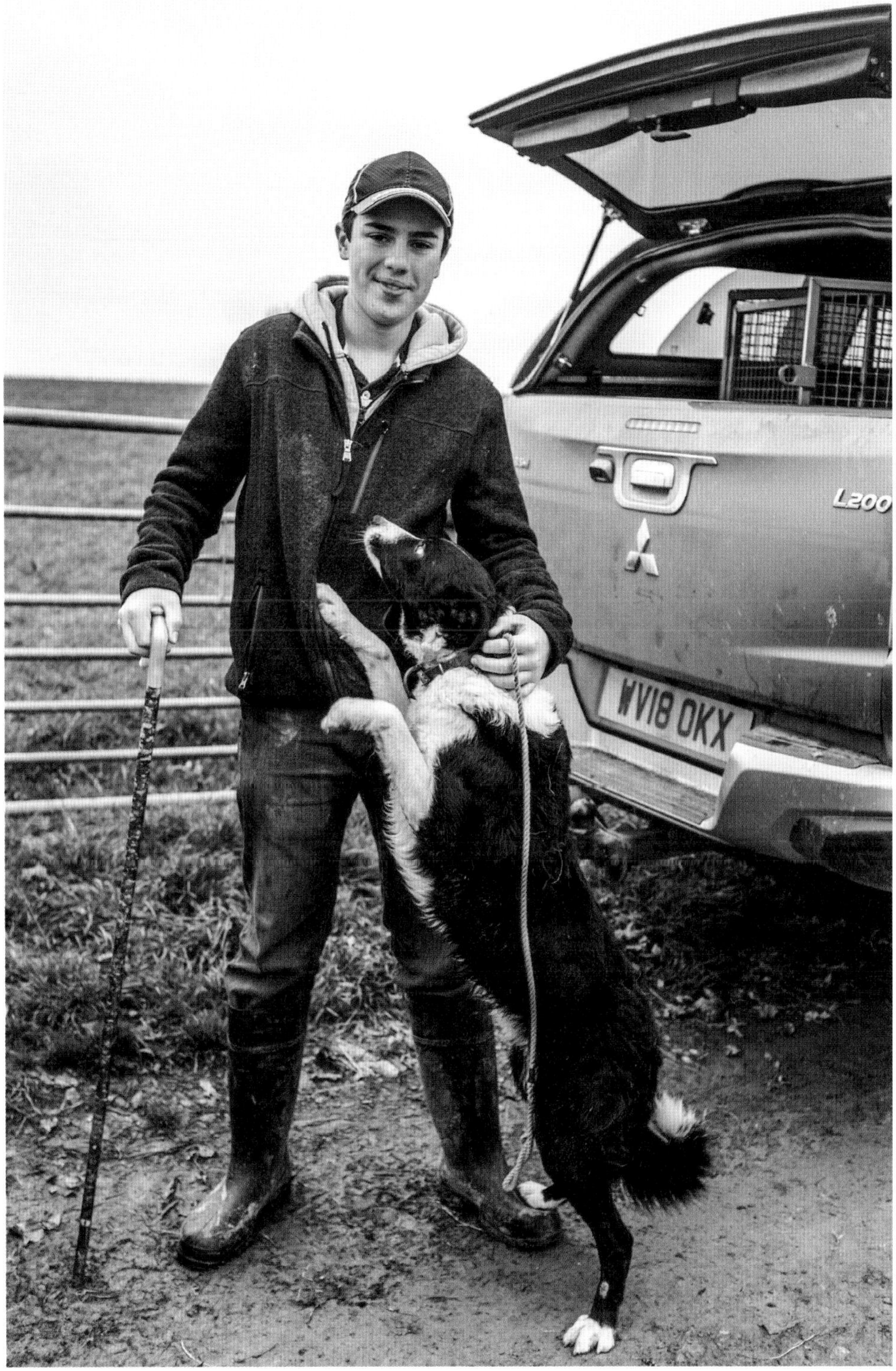
L200
WV18 OKX

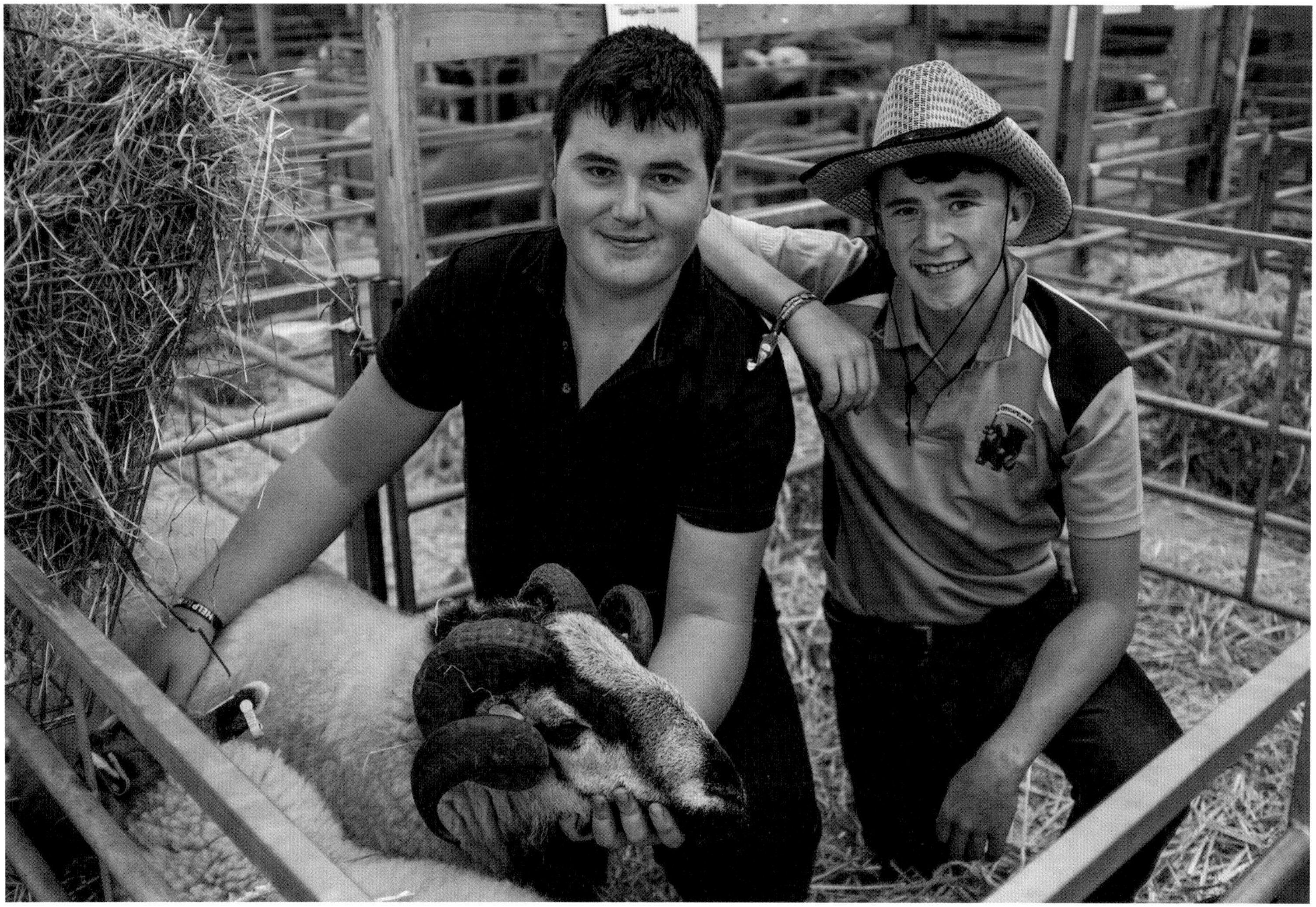

Afterword

The process of producing this book entailed an education for me, regarding a country that I felt I already knew. The world of shepherding in Wales has been going on for millenia, in one form or another. It is a world quite distinctly different from that of those who live in the cities, or even the towns, of this nation.

I was privileged to be given access into the privacy of rural families, in order to record and photographically document a way of life that is imminently under threat from the tsunami of social and economic change that seems sure to follow our exit from the European Union. My welcome, once I had been vouched for by known and trusted members of the shepherding network, was uniformly warm and generous. Families allowed me into their homes, fed me, and trusted me with personal and financial information. It struck me forcibly in the course of this project that all of the families I met, without exception, needed the income from outside work to supplement their farming income. They allowed me to portray them at work in a frank and honest manner which is not usual in the "Instagram" orientated world of today. I hope that I have not given anyone cause to regret their openness to me.

I have striven to achieve a measure of fluency in Cymraeg, albeit with a strong hint of a Northern Ireland accent. This ability proved invaluable, in that I was able to receive direct communication from people in the language in which they lived their lives, and in which they felt most at home. Welsh Government statistics would have us believe that there is a comfortably sufficient number of Welsh speakers to ensure the ongoing health of the language, but I do wonder what proportion of that total are truly "mamiaith", fluent first language speakers. Linguistic experts are quite unequivocal that this group are the true barometer of the integrity of any language, and a highly disproportionate number of those who use Cymraeg as their first and preferred tongue are among the rural farming communities. Social fragmentation of these would have a significantly detrimental effect on a linguistic heritage which the government purports to foster and support. Agricultural policy which exclusively focuses on biodiversity outcomes, or offsetting carbon emissions, has the potential to catastrophically compromise the already fragile economic infrastructure of hill farming in particular. It has always been a subsistence model rather than a great generator of financial returns, and as such it is vulnerable in a system where "profit" trumps all other cards. I am sure that we would not wish to be remembered as the demographic cohort who knew the price of everything, and the value of nothing.

Historically Wales has always reverenced the "Gwerin", the country folk. On St. David's Day little boys don flat caps, collarless shirts and spotted neckerchiefs. Small girls sport lace trimmed bonnets, shawls, and dresses with little aprons. It would be a tragedy if this picturesque little tableau were left to play out year after year in the future if we do not now acknowledge the important role that rural communities play in perpetuating a distinctive, and genuine, Welsh identity.

The digital universe now permits remote working, and it is quite likely that the beautiful landscape and better quality of life that rural Wales can offer will draw people from afar to enjoy them. These incomers will relate primarily to their computer and their online employer, and while they may soon realise that they have little in common with the local population, the die will already have been cast regards their location. King Midas died of starvation when everything he touched turned to gold, and the same would happen to us if we try to depend on a diet of "virtual" food. Computers may generate money, but we need to keep physically producing what we eat. We need agriculture.

If the existing social and economic infrastructure of our countryside is reduced to a carbon sink, or a theme park to accommodate a low level tourism destination, the loss in terms of destroyed communities and national dignity will be immeasurable. As Joni Mitchell said in her 60s ballad, "Don't it always seem to show that you don't know what you've got 'til it's gone....". Regret will avail us little after the event. The South Wales valleys are a stark spectral reminder of what happens to an area when you remove the economic engine for its existence. Replicating this devastation right across the Welsh countryside should never be contemplated.

Change is coming to everywhere, though, and at an ever increasing rate. There is a broad consensus that in many cases governance and ordered application are unable to keep up with the rapid speed of technical and social innovation. We do need to react quickly and effectively to our fast mutating reality, or indeed virtual reality, but there is fatal potentiality that "the baby will be thrown out with the bathwater." Joined-up thinking has not been a conspicuous feature of Governmental decision making of recent times, and a holistic approach to the funding and support of rural areas is imperative if we are to avoid catastrophic consequences of unintentional social engineering. Farming and shepherding will have to follow the money, families need to eat every day, so how and where financial support is to be allocated will be critically important.

Of course we should take notice of our need to supplement global biodiversity, and the universal dilemma of climate change. In fact it is species rich grassland that is the rarest habitat in the UK, and where progress in biodiversity is most required. While trees have doubtless an important role to play in carbon reduction, they are economically inert in the short and medium term. Forestry does not foster the web of social and economic transactions that are the glue bonding together today's rural communities. To suggest that Wales should blanket the uplands with afforestation in order to offset the carbon emmissions of industrial neighbours, or to contribute to international carbon trading, is a catastrophic miscalculation. Some elements of tree planting, sensitively managed, could surely be accommodated within a regime that would not financially disadvantage rural farming communities in Wales already coping with a challenging economic situation. These are not the factory farmers or the grain barons who abuse the subsidies of the public purse.

My grannie in Ireland had a saying regarding any innovation that did not earn her approval. "It may be change, but it's not progress." We should do our best to ensure that incoming policy changes in our countryside are genuinely progressive rather than inadvertently damaging, and respectful of the many diverse important considerations that will be affected.

I leave the last word to a young shepherdess from Snowdonia, Teleri Fielden:

"We must keep the people linked to the land."

Acknowledgements

Many thanks to Erwyd Howells and David "Dai Coed" Evans for their kind and generous support in the initial stages of my research, which got this project off to a flying start. The benefit of their extensive networks formed the bedrock of the content. My grateful thanks to everyone in the shepherding community who kindly agreed to be photographed in their private spaces, and shared their thoughts and personal circumstances with me in their homes, and on their farms. Without them there would be no book.

Thanks to John Humphrys and Will Troughton for their supportive forewords, and thanks also to Will for his advice and encouragement over the years.

Any errors or misrepresentations in the book are mine, and they are an unintended consequence of my ignorance. I hope that no-one will have reason to regret their participation in this depiction of shepherding in Wales. Neither is this book intended to be a comprehensive record, for what is shown here is but a fragment of a greater countrywide whole.

Farewell, and thanks, to Mick Felton for his kind guidance through the world of books over a long period, as he is now retiring from Seren Publishing, and thanks to Sarah Johnson his very capable successor.

Lastly, but most importantly, love and gratitude to Val and my family.